T0214830

Practical Enterprise React

Become an Effective React Developer in Your Team

Devlin Basilan Duldulao
Ruby Jane Leyva Cabagnot

Apress®

Practical Enterprise React: Become an Effective React Developer in Your Team

Devlin Basilan Duldulao
Oslo, Norway

Ruby Jane Leyva Cabagnot
Oslo, Norway

ISBN-13 (pbk): 978-1-4842-6974-9
https://doi.org/10.1007/978-1-4842-6975-6

ISBN-13 (electronic): 978-1-4842-6975-6

Managing Director, Apress Media LLC: Welmoed Spahr
Acquisitions Editor: Louise Corrigan
Development Editor: James Markham
Coordinating Editor: Nancy Chen

Cover image designed by Freepik (www.freepik.com)

Distributed to the book trade worldwide by Springer Science+Business Media LLC, 1 New York Plaza, Suite 4600, New York, NY 10004. Phone 1-800-SPRINGER, fax (201) 348-4505, e-mail orders-ny@springer-sbm. com, or visit www.springeronline.com. Apress Media, LLC is a California LLC and the sole member (owner) is Springer Science + Business Media Finance Inc (SSBM Finance Inc). SSBM Finance Inc is a **Delaware** corporation.

For information on translations, please e-mail booktranslations@springernature.com; for reprint, paperback, or audio rights, please e-mail bookpermissions@springernature.com.

Apress titles may be purchased in bulk for academic, corporate, or promotional use. eBook versions and licenses are also available for most titles. For more information, reference our Print and eBook Bulk Sales web page at http://www.apress.com/bulk-sales.

Any source code or other supplementary material referenced by the author in this book is available to readers on GitHub via the book's product page, located at www.apress.com/9781484269749. For more detailed information, please visit http://www.apress.com/source-code.

Printed on acid-free paper

I dedicate this book to my wife. This book is a fruit of our labor for all the years of sacrifices we both made to get to where we are today. I will never forget that everything I have now would not be possible without you, our families, and friends back home in the Philippines. And to my Inmeta managers here in Norway, I will always be grateful to all of you for believing in me.

—*Devlin*

***

To my husband. I couldn't have done this without you. You make me want to become a better version of myself. So here's to a lifetime of an exciting roller-coaster ride with you. Jeg elsker deg, beber.

To my dad, Ruben, and my mom, Nitz, I love and miss you more than I could ever say. To my brother, RJ, and my sisters, Yang, Rina, Bang, and Cheng, who I know will always have my back and vice versa! Our constant group chats and video calls from across the globe help me keep my sanity! And of course, I gotta give high fives to my brothers-in-law and sisters-in-law for putting up with them!

To my nieces and nephews – Robyn, Isaac, Ynah, Elijah, Sam, Eren, Riley, Kairo, Mathieu, and Raikko – you light up my life and give me the best medicine in the world!

—*Ruby*

Table of Contents

About the Authors

Devlin Basilan Duldulao is a Filipino full-stack cloud engineer (web, mobile, back-end, cloud services developer) based in Norway. He is a Microsoft MVP, an Auth0 Ambassador, a corporate on-site trainer for the past four years, a Microsoft Certified Trainer, an international conference speaker, and a senior consultant at Inmeta. He loves going to universities and user groups after office hours or during the weekend to share his expertise. If he is not coding or speaking at conferences, he is probably traveling around the world with his wife, trying local foods in different cities. You can find him on Twitter at @DevlinDuldulao.

Ruby Jane Leyva Cabagnot is a serendipitous Filipina React.js developer with a wanderlust heart but currently living in Norway. She is based in Oslo, Norway, with about three years of experience as a developer and over ten years as a content writer/manager. She believes that one can still teach old dogs new tricks, even coding.

About the Technical Reviewer

Alexander Chinedu Nnakwue has a background in mechanical engineering from the University of Ibadan, Nigeria, and has been a front-end developer for over three years working on both web and mobile technologies. He also has experience as a technical author, writer, and reviewer. He enjoys programming for the Web, and occasionally, you can also find him playing soccer. He was born in Benin City and is currently based in Lagos, Nigeria.

Introduction

What to expect from this book?

First of all, this book is for developers who already have a bit of experience in front-end development or, at the very least, have dabbled a bit in React and are now looking to find a reliable and practical guidebook on building enterprise-level React applications.

In the first two chapters of this book, we will go through an overview of some key React concepts, why React is a vital library to add to your arsenal of software development weapons. In the second chapter, we will briefly discuss what Node.js is and how to run the Node Package Manager (NPM), the popular back-end framework we use to work with React.

But if you're already familiar with the essential React concepts, you might want to jump right away to Chapter 3, where we have the starting point for building our React project. This book will cover some standard and important React APIs, how to navigate React Router, how to manage your Store, and so many other exciting things!

Suffice it to say that we expect you to have experience or proficiency in the following programming tools: HyperText Markup Language (HTML), Cascading Style Sheets (CSS), JavaScript (JS) ES2015+, and, of course, React. Some knowledge of TypeScript (TS) would be beneficial also because TypeScript is increasingly becoming the preferred language for building enterprise apps.

We will be using TS, and as long as you already know ES6 or the modern JavaScript, no need to worry if you're not that familiar yet with TS because we will be explaining it as we go along. We promise you that in no time, you'll see the benefits of writing enterprise-level apps in TypeScript, and you'll be developing in no other way!

The book's structure is designed as a practical building guide for you and your team to developing real-world enterprise applications. Even if in the future some new shiny tools will come up (as is to be expected in this fast-changing technological age), you can still apply the technical concepts and guidelines that we've painstakingly put together in this book. We even devoted a section on how you can reuse your React skills in other platforms and frameworks.

We will be using TypeScript for building React enterprise applications and Redux Toolkit (RTK) for managing complex application states.

But before we get right into it, let's just briefly explain or define the tools that we will use here:

TypeScript (TS): It is defined as a strict syntactical superset of JavaScript (JS). Codes written in TS are automatically translated into JS. The essential features of TS are its static typing and object-oriented programming based on classes.

Redux: Its official website defines it as a "predictable state container for JavaScript apps." Redux is typically used for application state management. Other state management solutions are Easy Peasy, MobX, and Recoil.

Redux Toolkit: It is a package library developed as a standard guide to write and simplify the configurations of Redux applications, thereby speeding up your development process. It can be added to the start of a new project or an existing project.

We will go into the step-by-step process that you can follow along and get your hands dirty from the start. After all, we all know, as developers, that we learn much faster by doing it.

CHAPTER 1

Getting Ahead in React

This chapter will cover a short overview of some key React concepts, including the advantages and potential benefits of having React as part of your front-end development arsenal.

React Primer

React is an open source JavaScript library for creating interactive user interfaces (UIs) and front-end applications. And its ever-increasing number of users and the robust community around the world are probably a testament to the fact that React is fulfilling its raison d'être, developing user interfaces, in particular, *faster and interactive user interfaces*.

You "declare" how you want your UI to look like and how it should behave, and React will follow your instructions and render it in your browser as per your description.

Facebook created React in 2011, which became open source in 2013. React is technically a library, but many users glibly refer to it as a framework because of its behavior and capabilities. Perhaps, one way to describe or compare how React behaves is to think of it as the View in the popular architectural pattern Model-View-Controller (MVC).

Component-Based Architecture

At its core, a React application is made up of components. *Reusable components* to be more precise. It is a section or a piece of the user interface, and each element has its specific logic.

React's modular nature allows the application's features to be developed independently and reused within or outside the project. For example, in Figure 1-1, we can break down the web page into various components such as the navbar, the hero section, the footer, etc.

1

© Devlin Basilan Duldulao, Ruby Jane Leyva Cabagnot 2021
D. B. Duldulao and R. J. L. Cabagnot, *Practical Enterprise React*, https://doi.org/10.1007/978-1-4842-6975-6_1

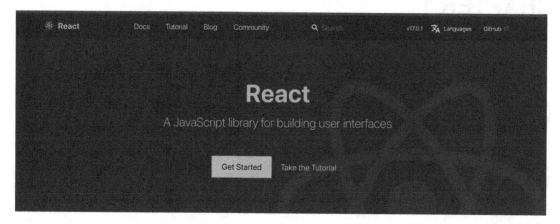

Figure 1-1. *A screenshot of a typical website. Source:* `www.reactjs.org`

A navbar component, as shown in Figure 1-2, contains the Page title and navigation elements. It is typically located at the top of the screen.

Figure 1-2. *An example of a navbar component*

As shown in Figure 1-3, a hero section component contains the images, usually large ones, designed to stand out from the visual field of a page and grab attention.

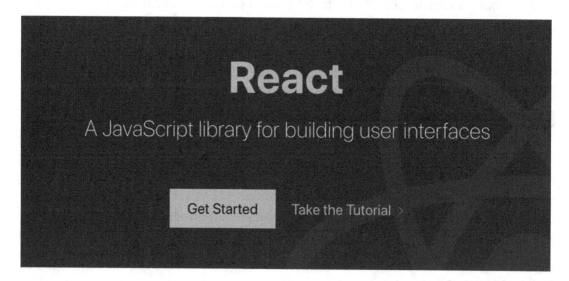

Figure 1-3. *An example of a hero section component*

So if you examine it closely, React components are small independent and self-contained blocks of reusable codes that we can put together to create complex user interfaces.

Yes, a React application is composed of many reusable components. Components can be thought of in any programming language as simple functions. The root of every React app is an element aptly called the root component that holds together the entire application, including all its child components.

Document Object Model (DOM)

Another concept worth understanding when learning React is its Virtual Document Object Model, or Virtual DOM for short.

Simply put, a Virtual DOM is merely a representation of the Real DOM.

A change in data or state is done first on the Virtual DOM. After the changes are computed, that's when the Real DOM is updated. The result? Overall fast performance and better user experience. React only re-renders the components and their children where an element of state has changed.

Essentially, the Virtual DOM works as follows:

- If the data changes, the entire UI in the Virtual DOM is re-rendered.

- The re-rendering creates a new Virtual DOM with the corresponding changes.

- Next, a comparison of the differences between the old and new Virtual DOMs is made or calculated.

- The Real DOM is then updated ONLY with the elements or states that have changed, not the whole DOM tree.

So, yes, the ingenious creation and use of the Virtual DOM is one of the reasons why React is fast.

The following are some visual representations to show how React's Virtual DOM works.

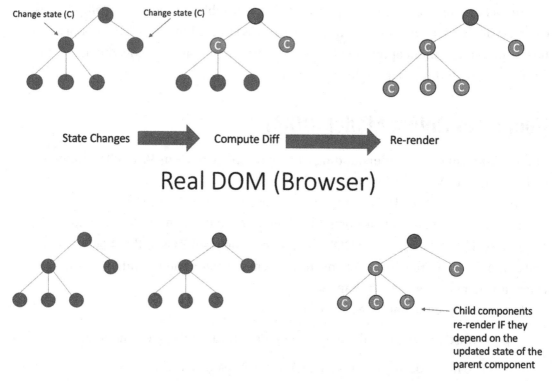

Figure 1-4. *Child components only re-render if their states depend on the parent component*

In Figure 1-4, changing the parent state will re-render the children IF the child components depend on the updated state of the parent component.

Virtual DOM

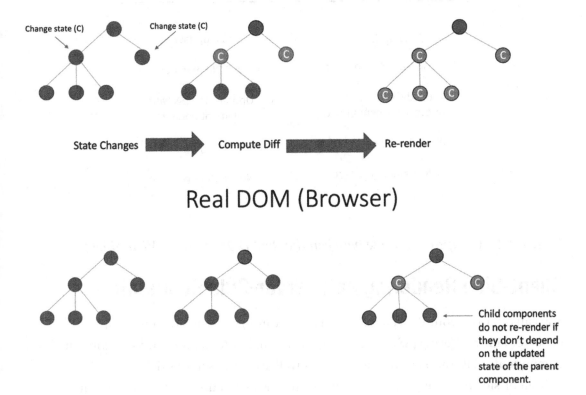

Real DOM (Browser)

Figure 1-5. *Child components do not re-render in the Real DOM if they don't depend on the updated state of the parent component*

In Figure 1-5, changing the parent state will NOT re-render the children IF the child components DO NOT depend on the updated state of the parent component.

Performance-wise, accessing or creating the Virtual DOM is cheap compared with building or re-rendering in the Real DOM.

Figure 1-6 provides a summary comparison between the Real DOM and the Virtual DOM.

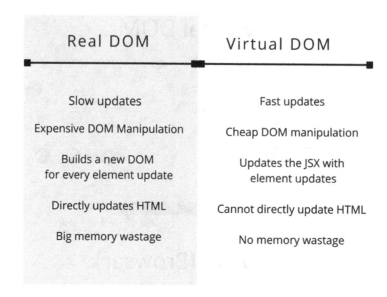

Figure 1-6. *Comparison table between the Real DOM and the Virtual DOM*

Client-Side Rendering and Server-Side Rendering

You can opt to do your React application either through client-side rendering (CSR) or server-side rendering (SSR). Developers can build independent and self-contained components of the app on the client side as well as on the server side.

Client-side rendering (CSR), a relatively new way to render websites, is about displaying content in the UI using JavaScript. There are certain performance advantages when you run your code on the client side, including making your interface much more interactive every time you make changes to your code. When data change, React will efficiently update and re-render our components.

The initial page load on CSR is supposedly slower, but page reuploads can become very fast because the entire UI is not called on the server.

React server-side rendering (SSR) means components are rendered on the server, and the output is HTML content. One argument for doing SSR is that it has a better application performance, especially for content-heavy apps; another one is that the HTML output is more SEO-friendly compared with doing CSR.

Unidirectional Flow/One-Way Data Binding

React is made more for unidirectional flow or one-way data binding. The downward data flow is one of the things that allow for faster and more efficient (not to mention easily testable code) developing times in React.

The unidirectional data binding allows you to control your application development better because components are supposedly immutable and data within them cannot be changed. To edit any element directly, one has to use the callback function.

Why React?

React has not only a fast-learning curve compared with other frameworks, libraries, or programming languages; it is also back end agnostic, which allows for users to use it whatever their stack is. JavaScript developers, in particular, can quickly become proficient in React development.

A big bonus point is a well-written documentation on its official site that is easy to follow and understand. You can think of React as the WordPress of the CMS (Content Management System) world because most of your problems can be solved by installing open source libraries.

React is also considered SEO-friendly, meaning that React components are more straightforward for Google to index. And this is a big deal for businesses.

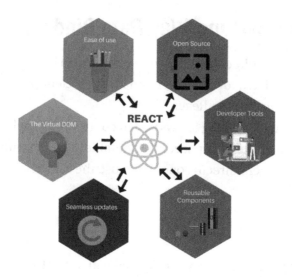

6 Reasons to Learn React

Figure 1-7. *Reasons to learn and use React*

Figure 1-7 illustrates why React has become a favorite of developers and many prominent business brands.

Some reasons to learn and use React and why it will be relevant for many years:

- The power of the Virtual DOM in React. It updates and renders only the elements that likewise update and generate in the DOM.

- Quick rendering and reusable components. Create encapsulated, independent components that can be reused within or outside the project.

- React can be rendered on a server using Next.js.

- To develop mobile apps, you can use React Native, a mobile app development framework using React. Moreover, you can reuse business logic parts of a React web app in your React Native mobile app.

- React is relatively easy to learn compared with other JavaScript frameworks or even other front-end frameworks such as Angular or Ember.js.

- A wide array of tools to choose from, including React DevTools, Redux DevTools, and MobX DevTools.

- React is open source with a robust ecosystem of active communities or groups around the world.

The last one, the big React community and support, is a significant factor, whether you believe it or not. This active community also translates to developers creating many tools and third-party libraries to help you in your developing experience.

Based on personal experiences, we have turned for help to many React groups like Slack, Gitter, Facebook groups, Discord, Spectrum, and Twitter. Or we reach out to a particular individual whenever we get stuck on something or need a bit of clarification.

Almost always, we get an answer from someone, and usually in less than an hour in our experience, maybe because the active members are based globally and in different time zones.

Career Opportunities in React

Interest in React is higher than other popular front-end frameworks and libraries such as Vue.js and Angular (Figure 1-8). If you do a quick job search for a front-end developer, you'll see many companies looking for proficient React developers or those who have experience in React. And we believe that this trend will continue for years to come.

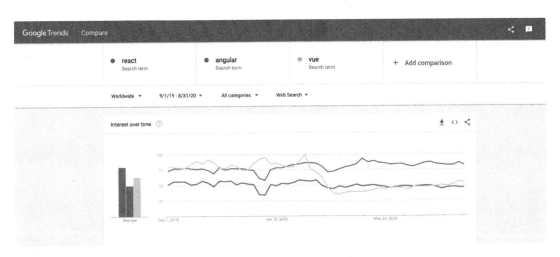

Figure 1-8. *Interest overtime in React, Angular, and Vue. Source:* `https://trends.google.com/trends/explore?date=2019-09-01`

If you want to expand your hiring desirability as a front-end developer and a full-stack developer, mastering React is the way to go.

React developers currently have a high job market demand and in the foreseeable future. Yes, it might be understandable that you could have a favorite language or library or framework. Still, to be blunt about it, one of the criteria for learning a new language or a new programming tool should be how hirable you would be, whether as a freelancer or as part of a company.

Summary

This chapter covered an overview of crucial React concepts, including the advantages and benefits of learning React. We learned that the core of all React applications are its reusable components and how Virtual DOM allows for overall fast performance and better user experience.

Another reason why React has become so popular is because it gives developers the possibility to build and render independent and self-contained components on the client side and the server side. Lastly, we showed that React skills are a good career move as interest and demand continue to grow.

In the next chapter, we will begin to download and install software packages that we will need to build our React application.

CHAPTER 2

Getting Started with the Node Package Manager

Before we can get React up and running, we need an installer to download and manage our JavaScript software packages. One of the most popular package managers is the Node Package Manager (NPM). Another one is Yarn, a newer package manager that supposedly drew a lot of inspiration from NPM. For our project, we opted to use NPM instead of Yarn. You can use Yarn if you prefer.

Our project will be using NPM, so this chapter will go through some of the most pertinent NPM commands and shortcuts, including semantic versioning and NPM scripts. We will just briefly discuss Yarn and go through some commonly used Yarn commands.

Don't worry about following the commands here for now because we would be doing it step-by-step in the succeeding chapters once we begin building our project.

Node Package Manager Overview

Before we get started, let's review what NPM is and how we use it in our app. NPM is similar to other package managers, such as RubyGems in Ruby on Rails or PIP in Python.

Released in 2010, NPM is JavaScript's package library manager, usually preinstalled with Node.js, an environment for building server-side applications. If you don't have Node.js installed yet, go to their website at `www.nodejs.org` (Figure 2-1).

11

© Devlin Basilan Duldulao, Ruby Jane Leyva Cabagnot 2021
D. B. Duldulao and R. J. L. Cabagnot, *Practical Enterprise React*, https://doi.org/10.1007/978-1-4842-6975-6_2

Node.js® is a JavaScript runtime built on Chrome's V8 JavaScript engine.

#BlackLivesMatter

New security releases to be made available Nov 16, 2020

Download for macOS (x64)

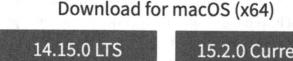

14.15.0 LTS	15.2.0 Current
Recommended For Most Users	Latest Features

Other Downloads | Changelog | API Docs   Other Downloads | Changelog | API Docs

Or have a look at the Long Term Support (LTS) schedule.

Figure 2-1. *Node's website*

Make sure to install the Long Term Support (LTS) version because it is more stable than the current version. If you already have Node installed, you can check the version:

```
$ node -version
```

Speaking of Node versioning, let me introduce you – if you're not familiar with it yet – to Node Version Manager, or nvm for short.

Node Version Manager

Node Version Manager (NVM) is a tool for managing different versions of the Node.js runtime.

You can easily downgrade or upgrade the Node.js version, which will come in handy if you face a legacy application or a JavaScript library that is only compatible with a specific range of Node.js versions.

12

Install nvm with a single command:

```
curl -o- https://raw.githubusercontent.com/nvm-sh/nvm/v0.34.0/install.sh | bash

#or

wget -qO- https://raw.githubusercontent.com/nvm-sh/nvm/v0.37.0/install.sh | bash
```

For a complete installation of NVM in Mac and Linux, go here https://github.com/nvm-sh/nvm.

Unfortunately, nvm does not support Windows, but it's possible to do it in Windows Subsystem for Linux (WSL) depending on the WSL version.

To download and install NVM in Windows, go here https://github.com/coreybutler/nvm-windows.

After installing NVM, you can install a specific version of Node:

```
$ nvm install 14
$ nvm use 14
```

The preceding commands will install and use the latest minor version of Node v14. Now, if there's a JavaScript project or library that only runs in Node v12, you can easily switch to that version:

```
$ nvm install 12
$ nvm use 12
```

The preceding commands will install and use the latest minor version of Node v12.

Another indispensable resource for any JavaScript developer is the npmjs website, where we can search for libraries or frameworks that we need to install for our project.

Installing Packages

You can use NPM to install just about any library or framework available in the NPM registry. You can head to www.npmjs.com to see more. If you already have an older version, you can update as follows.

For Mac and Linux users:

```
$ npm install -g npm@latest
```

Node Packaged Modules

Packages are either installed in local or global mode. Global mode packages are available from the command-line interface (CLI), while packages in local mode are installed in a node_modules folder of the parent working file.

Set up a new or an existing NPM package:

```
$ npm init
```

```
$ npm init --y
```

Fill in the blanks or just press Enter to accept the default values or add the flag --y to quickly generate a package.json file.

If you want to clone someone else's code, run the following command in the project root:

```
$ npm install or npm i
```

This will automatically fetch all the declared packages needed for you to run the app. The declared packages are located in the package.json file.

Package.json and Package-lock.json

Package.json is an important manifest file when using NPM and Node applications. It contains all of your app info, particularly the dependencies or modules that your app requires to run correctly. This manifest file is also the first thing that many developers would look at to run their local versions of your project.

Package-lock.json is a replica, versioned dependency tree of your package.json file.

A package.json file as shown in Listing 2-1 was automatically created when we did the npm install command in the terminal. This is just a sample object structure of a package.json file, including the dependencies and devDependencies. We will start installing the packages and libraries for our app in Chapter 4.

Listing 2-1. A Sample of a package.json File

```
{ "name": "npmproject",
   "version": "1.0.0",
   "private"
   "description": "NPM commands",
```

```
    "main": "index.js",
    "scripts": {
        "start": "react-scripts start",
        "build": "react-scripts build",
        "test": "react-scripts test",
        "eject": "react-scripts eject",
    "backend": "json-server --watch db.json --port 5000 -- delay=500",
    "start:fullstack": "concurrently \"npm run backend\" \"npm run start\""
},
    "author": "Devlin Duldulao",
    "license": "MIT",
    "dependencies": {
    "react": "^16.8.6",
                "react-dom": "^16.8.6",
},
"devDependencies": {
    "husky": "^4.3.0",
    "json-server": "^0.16.2",
    "lint-staged": "^10.4.0",
    "mobx-react-devtools": "^6.1.1",
    "prettier": "^2.1.2"
  },
 }
```

While package.json is used for dependencies such as project properties, author, version, description, scripts, license, etc., package-lock.json is likewise automatically created to lock dependencies to a specific version number.

As shown in Listing 2-1, the scripts object is the first thing I always read in an existing project because the scripts tell us what commands to run in order to run the project or build the project. The scripts object also helps us run shorter commands through its key and value pair. Another cool thing you can do in your scripts is to customize it.

Let's say you want to simultaneously use the scripts 'npm run backend' and 'npm run start'. Then you could just add a shortcut in your script such as 'npm start:fullstack' and run it:

```
"start:fullstack": "concurrently \"npm run backend\" \"npm run start\""
```

If you want to try for yourself the start:fullstack command, you can npm install concurrently. Concurrently is a very convenient tool that lets us run multiple commands at the same time:

```
$ npm i concurrently
```

The Dependencies, which is in our example just initially contains the bare minimum such as react and react-dom, are libraries that we require for our application in runtime. But take note also of the devDependencies object. The devDependencies object contains JavaScript libraries that you want to be added only during local development and testing because you don't need them in production. Some good examples include Gulp, Prettier, and ESLint.

Semantic Versioning or Semver

There are several types of versioning, but semantic versioning or semver is one of the most popular.

There are three version numbers to consider in so-called semantic versioning. On its official website, www.semver.org/, we can see the following summary:

Given a version number MAJOR.MINOR.PATCH, increment the:

MAJOR version when you make incompatible API changes,

MINOR version when you add functionality in a backward-compatible manner, and

PATCH version when you make backward-compatible bug fixes.

Additional labels for pre-release and build metadata are available as extensions to the MAJOR.MINOR.PATCH format.

An example of semantic versioning is "^3.2.1".

The first number (3) is the major version, (2) is the minor version, and (1) is the patch version.

The caret ^ tells NPM that we will take in the major version of that scheme; the minor and patch versions can vary. Another way to write this is, for example, 2.x, with 2 being the major version.

In some cases, you will see the tilde ~ (i.e., "~3.2.1"). This particular versioning can be read as "we will take the major version to be 3 and the minor version to be 2, but the patch version can be any number." You could also write this as 3.2.x.

In case you need the specific numbers for all three versions, simply remove the caret or tilde character.

Yarn

Yarn is *a new package manager for JavaScript*. Yarn, released in 2016 by Facebook, was designed to supposedly address some performance and security issues hounding NPM (at that time!). As stated earlier, we will not be using Yarn, but you can use it instead of NPM. In the following, we highlight some of the similarities and differences in syntax between the two.

Tables 2-1 and 2-2 highlight the similarities and differences between the two package managers.

Table 2-1. *Common Commands Between NPM and Yarn*

Command	NPM	Yarn
To initialize a project	npm init	yarn init
To set up the defaults	npm init -y	yarn init -y
To check if any package is outdated	npm outdated	yarn outdated
To clear local cache	npm cache clean	yarn cache clean
To run a script	npm run build	yarn run
To see a list of installed dependencies	npm list	yarn list

Table 2-2. *Different Commands Between NPM and Yarn*

Command	NPM	Yarn
To install dependencies	npm install	yarn install
To install packages	npm install[package-name]	yarn add [package-name]
To uninstall packages	npm uninstall [package-name]	yarn remove [package-name]
To install packages globally	npm install –global [package-name]	yarn global add [package-name]
To uninstall packages globally	npm uninstall –global [package-name]	yarn global remove [package-name]
*To update packages * for updating minor and patch releases only*	npm update [package-name]	yarn upgrade [package-name]
To install only regular dependencies	npm install --production	yarn --production
To show only the top-level dependencies	npm list -g --depth 0	yarn list --depth=0
To install and save packages in devDependencies	npm install --save-dev [package-name	yarn add [package-name] -D

Tips in using NPM:

1. To generate a package.json file quickly, use `npm init --y`.

2. Add `private: true` to package.json to prevent accidental publishing of any private repo.

3. Add packages (i.e., transpiling code or running tests) used for development purposes in your devDependencies.

4. Don't delete the package.json, but you can delete the package-lock.json before committing it.

5. If you encounter yarn.lock and want to use NPM instead, just delete the yarn.lock and do an npm install to automatically create a package-lock.json in your application.

6. You need to run npm install after cloning a project from a Git repository.

7. It is not recommended to push node_modules to your source control repo such as Git.

Summary

In this chapter, we have discussed how to get started with NPM including the various key commands that you need to understand going forward. We've also looked into using nvm to easily switch from one Node version to another. In the next chapter, we will talk about the various React components and how we use them in our application.

CHAPTER 3

Getting Started with React Function Components and TypeScript

In the previous chapter, we learned how to use the Node Package Manager or NPM, the command-line tool that allows us to install and update our application packages.

This chapter will examine React function components, which have become the status quo of writing up-to-date React apps, and the syntax to define the props we use for our function components using TypeScript. Simply put, React function components are essentially JavaScript functions that return JSX or JavaScript XML.

We'll set up a basic create-react-app (CRA) app with TypeScript and examine some key features with the CRA TypeScript template. TypeScript, a strongly typed superset of JavaScript, brings with it intuitive features that extend JS in powerful ways, such as defining the structure of an object in a lot of ways.

We will discuss the apparent benefits of using typings in TypeScript, especially in building large-scale enterprise-level applications. Furthermore, we will write React function components, or React.FC for short, and touch on two commonly used React Hooks: useState and useEffect.

Creating a create-react-app App

create-react-app (CRA) is the most popular as well as the easiest way to start building a single-page application (SPA). It is also Facebook's official boilerplate generator to create a simple or starter React application.

© Devlin Basilan Duldulao, Ruby Jane Leyva Cabagnot 2021
D. B. Duldulao and R. J. L. Cabagnot, *Practical Enterprise React*, https://doi.org/10.1007/978-1-4842-6975-6_3

CRA, which uses a preconfigured webpack build for development, gives us the capability to dive immediately into our code and build our React application without the need to manually set up and configure our local development environment and production build.

Minimum requirements are Node >= 8.10 and NPM >= 5.6.

First, in your terminal, check if you already have NPX:

```
$ npx -v
```

Or you can install it separately by running

```
$ npm install -g npx
```

NPX (Node Package Execute) comes with NPM. NPX, which is useful for a single-time-use package, executes packages from the NPM registry without installing them locally.

Note   If you've previously installed create-react-app globally via npm install -g create-react-app, you need to uninstall it using

---

```
npm uninstall -g create-react-app
```

```
#or
```

```
yarn global remove create-react-app
```

This is to ensure that NPX always uses the latest version. Global install of CRA is no longer supported.

Now, let's create our first `create-react-app` app with the following commands:

```
$npx create-react-app <name-of-your-app> --template
typescript
```

```
cd <name-of-your-app>
```

```
npm start
```

The naming convention is to use all small letters and separate the words with a dash. The --template TypeScript flag tells CRA to use TS as the default syntax and add the required configurations. To start your development server, run either <npm start> or <yarn start>.

You can find the complete command scripts under "scripts" in your package.json.

After running the command, check your app in your browser – `http://localhost:3000` – and see the initial loading page of CRA with TypeScript as shown in Figure 3-1.

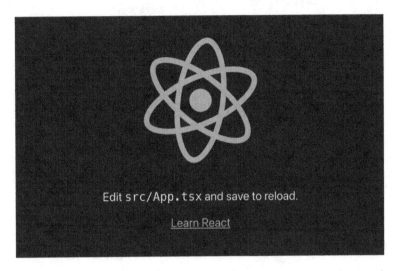

Figure 3-1. *Initial loading page of CRA with TypeScript*

And when you open your IDE or editor, you should be able to see the directories shown in Figure 3-2. We can see in the following the project or default folder structure that was automatically generated with CRA.

Figure 3-2. *Files initially created with create-react-app (CRA)*

Let's review some of the files generated with create-react-app. First, let's check out the two critical files for the project to be built:

public/index.html is the main page HTML template of our app that includes the React code and React to render context. Here's where you'll find the "root" to enable JavaScript to run the application. It is also known as the mounting point for React apps:

```
<!DOCTYPE html>
<html lang="en">
  <head>
    <meta charset="utf-8" />
    <link rel="icon" href="%PUBLIC_URL%/favicon.ico" />
    <meta name="viewport" content="width=device-width,
    initial-scale=1" />
    <link rel="manifest" href="%PUBLIC_URL%/manifest.json" />
    <title>React App</title>
```

```
  </head>
  <body>
    <section id="root"></section>
  </body>
</html>
```

src/index.tsx holds the main render call from the React DOM. It imports our App.
tsx component, which tells React where to render it:

```
import React from 'react';
import ReactDOM from 'react-dom';
import './index.css';
import App from './App';

ReactDOM.render(
  <React.StrictMode>
    <App />
  </React.StrictMode>,
  document.getElementById('root')
);
```

The following is a short definition and usage of some of the files and folders included
with CRA:

node_modules: It contains the JavaScript libraries and some dependencies of the
libraries that we've installed. We don't typically include this folder in our Git repository
because it's quite large, around 100mb–500mb, depending on how many packages we've
installed in the app.

public/manifest.json: This is a default file included with CRA. When building a
Progressive Web App (PWA) off your current React app, the configuration file is needed.

A simplistic explanation of a PWA is that it lets you run your application offline or
without Internet connectivity. What it does is that it caches the data or content of your
app so you can still see what's inside your website if the app is offline. FYI, you will never
see the T-Rex again when you don't have Internet connectivity. I'm sure all of us have
seen (you can even play it!) that dinosaur, right?

public/robots.txt: Also known as the **robots** exclusion protocol or standard. You can declare here the pages or HTML that you want to hide from Google's search results. Sample pages include the admin page because your users don't need to know your app's admin page. You can likewise specify here which search engine you want or don't want to index your site.

src: Contains the app UI code, including components and CSS styling. This is the core of the React app. We can also see the App.tsx, our application's entry point, and index.tsx, which bootstraps our app.

gitignore: A text file located at the root file; this is where you put files you want Git to ignore, such as your node_modules and .env files. Files already tracked by Git are not affected. Use the command git rm -cached to stop indexing a file that's already been tracked.

package-lock.json: If you've installed Yarn in your machine, by default, CRA will search for the Yarn package manager, but if it's not available, it will fall back to NPM. If you're using Yarn, then you'll see the yarn-lock.json file instead.

package.json: We've already discussed package.json in the previous chapter, but to recap, it manages dependencies, scripts, versions, and other metadata of our project app.

tsconfig.json: This file in the directory root indicates that the said directory is the TypeScript project root.

Inside the tsconfig.json is the compilerOptions object with some of the following configurations:

- "target": "es5": Modern browsers support all ES6 features, but you want your code to be backward-compatible to the ECMAScript 2009 or older environments.

- "lib": The standard type definition to be included in the type-checking process.

- "strict": true: This is the strict compiler option in TypeScript; it means you are opting for a strict-by-default mode of type safety without having to enable each compiler option separately.

- "module": "esnext": Specifies the code generation.

- "noEmit": true: Do not emit JavaScript source code, source maps, or declarations and instead use Babel.

- "jsx": Whether to support JSX in .tsx files.

- "include": The files and folders for TypeScript to check.

Declaration Files for TypeScript with React

Declaration files also called .d.ts files are prefixed with @types.

Using declaration files – also known as definition files – we avoid mishandling libraries and get the ever helpful and powerful "IntelliSense" or autocompletion in our editor.

Let's take a quick look at our package.json file to see the .d.ts files included with our CRA TypeScript template:

```
@testing-library/jest-dom":
"@testing-library/react":
"@testing-library/user-event":
"@types/jest":
"@types/node":
"@types/react":
"@types/react-dom":
```

To determine if we need a declaration file (@types) for the library we've recently installed, we go to the GitHub repository called DefinitelyTyped, where declaration files are being hosted. Another way is to simply go to www.npmjs.com and prefix the library name with @types/ in the search box. Fortunately, many people have already written declaration files for the most common and popular JavaScript libraries out there.

You will get errors or your IDE will complain if you're using an external library that requires a type declaration file and you fail to install it.

The Typings in TypeScript

The typings in TypeScript serve as documentation itself. Yes, it may seem to be a bit of extra work at first, but it pays off with a significant return in the long run. Many React developers who couldn't see its value initially say they now cannot imagine not using it.

Consider the following example. We explicitly define what type each variable is – name is a string, age is a number, and so on:

```
const name: string = "Jane Doe",
    age: number = "18",
    isStudent: boolean = true;
```

You'll note that the description of the code is part of the code itself when you write the TypeScript yourself.

If you're familiar with JavaScript, you know that it is untyped. JavaScript is probably the only programming language that is equally loved and hated for being flexible – maybe a bit too much sometimes – in its "rule" to pass around data and objects as we want or how we want it.

Now, imagine building an application with thousands of codes with a bunch of people in a team. Codes can quickly get messy and convoluted. You'll likely encounter methods being called in an object that doesn't exist or variables that were never declared.

But in TypeScript, we are required to define our objects and data format. In doing so, the compiler can then search or detect our code intelligently and catch potential errors such as calling a function with the wrong kind of argument or referencing a variable that's not available in the current scope.

Significant benefits of using TypeScript include having enhanced tooling options such as autocompletion, refactoring, and finding usages in our entire application. You can read up more on TypeScript here: `www.typescriptlang.org/docs/handbook/basic-types.html`.

Understanding React Function Components with Props

A React function component (React.FC) is a JavaScript/ES6 function that accepts arguments as properties of the component and returns valid JavaScript XML (JSX). It also takes props as a parameter if needed.

The following is a simple function component with props:

```
function Message(props) {
  return <div>{props.message}</div>
}
```

Now let's create a React function component. In the src folder, create a directory named components, and inside the folder components, create a file named Customer.tsx.

Before we proceed, let's define first our props using the type aliases of TypeScript. Another way of doing this is by using the interface, but we prefer the type alias in determining our properties:

```
import React from "react";

type Person = {
  firstName: string;
  lastName: string;
  age: number;
  isLegal: boolean;
};
```

Note here that we defined a type named Person that specifies the properties our components will take. firstName and lastName are required strings, while age is a required number and isLegal is a required boolean.

By creating a type, we can now then use it anywhere in our project as if it were a string, number, or any of the primitive or reference types.

Use the type Person as the model or shape of the props in our newly created component. See the following:

```
const Customer = (props: Person) => {
  const { firstName, lastName, age, isLegal } = props;

  return (
    <div>
      <h1> Hello React</h1>
    </div>
  );
};

export default Customer;
```

We can see that Customer is a stateless function component that takes a props object and destructures all the required properties of <Person>.

Now that we have our function component with props, let's get to our App.tsx to render it.

First, we need to import the component like so:

```
import Customer from "./components/Customer";
```

And in our return call:

```
function App() {
  return (
    <div className="App">
      <Customer
        firstName="Jane"
        lastName="Doe"
        age={21}
        isLegal={true} />
    </div>
  );
}

export default App;
```

Creating the type definition is also useful when we are using the Code IntelliSense feature in the code editor.

The Added IntelliSense in the Code Editor

Another beauty of creating a type for our props and declaring the parameters of our components is the so-called IntelliSense or code suggestions we get in our editor. IntelliSense is supported out of the box in VS Code.

```
return (
  <div className="App">
    <Customer />
```

e) age: numbe ×	🔧 age
	🔧 firstName
	🔧 isLegal
	🔧 lastName
	🔧 address?
	🔧 key?

Figure 3-3. *Code suggestion/IntelliSense in the editor*

And guess what? You get a TypeScript error if you write the Customer component without passing all the required values. Even before you run it, you'll already see the red squiggly line in <Customer /> to indicate an error or a stern warning.

```
TypeScript error in /Users/macbook/Desktop/React Book/ReactDemo/react-demo/src/App.tsx(16,8):
Type '{ firstName: string; lastName: string; }' is missing the following properties from type 'P
erson': age, isLegal  TS2739

   14 |     return (
   15 |       <div className="App">
 > 16 |         <Customer firstName="Jane" lastName="Doe" />
      |          ^
```

Figure 3-4. *TypeScript error in the compiler*

But wait. What if you don't need to declare or use all the props? Well, you can make some props optional with the use of ? in your prop type:

```
type Person = {
  firstName: string;
  lastName: string;
  age: number;
  address?: string;     // the address is optional
  isLegal: boolean;
};
```

The point is you have an option not to define all of the typings in your component to achieve that excellent tooling of autocompletion and type safety features of TypeScript.

Yes, it might take a bit of effort, in the beginning, to set up and get used to using typings in your variables and functions. Still, it would give us a better developer experience and a maintainable app in the long run.

Before we proceed, let's talk a bit more about React Hooks and two popular Hooks, namely, useState and useEffect.

React Hooks

React Hooks, which are essentially JavaScript functions, are a "new addition in React 16.8. They let you use state and other React features without writing a class."

Keep in mind also that Hooks don't work inside classes. Hooks are a big topic, but we will learn the fundamental concepts as we go along and build our app. But for now, here are the three important rules of Hooks to remember:

1. Call Hooks only at the top level of your React functions.

2. Call Hooks only from React function components – not from regular JavaScript functions.

3. Call Hooks only from custom Hooks.

React Hooks: useState

useState is a Hook that will allow state variables in function components. useState is also most likely the one we will be using a lot.

Let's say we want to update a state in our JSX. How do we do that inside our function component? Well, we use useState for that!

Create a local state inside a component and pass a default value. Note that useState is a named export from React:

```
import React, { useState } from "react";
import "./App.css";

function App() {
  const [title, setTitle] = useState("Practical React Enterprise");
```

The state variables inside the square brackets are a JavaScript syntax called array destructuring. The first variable, [title], which is the getter, is positioned as the first value returned by useState, and [setTitle] is a setter or set function that lets us update it.

And how to use the state variable or local state inside our JSX (HTML element)? In React, since our useState is in JavaScript, we need to wrap our getter in curly braces {} to read its value inside the JSX or HTML div:

...

```
<div className="App">
<h1
  style={{
    color: "blue",
    marginBottom: "5rem",
  }}
>
  {title}
</h1>
```

Practical React Enterprise

Figure 3-5. *Screenshot of rendering the UI using the local state*

Now we have the local value, but how to update the value [title]? That's the job of the setter function [setTitle]. Btw, if you're asking about the className in the div here, we use className in React instead of class to prevent name clashing because the latter is a reserved keyword in modern JavaScript and TypeScript.

Before we go on, we need to discuss briefly what is JSX or JavaScript XML. In React JSX, we can write HTML and JavaScript combined together. We can run JS code (logic, functions, variables, etc.) inside the HTML directly by using curly braces {}, like when we declare {title} or {setTitle()}.

Next, we need an event to trigger the setter function `setTitle` within the JSX. So how do we find an event? If you do <control -space> prefixed with the character "on" in your base code <h1> (see Figure 3-6), a window will appear with all the available events:

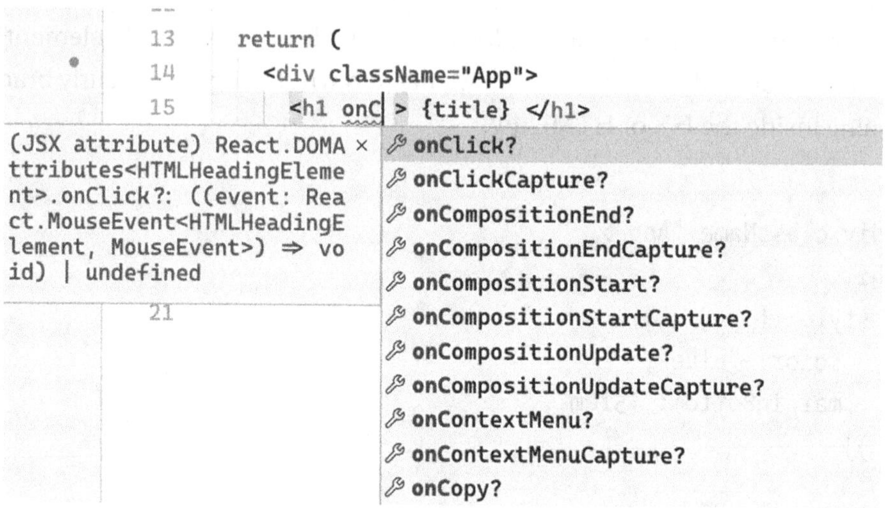

```
13      return (
14          <div className="App">
15              <h1 onC > {title} </h1>
```

(JSX attribute) React.DOMA ×
ttributes<HTMLHeadingEleme
nt>.onClick?: ((event: Rea
ct.MouseEvent<HTMLHeadingE
lement, MouseEvent>) ⇒ vo
id) | undefined

21

🔧 **onClick?**
🔧 **onClickCapture?**
🔧 **onCompositionEnd?**
🔧 **onCompositionEndCapture?**
🔧 **onCompositionStart?**
🔧 **onCompositionStartCapture?**
🔧 **onCompositionUpdate?**
🔧 **onCompositionUpdateCapture?**
🔧 **onContextMenu?**
🔧 **onContextMenuCapture?**
🔧 **onCopy?**

Figure 3-6. *Code suggestion in the IDE*

```
return (
  <div className="App">
      <h1 onClick={() =>
   setTitle("Become an Effective React Developer from Day 1")
        }}</h1>
    </div>
  );
}

export default App;
```

Become an Effective React Developer from Day 1

Figure 3-7. *Updating the UI using the local state*

Go to your browser and click the title "Practical React Enterprise" to update the local state title.

We can also put events, for example, on a `<button>` or a `<div>`. Let's create a handleAlert function and put it on a <button> to pop up an alert message:

```
const handleAlert = () => {
  alert("I'm a button!");
};

return (
  <div className="App">
    <button
      style={{
        color: "#ffff",
        height: "5rem",
        width: "10rem",
        backgroundColor: "tomato",
        borderRadius: "5px",
        fontSize: "18px",
      }}
      onClick={handleAlert}
    >
      Click me
    </button>

  </div>
);
```

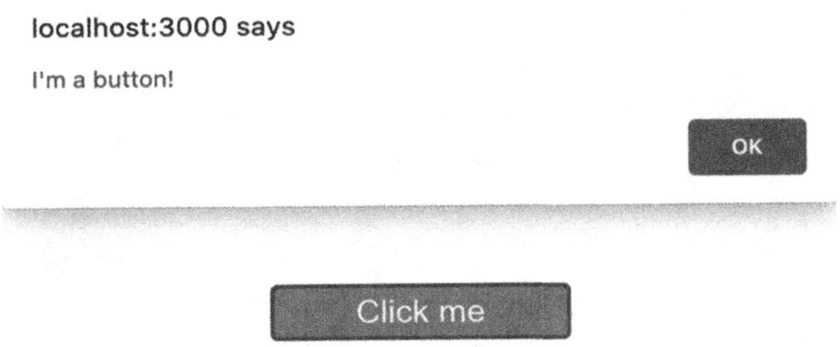

localhost:3000 says

I'm a button!

OK

Click me

Figure 3-8. *Alert message pop-up*

React Hooks: useEffect

useEffect is used for all side effects and essentially replaced the lifecycle methods we have worked with before (componentDidUpdate, componentDidMount, componentWillUnmount). This all-around Hook accepts two parameters – the first is a required function and the second an optional parameter for specific states.

Now, let's say we want to trigger an event as soon as the user lands on our app or trigger an event BEFORE everything in the UI gets rendered.

Yes, we have useEffect for that. We'll do a simple handleAlert message that pops up as soon as the user lands on the browser and without having to call it in our JSX:

```
import React, {useEffect, useState} from "react";
import "./App.css";

function App() {
  const [title, setTitle] = useState("Practical React Enterprise");

  const handleAlert = () => {
    alert("I'm a button!");
  };

  useEffect(() => {
    alert("Welcome to the Practical React Enterprise!");
  });

  return (
...
```

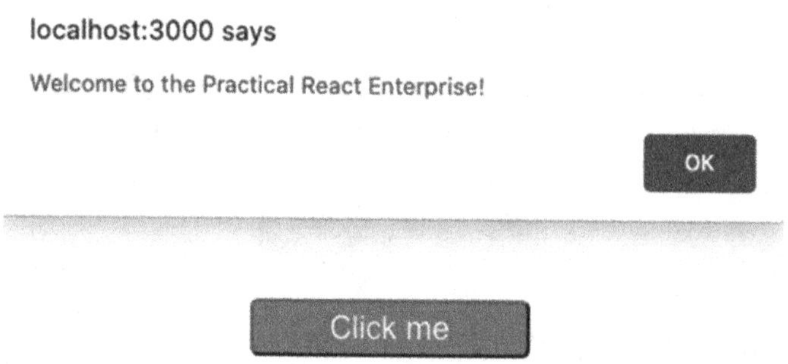

localhost:3000 says

Welcome to the Practical React Enterprise!

OK

Click me

Figure 3-9. *Alert message with useEffect*

A use case example of useEffect is when you want to send a request to a web service to get data of your user or a list of values like customer names, addresses, etc.

You can also put the setter inside useEffect, for example:

```
useEffect(() => {
  // handleAlert();
  setTitle("Updating the React Enterprise using useEffect");
}, []);
```

Noticed the square array brackets in the useEffect Hook?

1. The array brackets will prevent useEffect from running continuously on an infinite loop.

2. You can also add a state inside the array. And any change in the value of the state (i.e., title) will trigger useEffect to re-render:

```
useEffect(() => {
  //another state here
}, [title]);
```

Tips

1. Don't use the "eject": "react-scripts eject" command unless you need to expose the plumbing, such as Babel RC and Webpack, that CRA included at the start of the application. Do this only when you need to do some customization inside your React project. Keep in mind that you cannot go back to the original boilerplate structure of create-react-app once you eject.

2. Declare types before runtime code implementation. The types used within the current module must be seen at the top.

3. In the naming convention, components should be in PascalCase, while methods should be in camelCase.

Summary

In this chapter, we used a simple create-react-app boilerplate with TypeScript to show the easiest way for us to get up and running in building a React app. We learned some of CRA's essential elements with TypeScript and how they all go together to run our app correctly.

We also saw some of the benefits of using TypeScript in our React app, including

- The code suggestions and options to make it easier for us to read the code of others. And this allows for efficiency in team communication and consistency in the code base.

- IntelliSense and error catching early on and before running the code

Somehow, we managed to deconstruct the React function component with TypeScript.

But what we have touched here is just the tip of the iceberg, especially in understanding the full powers of TypeScript with React and what TS can bring to your JavaScript code.

As this book is about building a *practical* enterprise-level app, we will delve into it more in depth as we apply it to our code. In the next chapter, I will show you how to set up the foundations of our project app in a useful and efficient way so you'll become a productive React developer from day 1.

CHAPTER 4

Setting Up an Enterprise-Level App

Whether you're a newbie or an expert in the programming space, you must have wondered one way or the other how other developers set up and configure their starting project application, right?

So this chapter tackles an efficient and intelligent way to set up a production-ready boilerplate.

We'll look into how to choose the *right* boilerplate for our project with tools, frameworks, and modules that will allow us to manage the performance, styling, asynchrony, and other essential stuff we need to build an actual application.

Yes, we're not merely starting with the ubiquitous ToDo list app for learning a new framework or language. It is a project that you can be confident that you'd likely see – particularly the configurations and even the folder arrangement – in a lot of enterprise-level React apps. More importantly, it will be well architected and highly scalable.

First, we will look at the criteria that I use to find the right boilerplate for a particular application. And then, let's see the pros and cons of using a boilerplate.

How to Select a Good Boilerplate

Like many seasoned and "smart" developers that I know, I firmly believe in using a boilerplate, or at least being open-minded about it, right? The only trick – or maybe the hard part actually – is finding and selecting the ***right*** boilerplate for your project.

After deciding on a boilerplate, the first thing you need to do is to know every NPM package that you see in the package.json.

© Devlin Basilan Duldulao, Ruby Jane Leyva Cabagnot 2021
D. B. Duldulao and R. J. L. Cabagnot, *Practical Enterprise React*, https://doi.org/10.1007/978-1-4842-6975-6_4

Tip   Check out the libraries and tools included in the boilerplate before deciding if it is the right boilerplate for you.

One easy way to get a brief definition of a package or dependency is to go to www.npmjs.com and search for it there.

I have several criteria for deciding on what's the right boilerplate for a particular project, but the following are the three main ones:

1. **It contains MOST – if not all – of the core features I need**. This is the most crucial process. Search for a boilerplate that *practically* checks all the major features that you need so you don't have to do a lot of customization that could eat up a lot of your time. Always read the features and description of the boilerplate.

2. **It has a certain number of contributors or authors**. This is another critical part of what makes a boilerplate good. Many experienced and active developers are contributing to the boilerplate and maintaining it for updates and other stuff.

3. **It contains frequent updates or commits**. Check for the latest patch or commits on GitHub. A well-maintained template or boilerplate will have regular updates or commits from contributors.

Keep in mind that every project or even project team can mean many different boilerplate apps. Most of the time, the boilerplate you decide on would depend on the project itself, the people you work with, and even the client.

But the point is you would want to start from a standard base of code to get up and running quickly.

Pros of Using a Boilerplate

As a developer, I'm sure that you've experienced the seemingly endless torture of setting up all the libraries, themes, and required dependencies that you need at the get-go. It would take hours and hours just to configure them all up without any errors.

Trust me. If we were to implement ourselves the full suite of React, TypeScript, Redux, Redux Toolkit, the testing, and all the other essential stuff, it would take us a whole lot longer than the time we would like to spend. And this is assuming that everything works out smoothly as we install them one by one. No errors, and all the library versions integrate well together.

Here are some of the reasons why I say using the right boilerplate as a starting point for your app can make you a competent and *efficient* developer from day 1:

1. **You can reduce setup and development time**. As developers, we all know that it makes perfect sense to reuse codes or templates. Using a boilerplate reduces setup and development time using the same code pattern and avoiding rewriting from scratch.

2. **You can fork a boilerplate and customize it based on your needs**. When I was starting as a junior developer, one way for me to quickly learn a new library or a framework was to look at two or more popular apps. I would study and compare them, including all the dependencies used. Afterward, I'd build something based on my requirements.

3. **You can study the app's well-architected structure**. The boilerplate immediately introduces you to an excellent approach to design React projects. It's like having a lead architect handing you over the blueprint to build your app.

4. **You can benefit from experts' contributions in the field**. Having a boilerplate is just like having a senior developer or a front-end architect already giving you guidelines on starting your project. This is priceless, especially if you're just new to the team or particular tooling. You don't have to go down the rabbit hole of doing the research and testing everything before settling on something that works for you.

Cons of Using a Boilerplate

Like any other good thing, there's always an argument against it. Of course, there is, right? But the trick is recognizing and understanding the cons and weighing them against the pros in your list. That said, let's take a look at some of the reasons against the use of boilerplates in your app instead of building your project from scratch.

41

Let's take a look at some disadvantages of using a boilerplate:

1. **You might find yourself in a time sinkhole**. You *actually* still need to check and understand how things run under the hood. Of course, before choosing a particular boilerplate, you need to see what are the included core features. Sometimes, you may find yourself either putting in additional base features or scraping off the excess for modules you don't need.

2. **You might dig yourself into more complexity than necessary**. You might get more features than you need and higher complexity than necessary.

After considering all the preceding points, it is now time to set up our chosen boilerplate.

Cloning a Boilerplate

First, go to my GitHub and clone the project's starting point if you want to code along with the book. Make sure to start at Chapter-4/starter-boilerplate.

I forked this boilerplate just in case you'll be reading this book a year or two years from now, so you'll still have the same code base here in case you want to follow along with me. I'd recommend that you use my forked boilerplate to ensure that you get the same developing experience.

You'll find in Figure 4-1 the link to my GitHub where you should start if you want to code along with me.

webmasterdevlin/practical-enterprise-react

Contribute to webmasterdevlin/practical-enterprise-react development by creating an account on GitHub.

https://github.com/webmasterdevlin/practical-enterprise-react/tree/ma...

Figure 4-1. Practical Enterprise React from the source: https://github.com/ webmasterdevlin/practical-enterprise-react/tree/master/chapter-4/ starter-boilerplate

However, once you've finished this book and developed a good grasp of the process of building an enterprise-level React app, I strongly suggest that you go with the original boilerplate in Figure 4-2 when you're ready to make your application.

You can find the master copy of the React boilerplate CRA template in Figure 4-2.

React Boilerplate meets CRA

Crafted for **highly scalable & performant** and **easily maintainable** React.js applications with a focus on **best DX** and **best practices**.

build passing   test passing   release failing

coverage 100%   backers 27   sponsors 9

The official Create React App template of React Boilerplate   stars 27k

Figure 4-2. *React boilerplate CRA template from the source:* $https://github.com/react-boilerplate/react-boilerplate-cra-template$

Note   Don't forget to compare the versions of the libraries in the package.json to avoid any errors.

To be quite honest, you can even search for another boilerplate that suits your project specifications better.

My goal here is to provide you a step-by-step process of building a production-ready app and make you a more confident enterprise-level app developer by arming you with the right tools to use, or at least how to choose them.

React Boilerplate Meets CRA

Our chosen template for this project is an excellent collaboration of create-react-app (CRA), the most popular and well-liked starter template, and React boilerplate, including all the industry-standard tools: Redux, Redux Toolkit, TypeScript, and many more.

The following are reasons **why I chose** this particular boilerplate for our project:

- *create-react-app*: Built with the React boilerplate, it can be ejected to make customized configurations.

- *Redux*: A standalone library to manage the global state of the React app. The Redux store is the heart of the application. Redux is a much better implementation of a flux-like, unidirectional data flow.

- *TypeScript*: Improves the developer's experience by catching errors *before* hitting refresh. TS also prevents costly bugs by enforcing type safety. Lastly, TypeScript is self-documenting because of the typings of parameters and models.

- *Jest*: A test runner that is quite popular in the React ecosystem.

- *Reselect*: Used to slice Redux state and provide just the necessary subtree to a React component.

- *react-router*: Used for routing in this boilerplate.

The following are additional libraries needed to install on our boilerplate. npm install the following packages that we will be using:

- Material-UI is developed by Google in 2014 and offers an optional CssBaseline component for faster web development. It uses grid-based layouts, animations, transitions, padding, and many more.

- clsx is a small utility for constructing className strings conditionally.

- Formik is a very popular open source form library for React and React Native.

- Yup is a JavaScript schema builder for value parsing and validation.

- axios is a library that allows us to make HTTP requests to external resources.

For dependencies:

```
$ npm i [package name]
```

```
@material-ui/core
@material-ui/icons
@material-ui/lab
@material-ui/pickers
@material-ui/styles
clsx
formik
@types/yup
yup
axios
```

For devDependencies:

```
$ npm i -D [package name]
```

```
cypress
concurrently
json-server
json-server-auth
```

Before we proceed, it is essential to understand the different tools and technologies that converge together to form a single working application.

Husky

In my opinion, Husky is a great tool to add to our application. It essentially prevents you from committing or pushing bad commits or code with errors; it adds protection alongside TypeScript's typings:

```
"husky(remove-everything-in-these-parentheses.See-the-issue-#29)": {
    "hooks": {
      "pre-commit": "npm run checkTs && lint-staged"
    }
},
```

Dependencies

Open up the project in your IDE and open the package.json file to check if you've got all the dependency libraries installed:

```
"dependencies": {
  "@material-ui/core": "4.11.1",
  "@material-ui/icons": "4.9.1",
  "@material-ui/lab": "4.0.0-alpha.56",
  "@material-ui/pickers": "3.2.10",
  "@material-ui/styles": "4.11.1",
  "@reduxjs/toolkit": "1.4.0",
  "@testing-library/jest-dom": "5.11.6",
  "@testing-library/react": "10.0.1",
  "@types/fontfaceobserver": "0.0.6",
  "@types/jest": "25.1.4",
  "@types/node": "13.9.3",
  "@types/react": "16.9.25",
  "@types/react-dom": "16.9.3",
  "@types/react-helmet": "5.0.15",
  "@types/react-redux": "7.1.11",
  "@types/react-router-dom": "5.1.6",
  "@types/react-test-renderer": "16.9.2",
  "@types/styled-components": "5.1.4",
  "@types/testing-library__jest-dom": "5.9.5",
```

```
"@types/webpack-env": "1.15.3",
"@types/yup": "0.29.9",
"axios": "0.21.0",
"clsx": "1.1.1",
"cross-env": "7.0.2",
"eslint-config-prettier": "6.15.0",
"eslint-plugin-prettier": "3.1.4",
"fontfaceobserver": "2.1.0",
"formik": "2.2.5",
"husky": "4.3.0",
"i18next": "19.8.4",
"i18next-browser-languagedetector": "4.0.2",
"jest-styled-components": "7.0.3",
"lint-staged": "10.5.2",
"node-plop": "0.26.2",
"plop": "2.7.4",
"prettier": "2.2.0",
"react": "16.13.0",
"react-app-polyfill": "1.0.6",
"react-dom": "16.13.0",
"react-helmet-async": "1.0.7",
"react-i18next": "11.7.3",
"react-redux": "7.2.2",
"react-router-dom": "5.2.0",
"react-scripts": "4.0.1",
"react-test-renderer": "16.13.0",
"redux-injectors": "1.3.0",
"redux-saga": "1.1.3",
"reselect": "4.0.0",
"sanitize.css": "11.0.0",
"serve": "11.3.2",
"shelljs": "0.8.4",
"styled-components": "5.2.1",
"stylelint": "13.8.0",
"stylelint-config-recommended": "3.0.0",
```

```
    "stylelint-config-styled-components": "0.1.1",
    "stylelint-processor-styled-components": "1.10.0",
    "ts-node": "8.8.2",
    "typescript": "3.9.7",
    "yup": "0.31.0"
},
```

A Closer Look at Some Dependencies

"cross-env": Runs scripts that set and use environment variables across various platforms

    "eslint-config-prettier": Turns off all rules that might conflict with Prettier

    "eslint-plugin-prettier": Runs Prettier and ESLint rules and logs differently

    "fontfaceobserver": Monitors when a web font is loaded

    "husky": Prevents bad commits or push

    "i18next": An internationalization framework for any JavaScript environment or browser

    "i18next-browser-language detector": Detects a user language in the browser

    "jest-styled-components": Improves the testing experience

    "lint-staged": Helps ensure that no errors go into the repository by enforcing the set code style

    "node-plop": Helps automate code generations without using the command line

    "plop": Facilitates the easy creation of files uniformly across the team

    "prettier": Enforces consistency in style and code

    "react-app-polyfill": Polyfills for various browsers including commonly used language features

    "react-dom": React package for working with the DOM

    "react-helmet-async": A fork of React Helmet

    "react-i18next": Internationalization for React

    "react-redux": Official React bindings for Redux

    "react-router-dom": DOM bindings for React Router

    "react-scripts": Configurations and scripts used by CRA

    "react-test-renderer": React package for snapshot testing

    "redux-injectors": Loads Redux reducers and redux-saga only as necessary and not as all at once

"redux-saga": Saga middleware for Redux to handle side effects

"sanitize.css": Ensures consistent styling of HTML elements and other style defaults

"serve": Gives a clean interface for listing the directory's contents

"shelljs": A portable (Windows/Linux/OS X) implementation of Unix shell commands on top of the Node.js API

"stylelint": Helps prevent errors and ensures style conventions

"ts-node": TypeScript execution environment and REPL for Node.js, with source map support

"Cypress": For end-to-end testing

Insert inside the script: "cypress:open": "cypress open"

```
$ npm run cypress:open
```

Types Dependencies

These are TypeScript definitions:

```
"@material-ui/core": "4.11.1",
"@material-ui/icons": "4.9.1",
"@material-ui/lab": "4.0.0-alpha.56",
"@material-ui/pickers": "3.2.10",
"@material-ui/styles": "4.11.1",
"@reduxjs/toolkit": "1.3.2",
"@testing-library/jest-dom": "5.1.1",
"@testing-library/react": "10.0.1",
"@types/fontfaceobserver": "0.0.6",
"@types/jest": "25.1.4",
"@types/node": "13.9.3",
"@types/react": "16.9.25",
"@types/react-dom": "16.9.3",
"@types/react-helmet": "5.0.15",
"@types/react-redux": "7.1.7",
"@types/react-router-dom": "5.1.3",
"@types/react-test-renderer": "16.9.2",
"@types/styled-components": "5.0.1",
```

```
    "@types/testing-library__jest-dom": "5.0.2",
    "@types/webpack-env": "1.15.1",
    "@types/yup": "0.29.9",
```

Check out the "scripts" here. It's pretty amazing because they've included many scripts, so you don't have to do it yourself:

```
"scripts": {
    "start": "react-scripts start",
    "build": "react-scripts build",
    "test": "react-scripts test",
    "eject": "react-scripts eject",
    "test:generators": "ts-node --project=./internals/ts-node.tsconfig.json
    ./internals/testing/test-generators.ts",
    "cypress:open": "cypress open",
    "start:prod": "npm run build && serve -s build",
    "checkTs": "tsc --noEmit",
    "eslint": "eslint --ext js,ts,tsx",
    "lint": "npm run eslint -- src",
    "lint:fix": "npm run eslint -- --fix src",
    "lint:css": "stylelint src/**/*.css",
    "generate": "cross-env TS_NODE_PROJECT='./internals/ts-node.tsconfig.
    json' plop --plopfile internals/generators/plopfile.ts",
    "prettify": "prettier --write"
  },

"engines": {
    "npm": ">=6.4.1",
    "node": ">=10.13.0"
  },
  "lint-staged": {
    "*.{ts,tsx,js,jsx}": [
      "npm run eslint -- --fix"
    ],
    "*.{md,json}": [
      "prettier --write"
    ]
```

```
  },
  "husky": {
    "hooks": {
      "pre-commit": "npm run checkTs && lint-staged"
    }
  },
"jest": {
    "collectCoverageFrom": [
      "src/**/*.{js,jsx,ts,tsx}",
      "!src/**/*/*.d.ts",
      "!src/**/*/Loadable.{js,jsx,ts,tsx}",
      "!src/**/*/types.ts",
      "!src/index.tsx",
      "!s rc/serviceWorker.ts"
    ],
  "devDependencies": {
    "concurrently": "5.3.0",
    "cypress": "6.0.0",
    "json-server": "0.16.3",
    "json-server-auth": "2.0.2"
  }
}
```

The preceding packages are not the only packages that we need in our application. We will be installing some third-party JS libraries along the way.

Tip   You may go to my GitHub at `https://github.com/webmasterdevlin/` `practical-enterprise-react/` to check if we are working on identical installed package versions.

Now let's set up your VS Code, but you can use your preferred IDE if you wish to do so.

Setting Up Your Visual Studio Code (Hybrid Text Editor)

We need to familiarize ourselves with our text editor, VS Code, to help us achieve an optimum developer experience.

Install the extensions available in the VS Code Extension Marketplace to customize your IDE according to your preferences:

- *vscode-icons*: For light theme.

- *Material icon theme*: For dark theme.

- *Code spell-checker*: Helps you catch common spelling errors. One of the leading causes of bugs is a typo error.

- *Import cost*: This gives you an idea of the file size of your library.

- *Version lens*: Gives you an easy way to update your packages and check if there are available updates. Be careful in making updates to major versions so as not to break your code. Minor versions or patches are likely safe:

  - Click the up arrow to update. After making the changes, run the npm install again.

- *Path autocomplete*: Offers path autocompletion for VS Code.

- *ES7 React/Redux/GraphQL/React-Native snippets*: Gives you confidence in your syntax as it provides snippers as you code.

- *Live Share*: Allows you to collaboratively edit and debug with others in real time regardless of programming language or tools being used or developed.

- *ESLint*: An excellent linter that detects and warns you of syntax errors before you run your code.

- *Debugger for Chrome*: A VS Code extension to debug JS code in the Google Chrome browser or any target that supports the Chrome DevTools Protocol.

Summary

Let's summarize what we've learned so far in this chapter.

We installed various extensions for our VS Code to help us achieve a better developer experience while building our application.

We discussed how to select the right boilerplate, the advantages and the disadvantages of using one when starting to build your application, and why we opted to use the React boilerplate CRA template for our app.

And last but not least, we listed all the installed package libraries with their corresponding version numbers to ensure that you would be using the same when coding along with the book.

In the next chapter, we will continue with React Router, the standard routing library for React, and create SPAs, or single-page apps, with dynamic routing capabilities.

CHAPTER 5

Navigating React Router

This chapter deals with navigation using React Router, a specific library for handling and managing routes within a web app, which we would do so as follows:

1. Create a JavaScript file, router.js, in the root directory. For a TS file, we will use router.tsx.

2. Use the Route from react-router-dom to define the path and component associated with the path, for example:

   ```
   <Route path={"/hello"} component={HelloComponent}/>
   ```

3. Wrap all the Route that we created inside the Switch from react-router-dom, for example:

   ```
   <Switch><Router .../> and more...</Switch>
   ```

4. Navigate successfully to any page using the Link from react-router-dom, for example:

   ```
   <Link to="/hello">Hello</Link>
   ```

Along the way, we will learn how to use our preferred design library in the application we are building, which is Material-UI.

We will also touch on lazy loading or code-splitting our component to speed up initial loading time and improve user experience. In many relatively small React SPAs (single-page applications), the concept of code-splitting may not be necessary or may not have that much impact on performance. However, if we have a huge application with, let's say, an admin dashboard as well as a customer portal, it is not a good idea to try to load the complete application at initial loading times.

© Devlin Basilan Duldulao, Ruby Jane Leyva Cabagnot 2021
D. B. Duldulao and R. J. L. Cabagnot, *Practical Enterprise React*, https://doi.org/10.1007/978-1-4842-6975-6_5

Why React Router?

React Router is a dynamic routing library for React. It is composed of the following packages: react-router, react-router-dom, and react-router-native. The core is the `react-router`, while the other two are environment specific. `React-router-dom` is for web apps, and `react-router-native` is for mobile apps using React Native.

The router manages the URLs whenever we need to navigate through our React app with multiple views. React Router keeps our app UI and URL in sync with each other. The benefits include the following:

- It is compostable.

- It is easy to add links to the web page.

- It can add routing to several different pages on SPAs.

- It conditionally renders components based on the route from the URL.

Why Material-UI?

One of the fundamental reasons for using a UI library is that it saves us time styling our app. We don't need to reinvent the wheel, and we can just use something readily available, and more importantly, it's already battle-tested by the community.

Choosing a UI design depends on your project specifications, of course. Still, usually, I'd look first at the most recommended and popular among other developers, like in the case of Material-UI. Again, I'd look at the active contributors on GitHub, contributors helping to maintain the project. In `npmjs.com`, Material-UI has about 1.4 million weekly downloads.

There's also a higher chance that any issues you might encounter in your applications have already been resolved and documented on Stack Overflow or other sites.

Other top UI designs worth checking out include Ant Design and React-Bootstrap. We would talk more about styling React components in later chapters.

Getting Started

Let's start building our React Router navigation for our application. First, let's make a few edits to some default files, and let's build it up again in a step-by-step process.

In your src/app/ folder, delete the following two directories: containers/ HomePage and components/NotFoundPage. See Figure 5-1.

Figure 5-1. *Deleting folders: containers and components*

It should break something in the app. So open the file src/app/index.tsx and update the file with the following line of code:

Listing 5-1. Updating index.tsx

```
export function App() {
  return (
    <BrowserRouter>
      <Helmet
        titleTemplate="%s - React Boilerplate"
        defaultTitle="React Boilerplate"
      >
```

```
      <meta name="description" content="A React Boilerplate application" />
    </Helmet>

    <Switch>
      <Route exact path= '/' component={} />

    </Switch>
    <GlobalStyle />
  </BrowserRouter>
 );
}
```

Next, under the app directory, create another folder named views. And under views, create another folder named pages. Lastly, within the pages directory, create a new file and call it Home.tsx. See Figure 5-2 for the folder structure.

```
App
  views
    pages
      Home.tsx
```

Figure 5-2. *New folder structure*

Open the file Home.tsx and type the snippet rafce (short for react arrow function export component) if you're using VS Code. In WebStorm, the snippet is rsc (short for React stateless component without prop types and ES6 module system).

Figure 5-3 shows how to use code snippets in our code editor. Ensure you have already installed the extension ES7 React/Redux/GraphQL/React-Native snippets from the VS Code Marketplace.

app > views > pages > ⊛ Home.tsx

```
1    ra
2        ☐ rafce              reactArrowFunctionExportComp...    Creates a React Arrow Functio
3        ☐ rafcp              reactArrowFunctionComponentW...    omponent with ES7 module syst
4        ⊗ randomBytes                                          (ES7 React/Redux/GraphQL/Reac
5        ⊗ randomFill                                           ative snippets)
6        ⊗ randomFillSync
7        ⊗ rawListeners                                         import React from 'react'
8        [⊚] RadioNodeList
         [⊚] RandomSource                                       const  = () ⇒. {
         [⊚] Range                                                  return (
         [⊚] RangeError                                                 <div>
         ⊗ removeAllListeners                                           </div>
         ⊗ removeAllListeners                                        )
                                                               }

                                                               export default
```

Figure 5-3. *Typing the rafce snippet, short for react arrow function export component*

Add the heading in the return statement <h1>Home Page</h1> as shown in Listing 5-2.

Listing 5-2. Adding h1 Heading to the Home Page

```
import React from 'react';

const Main = () => {
  return (
    <div>
      <h1>Home Page</h1>
    </div>
  );
};

export default Main;
```

In our app/index.tsx file, we add the Home component to our Route path, as shown in Listing 5-3.

Listing 5-3. Adding the Home Component to routes.tsx

```
export function App() {
  return (
    <BrowserRouter>
      <Helmet
        titleTemplate="%s - React Boilerplate"
        defaultTitle="React Boilerplate"
      >
        <meta name="description" content="A React Boilerplate application" />
      </Helmet>

      <Switch>
        <Route exact path="/" component={Home} />
      </Switch>
      <GlobalStyle />
    </BrowserRouter>
  );
}
```

When you run the app and go to your default localhost:3000, you should see the rendered page.

Figure 5-4 is the Home Page being rendered in the UI.

Home Page

Figure 5-4. *Rendering the Home Page to the UI*

What did we do here? We've shown a straightforward way of navigating our app using React Router.

Next, let's create another file and name it material-buttons.tsx, and the path shall look like this: app/components/material-buttons.tsx.

Here we'll render some buttons in the UI. We will use the design coming from Material-UI that we've imported earlier. Go to the website of Material-UI, specifically the Button component.

Figure 5-5 shows the link to the Material-UI website.

React Button component - Material-UI

Buttons allow users to take actions, and make choices, with a single tap.
Buttons communicate actions that users can take. They are typically placed

https://material-ui.com/components/buttons/

Figure 5-5. *Using the Material-UI Button component*

Choose the Contained Buttons design. Make sure to choose the TypeScript option
and copy the complete source code and paste it in our `material-buttons.tsx` file.

Important Note   Rename the file from `ContainedButtons` to
`MaterialButtons`.

Afterward, go to the `Home.tsx` to use the newly created Material-UI Button
component, as shown in Listing 5-4.

Listing 5-4. Copying the Material-UI Button Component

```
import React from "react";
import MaterialButtons from 'app/components/material-buttons';

const Home = () => {
  return (
    <div>
        <h1>Main Page</h1>
        <MaterialButtons/>
    </div>
  );
};

export default Home;
```

In your localhost, you should see the following changes, as shown in Figure 5-6.

Home Page

Figure 5-6. *Rendering the Material-UI Button component*

Now that we have a proof of concept that we can use the Material-UI library in our design, we can look to configuring a router and then navigation.

But first, let's quickly recap the React Router installation.

Basics Recap

With the installation of `react-router-dom` as part of our boilerplate, we gained access to the following three components in our `index.tsx`: `<BrowserRouter>`, `<Route>`, and `<Switch>`.

Open your `index.tsx` file, and let's discuss each one:

`<BrowserRouter>` is the base configuration. It wraps the other components and keeps them in sync with the URL.

`<Switch>` is the dynamic part of the web application. As the name suggests, it will change or dynamically switch based on the URL. The Switch component makes sure that the first Route child component that matches the URL location will render.

`<Route>` needs a "path prop" and is rendered when it gets the matched or exact URL path.

Now let's see how we navigate the URL paths in our application to get from one component to the next.

`React-router-dom` allows us a few ways of changing paths, including the most common one called the `<Link>` tag, which we would be using a lot here in our app. For a cleaner code and for separation of concerns, we shall create a new file in the app directory and name it routes.tsx.

Creating routes.tsx

Our Route path will likely become more extended, so instead of building all the routes in our app/index.tsx file, we will create a new file and name it routes.tsx.

Here's the file path:

app ➤ routes.tsx

Next, we will then move the <Switch> and <Route> components from the index.tsx to our newly created routes.tsx, as shown in Listing 5-5.

Listing 5-5. Moving Switch and Route Components to routes.tsx

```
import React, { lazy, Suspense } from 'react';
import { Switch, Route } from 'react-router-dom';
import Home from './views/pages/Home';

const Routes = () => {
  return (
     <Switch>
       <Route exact path="/" component={Home} />
     </Switch>
);
}
export default Routes;
```

Now we need to use our newly created <Routes /> back at index.tsx, as shown in Listing 5-6.

Listing 5-6. Using the Routes in index.tsx

```
export function App() {
  return (
    <BrowserRouter>
      <Helmet
        titleTemplate="%s - React Boilerplate"
        defaultTitle="React Boilerplate"
      >
```

```
        <meta name="description" content="A React Boilerplate application" />
      </Helmet>
      <Routes/>
      <GlobalStyle/>
    </BrowserRouter>
  );
}
```

Let's create another view page and name it AboutPage.tsx under the path views/pages. Add an <h1>This is the About Page</h1>.

Listing 5-7 is the About Page component.

Listing 5-7. Creating AboutPage and Adding h1 Heading

```
import React from 'react';

const AboutPage = () => {

return (
  <div>
   <h1>This is the About Page</h1>
  </div>
);
 };
export default AboutPage;
```

Don't forget to add the new component in the routes.tsx as well as import the About Page component on top:

```
<Route exact path="/about" component={AboutPage} />
```

Check your localhost:3000/about to see if it's still working.

Note   When building an application, I usually gather the requirements before writing any code. I always check whether I need to create a dashboard for the application or an admin dashboard. As much as possible, we make the routing first and determine if there are nested routes or not.

Now we can navigate the URL paths in our application. The first task is to build a dashboard.

Building a Dashboard

Go to the website of Material-UI and search for a navigation bar or app bar. They're the same. Grab the TS source code of Simple App Bar. See a screenshot of Simple App Bar in Figure 5-7.

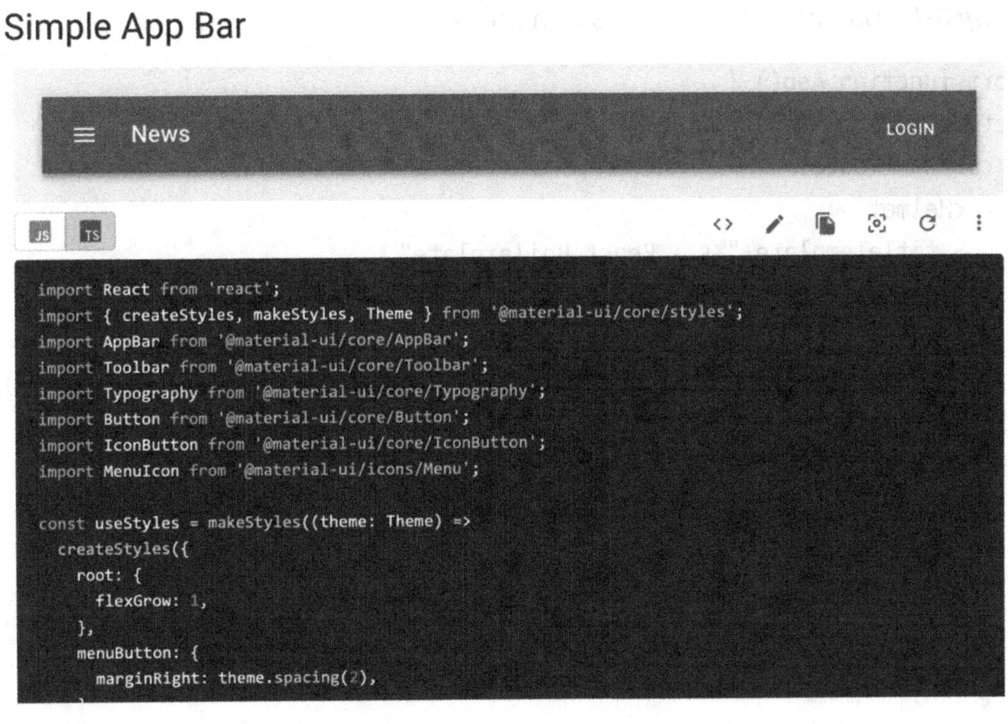

Simple App Bar

Figure 5-7. Screenshot of Simple App Bar at the Material-UI website

Navigation Bar

The navbar component is what we place on top of the app and allows us to switch between different pages such as Home, About, Login, etc.

Create a new file under the folder components and name it navigation-bar.tsx.

Paste the source code that you grabbed from Material-UI Simple App Bar (see Figure 5-8). Don't forget to change the default filename from ButtonAppBar to NavigationBar.

At this point, let's just delete the file material-buttons.tsx since we don't need it anymore. We just created it to quickly show how we can use the Material-UI designs in our component pages.

After that, open again the app/index.tsx and render the NavigationBar. Make sure to put it on top of or before the <Routes/> component to permanently position the navigation bar on the web app's top area, as shown in Listing 5-8.

Listing 5-8. Using the NavigationBar in index.tsx

```tsx
export function App() {
  return (
    <BrowserRouter>
      <Helmet
        titleTemplate="%s - React Boilerplate"
        defaultTitle="React Boilerplate"
      >
        <meta name="description" content="A React Boilerplate application" />
      </Helmet>
      <NavigationBar />
      <Routes/>
      <GlobalStyle/>
    </BrowserRouter>
  );
}
```

Check your localhost:3000 to see the navbar in the UI.

Home Page

Figure 5-8. *Showing the NavigationBar at the browser*

We will discuss in detail the various React styling methods in the following few chapters. But in the meantime, I just want to point out that the styling solution of Material-UI comes from many other styling libraries, such as styled-components.

At its core, Material-UI uses CSS-in-JS that works at runtime and server-side. We will talk more about CSS-in-JS in a later chapter.

Take a look at the navigation bar styling components from Material-UI. We are using makeStyles, which basically allows us to create multiple style rules per stylesheet. The returned function, useStyles, we will then call inside the NavigationBar component:

```
const useStyles = makeStyles((theme: Theme) =>
  createStyles({
    root: {
      flexGrow: 1,
    },
    menuButton: {
      marginRight: theme.spacing(2),
    },
    title: {
      flexGrow: 1,
    },
  }),
);
```

In my opinion, Material-UI is one of the best styling libraries, especially for React apps. The components are reusable, fast, and declarative. On its GitHub, it also has over 63K stars, which means I'm not alone, in my opinion.

Adding Navigation Links

Let's add some buttons and navigation links in our navigation bar and name them as follows – <Home> <About> <Dashboard> – as shown in Listing 5-9.

Don't forget to import the named component from "react-router-dom":

```
import { Link } from 'react-router-dom';
```

Note   We will discuss in detail later in this chapter the different navigation paths we can use for our React app, but for now, let's build our components first.

Listing 5-9. Adding Navigation Links to the navbar

```
import React from 'react';
import { createStyles, makeStyles, Theme } from '@material-ui/core/styles';
import AppBar from '@material-ui/core/AppBar';
import Toolbar from '@material-ui/core/Toolbar';
import Button from '@material-ui/core/Button';
import { Link } from 'react-router-dom';
import { colors } from '@material-ui/core';

export default function NavigationBar() {
  const classes = useStyles();

  return (
    <div className={classes.root}>
      <AppBar position="static">
        <Toolbar>
          <Link className={`${classes.link} ${classes.title}`} to={'/'}>
            LOGO
          </Link>
          <Button color="inherit">
            <Link to={'/'}>
              Home
            </Link>
          </Button>
          <Button color="inherit">
              About
          </Button>
          <Button color="inherit">
              Dashboard
          </Button>
          <Button color="inherit">
              Login
          </Button>
        </Toolbar>
```

```
      </AppBar>
    </div>
  );
}
```

While at it, replace the word "News" with LOGO because that's where we're going to put our icon logo later.

We also added the link style object. See the edits in Listing 5-10.

Listing 5-10. Adding a link Style Object

```
const useStyles = makeStyles((theme: Theme) =>
  createStyles({
    root: {
      flexGrow: 1,
    },
    menuButton: {
      marginRight: theme.spacing(2),
    },
    link: {
     color: colors.lightBlue[50],
     textDecoration: 'none',
      },
    title: {
      flexGrow: 1,
      },
  }),
);
```

As you can see in Listing 5-11, we can now use it in our button navigation links using the reserved React word `<className>`.

First, we used the useStyles Hook by calling it and storing it in a variable. We named the variable classes for readability purposes:

```
const classes = useStyles();
```

And then let's add the navigation links to the rest of the buttons.

Listing 5-11. Adding the Navigation Links and CSS Class Objects in the NavigationBar

```
export default function NavigationBar() {
  const classes = useStyles();

  return (
    <div className={classes.root}>
      <AppBar position="static">
        <Toolbar>
          <Link className={`${classes.link} ${classes.title}`} to={'/'}>
            LOGO
          </Link>
          <Button color="inherit">
            <Link className={classes.link} to={'/'}>
              Home
            </Link>
          </Button>
          <Button color="inherit">
            <Link className={classes.link} to={'/about'}>
              About
            </Link>
          </Button>
          <Button color="inherit">
            <Link className={classes.link} to={'/dashboard'}>
              Dashboard
            </Link>
          </Button>
          <Button color="inherit">
            <Link className={classes.link} to={'/login'}>
              Login
            </Link>
          </Button>
        </Toolbar>
```

```
    </AppBar>
  </div>
  );
}
```

In our LOGO component, notice that we need to use the backticks `` `` `` to use two CSS class objects in our Button component.

Listing 5-12. Using Backticks for Two or More CSS Class Objects

```
Link className={`${classes.link} ${classes.title}`} to={'/'}> LOGO </Link>
```

Make sure to clean up any unused or grayed-out imported libraries.

Next, let's add another component under views/pages and name it NotFoundPage.tsx.

Type again the snippet "rafce" to conveniently create the stateless arrow component for us. And also add the heading <h1> 404 Page Not Found</h1>.

Listing 5-13. Creating a 404 Not Found Page

```
import React from 'react';

const NotFoundPage = () => {
  return (
      <div>
          <h1>404 Page Not Found</h1>
      </div>
      )
  }
export default NotFoudPage;
```

Don't forget to define the path of NotFoundPage after importing it in routes.tsx:

```
import NotFoundPage from './views/pages/NotFoundPage';
<Route exact path="/not-found"component={NotFoundPage} />
```

Navigating React Router: <Redirect >

In our `routes.tsx`, let's add `<Redirect />`, which is fortunately already built into the react-router-dom.

There are many use cases for redirecting our user to a particular page. In general, we use `<Redirect />` if we need to change the URL path without the user having to click a link to that path.

Here are a few conditions:

- When the user is accessing a restricted page.

- When the user is accessing a page that is not found or no longer exists.

- When the user typed an incorrect path into the address bar (typo error!).

- A successful login has occurred, and the user is now being directed to the home page or dashboard.

For now, let's create a `<Redirect />` for all paths that are not defined on the 404 page:

```
<Route path={'/not-found'} component={NotFoundPage} exact />
        <Redirect from={'*'} to={'/not-found'} exact />
```

Before we wrap up this section, let's just put a bit of styling on our pages, especially paddings and margins.

Adding the Container-Style Class Component

Go to `app/index.tsx`, and we're going to wrap our `<Routes/>` in a Container using Material-UI. Import the named component from Material-UI and directly use the <Container> to wrap the Routes component:

```
...
import { Container } from '@material-ui/core';

<Container>
    <Routes />
</Container>
```

Check the browser, and you'll notice, as shown in Figure 5-9, that the <h1> headings are no longer pushed out into the left corner. The styling applies to all the pages that were wrapped in `<Container> <Routes/> </Container>`.

Figure 5-9. *Using Container from Material-UI*

But don't worry too much about the specific styling for these pages. We're just showing you the easy convenience of using Material-UI to style our app.

Remember that this book's primary goals are to guide you to build an enterprise-level app and give you an idea of how developers develop their apps similarly. In the end, you still decide on how you will make your app based on your specific requirements.

So what about the dashboard? Let's build that up now.

Creating the Dashboard Layout

In the app folder, create a folder named `layouts,` and after which, make a subfolder and call it `dashboard-layout`.

In the dashboard-layout folder, create the file `dashboard-sidebar-navigation.tsx`.

The path is **app ➤ layouts ➤ dashboard-layout ➤ dashboard-sidebar-navigation. tsx**.

Let's populate the newly created file with the following code. First, import the following libraries.

Listing 5-14. Importing Libraries to dashboard-sidebar-navigation.tsx

```
import React, { useEffect } from 'react';
import { Link } from 'react-router-dom';
import { createStyles, makeStyles } from '@material-ui/core/styles';
import Drawer from '@material-ui/core/Drawer';
import Toolbar from '@material-ui/core/Toolbar';
import { useRouteMatch } from 'react-router';
```

Okay, let's briefly explain a couple of the unfamiliar libraries we imported here before we proceed. We will start with the long-overdue <Link> from react-router-dom and the other ways of navigating paths in our app.

Navigating Path: <Link>

The <Link> from react-router-dom allows users to navigate the application and have pages re-rendered without a refresh. It allows for a declarative and easy navigation path around our app.

Some common ways we can use it:

- to: string: Created by concatenating the location's pathname, search, and hash properties. For example: <Link to="/products/?sort=name" />.

- to: object: This can be any of the following props: pathname, search, hash, and state.

- replace: bool: When true, clicking the link replaces the current entry in the history stack instead of adding a new one. For example: <Link to="/products" replace />.

- to: function: The current location is passed as an argument, and location representation should be returned as an object or string. For example:

  ```
  <Link to={location => ({ ...location, pathname: "/products" })} />
  <Link to={location => `${location.pathname}?sort=name`} />
  ```

React Hook: useRouteMatch

useRouteMatch is a Hook that we typically need when we are using <Route>. useRouteMatch allows us to access to a <match> object and use it inside the component; so instead of rendering a <Route>, just use useRouteMatch.

Okay, now that we've discussed some of the libraries we've imported here, let's now create our DashboardSidebarNavigation component.

Listing 5-15. Creating the DashboardSidebarNavigation Component

```
const DashboardSidebarNavigation = () => {
  const classes = useStyles();
  const { url } = useRouteMatch();

  useEffect(() => {}, []);

  return (

      <div className={classes.root}>
        <Drawer
          className={classes.drawer}
          variant="permanent"
          classes={{
            paper: classes.drawerPaper,
          }}
          anchor="left"
        >
          <Toolbar
            style={{ width: '6rem', height: 'auto' }}
            className={classes.toolbar}
          >
            <Link to={`${url}`} className={classes.logoWithLink}>
              Logo
            </Link>
          </Toolbar>

        </Drawer>
      </div>

  );
};

export default DashboardSidebarNavigation;
```

We're using styling from Material-UI Drawer and Toolbar and using the <Link> component as our navigation path.

The styling components are coming from Material-UI.

Listing 5-16. Styling the dashboard-sidebar-navigation Using Material-UI

```
const drawerWidth = 240;
const useStyles = makeStyles(theme =>
  createStyles({
    root: {
      display: 'flex',
    },
    drawer: {
      width: drawerWidth,
      flexShrink: 0,
    },
    drawerPaper: {
      width: drawerWidth,
    },
    drawerContainer: {
      overflow: 'auto',
    },
    toolbar: theme.mixins.toolbar,
    content: {
      flexGrow: 1,
      padding: theme.spacing(3),
    },
    link: { textDecoration: 'none', color: 'inherit' },
    logoWithLink: {
      display: 'flex',
      alignItems: 'center',
      textDecoration: 'none',
      color: 'inherit',
    },
  }),
);
```

After finishing the dashboard-sidebar-navigation.tsx, create an index.tsx under the dashboard-layout folder and copy the following code.

Listing 5-17. Creating the Dashboard Component

```
import React from 'react';
import { Grid } from '@material-ui/core';

import DashboardSidebarNavigation from './dashboard-sidebar-navigation';

type Props = {
  children: React.ReactNode;
};

const Dashboard = ({ children }: Props) => {
  return (
    <Grid
      container
      direction="row"
      justify="flex-start"
      alignItems="flex-start"
    >
      <DashboardSidebarNavigation /> {children}
    </Grid>
  );
};
export default Dashboard;
```

Dashboard Component

So what's going on here? We have the main Dashboard component and its children props, which are the main content pages. The children props have routers for users to navigate successfully from one view or page to another.

Bear in mind that the children parameter in the Dashboard is the entry point for React components. For example, if we pass a Button component in the Dashboard, it will be rendered beside the DashboardSidebarNavigation component.

We now have a reusable layout of the Dashboard that contains a DashboardSidebarNavigation.

As for the `<Grid>`, it is used for the positioning of the layouts. The grid's responsive layout, which is based on a 12-column grid layout, is quite powerful because it can adapt to any screen size and orientation.

Now that we already have the layout, the next step is to create a dashboard default component, which is the first thing that users will see in the Dashboard.

In views, create a new dashboard folder, and inside that create two new files: `dashboard-default-content.tsx` and `settings-and-privacy.tsx`.

The path looks like this:

```
Views ➤ dashboard ➤ dashboard-default-content.tsx
Views ➤ dashboard ➤ settings-and-privacy.tsx
```

Type in the snippet "rafce" to create a stateless arrow component and return an `<h1>` with the title heading the same as the component's name. See the following sample.

Also, make sure to rename and use the Pascal naming convention in the component's name.

Listing 5-18. Creating the DashboardDefaultContent Component

```
import React from 'react';

const DashboardDefaultContent = () => {
  return (
    <div>
      <h1>Dashboard Default Content</h1>
    </div>
  );
};

export default DashboardDefaultContent;
```

Do the same thing to the `settings-and-privacy.tsx` file.

Listing 5-19. Creating the SettingsAndPrivacy Component

```
import React from 'react';

const SettingsAndPrivacy = () => {
  return (
```

```
    <div>
      <h1>Settings and Privacy</h1>
    </div>
  );
};
```

```
export default SettingsAndPrivacy;
```

For now, we're just setting up the Dashboard and navigation without the styling because we just want to show a proof of concept that we're able to navigate successfully from one page to the next.

Now, let's define the path in our `routes.tsx`. But in this case, we will be using render props.

Render Props

On the website `www.reactjs.org`, the term *render props* refers to "a technique for sharing code between React components using a prop whose value is a function."

Okay, simply, it means that our Route component has a render prop that takes a function as a value. The Route component then uses that function to render whatever the function provides – in our case, the Dashboard.

We're just reusing code, actually, in an efficient way.

Listing 5-20. Using the Render Props in routes.tsx

```
<Route path={'/dashboard'}
               render={(({match: {path}}) => (
                   <Dashboard>
                       <Switch>
                           <Route exact path={path + '/'}
                               component={DashboardDefaultContent}/>

    <Route exact path={path + '/settings-and-privacy'}
               component={SettingsAndPrivacy}/>

                       </Switch>
                   </Dashboard>
               )}>
  </Route>
```

In the React Router library, the `<Route />` carries the behavior of navigating to different views or pages. It renders the component when the path matches.

Next, let's update the `dashboard-sidebar-navigation.tsx` to add the settings and privacy button and a logout button.

For a bit of styling, first, let's import the components, as shown in Listing 5-21, from Material-UI to our `dashboard-sidebar-navigation.tsx`.

Listing 5-21. Importing the Material-UI Components to dashboard-sidebar-navigation.tsx

```
import { List, ListItem, ListItemIcon, ListItemText } from '@material-ui/
core';
import ExitToAppIcon from '@material-ui/icons/ExitToApp';
import SettingsIcon from '@material-ui/icons/Settings';
```

The additional styling components for the dashboard sidebar navigation are as shown in Listing 5-22.

Right after the </Toolbar> and still within the <Drawer />, add the following code:

Listing 5-22. Additional Components and Styling for dashboard-sidebar-navigation.tsx

```
<return (
        <div className={classes.root}>
          <Drawer
            className={classes.drawer}
            variant="permanent"
            classes={{
              paper: classes.drawerPaper,
            }}
            anchor="left"
          >
            <Toolbar
              style={{ width: '6rem', height: 'auto' }}
              className={classes.toolbar}
            >
```

```
      <Link to={`${url}`} className={classes.logoWithLink}>
        Logo
      </Link>
    </Toolbar>
    <div className={classes.drawerContainer}>
      <List>
        <Link className={classes.link} to={`${url}/settings-and-
        privacy`}>
          <ListItem button>
            <ListItemIcon>
              <SettingsIcon />
            </ListItemIcon>
            <ListItemText primary={'settings and privacy'} />
          </ListItem>
        </Link>
        <a className={classes.link} href={'/'}>
          <ListItem button>
            <ListItemIcon>
              <ExitToAppIcon />
            </ListItemIcon>
            <ListItemText primary={'logout'} />
          </ListItem>
        </a>
      </List>
    </div>
  </Drawer>
</div>

  );
};
```

If you click the Dashboard button in our UI, you should be able to see the following additional components:

settings and privacy

logout

Figure 5-10. *Dashboard Default Content UI*

If you click settings and privacy, you should successfully navigate to that page. The same goes for when you click Home, About, or Login – the last one is currently just a 404 page because we haven't built that one yet. Also, logout, for now, is just basically refreshing the page.

Going into React.lazy( )

But wait. We're not done yet. We can still improve our route navigation. And we can do this with the help of lazy loading, which is one of the most effective ways to speed up our bundles' loading times.

So what is lazy loading?

The concept of lazy loading is easy to understand. It is merely rendering first what is essential to the user interface while quietly loading nonessential sections or items as needed.

Lazy loading in React is a relatively new feature that was released in version 16.6.0. It has come about as applications have become more complex, powerful, and massive, leading to increased loading times and negatively impacting the user experience.

And as a best practice, we should always need to consider users, including those using mobile data and slow Internet connection.

Note   React.lazy(), which is now fully integrated into the core React library, has replaced a third-party library react-loadable.

But use react-loadable for server-side code-splitting since React.lazy () and Suspense are not yet available for server-side rendering.

React lazy loading allows us to load components slowly or gradually using **code-splitting** without installing additional libraries. This approach enables us to render the necessary or only critical interface items at initial loading times while lazily and quietly unrolling the other sections as needed.

According to the official React docs, the best way to do code-splitting in our React app is through the dynamic import () syntax. Eager loading is the default behavior of our web app, meaning if you download all the page resources, for example, the Home Page, then everything will be downloaded in one go.

The potential problem with this is that it can create a bottleneck if the application is huge – hence, we need to do code-splitting.

Let's show some sample codes before and after code-splitting.

Listing 5-23. Showing Eager Loading vs. Lazy Loading

```
import MyComponent from './MyComponent';

function OneComponent() {
    return (
        <div>
            <MyComponent />
        </div>
    );
}

const MyComponent = React.lazy(() => import('./MyComponent'));

function OneComponent() {
    return (
        <div>
            <MyComponent />
        </div>
    );
}
```

Note that components created using React.lazy() need to be wrapped in React. Suspense, so let's review that now.

React Suspense

Suspense acts like placeholder content while the lazy components are loaded. Note that we can wrap several lazy components at various hierarchy levels with just a single Suspense component.

A little caveat: In the official React docs, Suspense is still an experimental API and could still undergo some changes until such time when the React team says it's fully complete for production-ready work.

However, this notice, which has been on for a couple of years, has not deterred React developers from using React.lazy() and Suspense in big applications or production-level apps.

Tip: For the best user experience, wrap your lazy component in an error boundary `<ErrorBoundary />` if it fails to load.

Let's take a look at the DevTools and show the eager loading of the Home Page and About Page. Everything is loaded at one go, as shown in Figure 5-11.

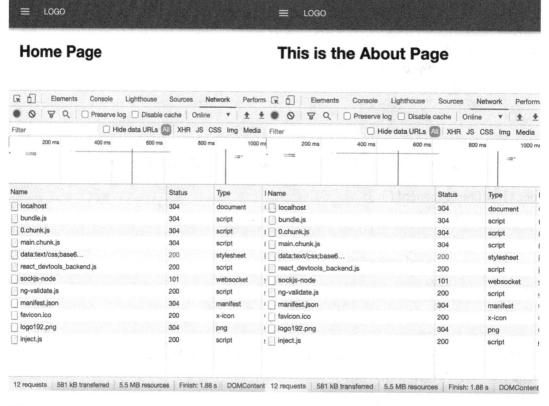

Figure 5-11. *A screenshot of eager loading of the Home Page and About Page in DevTools*

You'll see that ALL components are loaded even at the app's initial loading. This means that even if you navigate from the Home Page to the About Page, nothing new is added.

So now, let's see the difference between a component that is eager loading and one that is lazy loading.

Eager Loading vs. Lazy Loading

Now, let's compare a component that is wrapped in lazy loading against an eager loading component.

In our routes.tsx, import the named components:

```
import React, {lazy, Suspense}from 'react';
```

But before we can compare the two components, we need to wrap our lazy component with React Suspense. So let's do that now.

Next, for our comparison, we will put on lazy load the following components: **About and Dashboard**.

Listing 5-24. Lazy Loading the Components About and Dashboard for Comparison

```
const Routes = () => {
  return (
    <Suspense>
    <Switch>
      {/*eager loading */}
      <Route exact path="/" component={Home} />

      {/*lazy loading */}
      <Route exact path="/about" component={AboutPage} />

      {/*lazy loadings*/}
        <Route
         exact path={'/about'}
          component={lazy(() => import('./views/pages/AboutPage'))}
          />
```

```
<Route
    exact path={'/dashboard'}
  render={(({ match: { path } }) => (
    <Dashboard>
      <Switch>
        <Route
          path={path + '/'}
          component={lazy(
            () => import('./views/dashboard/dashboard-default-
            content'), )}
        />

        <Route
          exact
          path={path + '/settings-and-privacy'}
          component={SettingsAndPrivacy}
        />
      </Switch>
    </Dashboard>
  )}
></Route>

<Route exact path="/not-found" component={NotFoundPage} />
<Redirect from={'*'} to={'/not-found'} exact />
</Switch>

</Suspense>
  );
};
```

BUT wait. If you look at the browser, you'll see the following error.

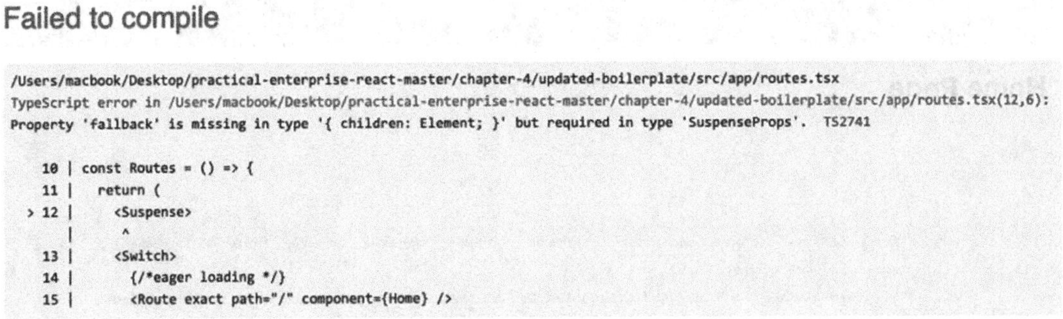

Failed to compile

```
/Users/macbook/Desktop/practical-enterprise-react-master/chapter-4/updated-boilerplate/src/app/routes.tsx
TypeScript error in /Users/macbook/Desktop/practical-enterprise-react-master/chapter-4/updated-boilerplate/src/app/routes.tsx(12,6):
Property 'fallback' is missing in type '{ children: Element; }' but required in type 'SuspenseProps'.  TS2741

    10 | const Routes = () => {
    11 |   return (
  > 12 |     <Suspense>
       |      ^
    13 |     <Switch>
    14 |       {/*eager loading */}
    15 |       <Route exact path="/" component={Home} />
```

Figure 5-12. *Failed to Compile React Suspense*

This is because Suspense requires the property "fallback."

React looks up the tree, encounters the first <Suspense> component, and renders its fallback.

Use the required Suspense prop called fallback and don't forget to import the named component too. The LinearProgress bar is from Material-UI.

Listing 5-25. Using the Suspense Prop fallback

```
...
import { LinearProgress } from '@material-ui/core';

export const Routes = () => {
  return (
    <Suspense fallback={<LinearProgress style={{ margin: '10rem' }} />}>
```

Okay, that should make our Suspense component working now. You can also lazy load the settings and privacy, but make sure to leave the Home Page on eager loading so we can see the comparison.

Refresh the browser. Open the DevTools while refreshing the Home Page, as shown in Figure 5-13.

Home Page

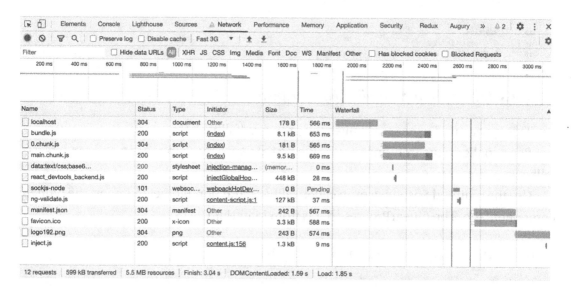

Figure 5-13. *Eager loading of the Home Page at initial loading time*

But when you click the lazy-loaded About Page, you can see that the highlighted portions are just the ones added. The highlighted parts were not initially rendered on the Home Page because they were not needed yet. See Figure 5-14.

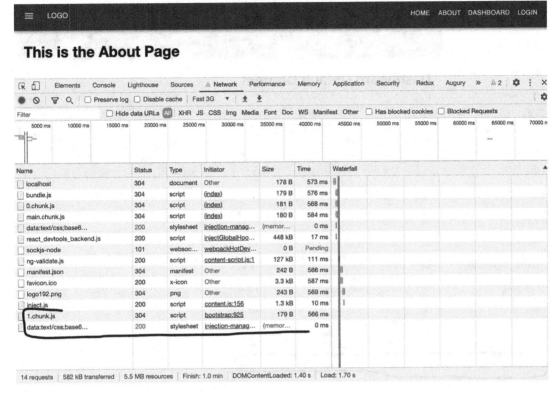

Figure 5-14. *Lazy loading the About Page*

You'll notice the same when you click the lazy-loaded Dashboard. See Figure 5-15.

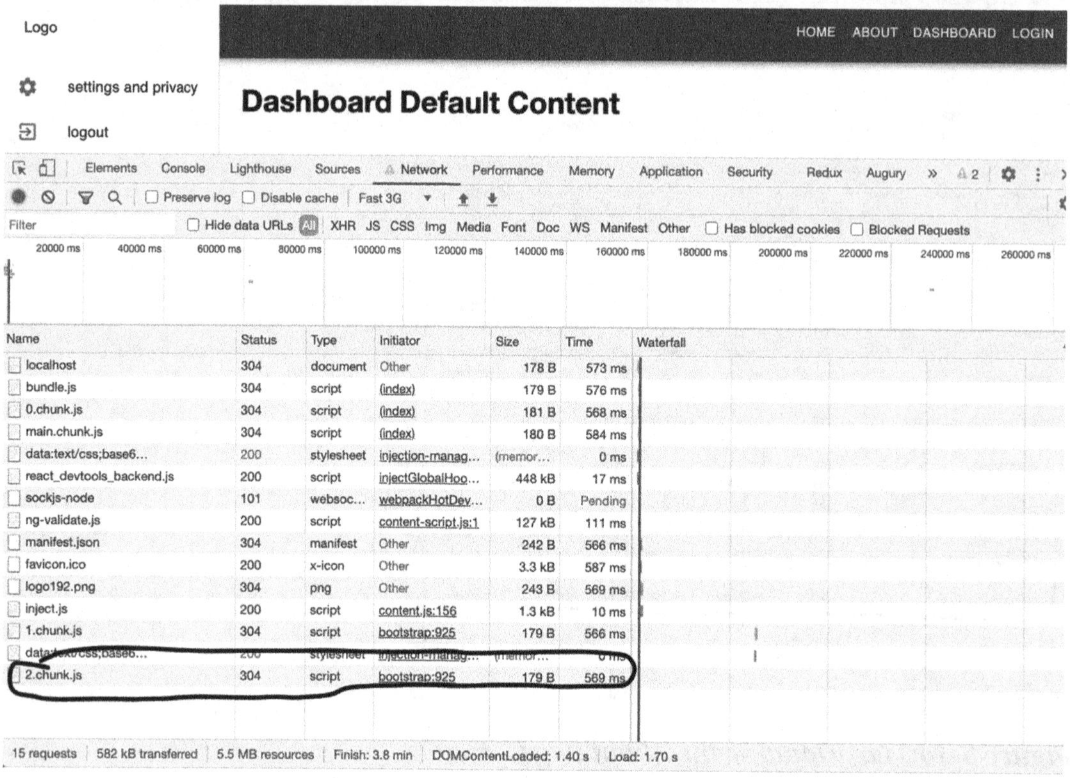

Figure 5-15. *Lazy loading the Dashboard*

The highlighted portion was the only thing loaded when we navigated from the About Page to the Dashboard page.

You might think that the file and time to load may be insignificant or small, but imagine if your app already got massive lines of codes and you've got 50 pages or more. Your user, especially on a mobile app or a slow Internet connection, would feel it.

Summary

I hope by now you have a fair idea of how client-side routing works in general and how to implement routing in React using the React Router library. We've also touched on how to use lazy loading in our app to turbo-charge our initial loading times with the end goal of improving user experience.

In the next chapter, we will tackle writing local states, sending HTTP requests, and using ApexCharts.

CHAPTER 6

Writing Local States, Sending HTTP Requests, and ApexCharts

In the previous chapter, we tackled navigation using `react-router`. Now, we'll be writing local states, sending HTTP requests using Axios, and installing ApexCharts to help us create an interactive chart in our app.

HTTP requests are essential parts of any web app communicating with a back-end server; meanwhile, a local state in React, as the name suggests, is handled locally or in isolation within a component. Any change in the state must be set or the state will be re-rendered using the setState function.

Axios and Fetch API are two of the most popular methods of how we can consume REST APIs. Axios is a promise-based HTTP client, while Fetch API is native to JavaScript and a built-in HTTP client in modern browsers.

In this chapter, we will do our best to stay organized and DRY (short for Don't Repeat Yourself) using Axios for API requests. The DRY concept in programming is the process of abstraction to avoid repetition of code. Since, technically, we don't have a back-end server, we will also create a fake Rest API using a JSON server.

ApexCharts is an open source charting library that we will be using to create modern-looking and interactive visualizations for our web page.

But before we start writing local states and sending HTTP requests, we will do some refactoring in our compiler options in TypeScript.

This is more for our personal preferences when using TypeScript in our application. Yes, we love the type safety features that TypeScript gives us that JavaScript cannot; however, we also do not want to lose the flexibility that JavaScript provides when developing our application. In short, we want the best of both worlds.

91

© Devlin Basilan Duldulao, Ruby Jane Leyva Cabagnot 2021
D. B. Duldulao and R. J. L. Cabagnot, *Practical Enterprise React*, https://doi.org/10.1007/978-1-4842-6975-6_6

It is up to you whether you will opt out of the default strict type-checking options in TypeScript or not. There are two ways we can go about it.

Strict Type-Checking Options in TypeScript

As mentioned, there are two ways on how we personally use or set the type-checking options in TypeScript in our application.

The first one is to set or change the value to "false." And to do this, in your project app, open the tsconfig.json file and look under the "compilerOptions". Set the strict value flag to false.

Listing 6-1. tsconfig.json File

```
{
  "compilerOptions": {
    "target": "es5",
    "lib": ["dom", "dom.iterable", "esnext"],
    "allowJs": true,
    "skipLibCheck": true,
    "esModuleInterop": true,
    "allowSyntheticDefaultImports": true,
    "strict": false,
    "forceConsistentCasingInFileNames": true,
    "module": "esnext",
    "moduleResolution": "node",
    "resolveJsonModule": true,
    "isolatedModules": true,
    "noEmit": true,
    "noFallthroughCasesInSwitch": true,
    "jsx": "react",
    "baseUrl": "./src"
  },
  "include": ["src"]
}
```

By default, the strict mode in the compilerOptions in tsconfig.json is set to true. It means all codes or files in the application will be validated or type-checked using the strict mode.

You can check out www.typescriptlang.org/tsconfig for more tsconfig reference.

But Figure 6-1 is a brief description of the type-check flags.

```
/* Strict Type-Checking Options */
"strict": true
/* Enable all strict type-checking options. Setting. all the flags below to true */

// "noImplicitAny": true,
/* Raise error on expressions and declarations with an implied 'any' type. */

// "strictNullChecks": true,
/* Enable strict null checks. Null and undefined values are not valid values in types

// "noImplicitThis": true,
/* Raise error on 'this' expressions with an implied 'any' type. */

// "alwaysStrict": true,
/* Parse in strict mode and emit "use strict" for each source file. */
```

Figure 6-1. *Type-checking option flags*

The second way is to sometimes opt out of the type-checking options in TypeScript and to allow the default value of strict, which is true, but add the following to the compilerOptions:

```
"noImplicitAny": false,
"strictNullChecks": false,

    ...
    "strict": true
```

TypeScript Tips

⚠ Typescript recommends putting on the strict mode **true** especially for new projects.

⚠ For JS projects migrating to Typescript, strict mode set to **true** can be used while the rest of flags set to **false**, especially if you're getting a lot of type errors.

Adding Fake Data Using json-server

The main benefit of using our own fake REST API is decoupling the front-end and back-end development work. If separate teams were working on the front end and the back end, the teams would only need to discuss and agree on JSON structures before they can work independently on their ends.

On the front end, using fake data can speed up the development process; no need to wait for the back end to finish building the real APIs.

And the setup? It lets us serve JSON from our file system through a local server.

Let's go to our `package.json` file to check on our `json-server` as a devDependency:

```
"devDependencies":{
"concurrently": "5.3.0",
"cypress": "6.0.0",
"json-server": "0.16.3",
"json-server-auth": "2.0.2" } }
```

`Json-server` is a fake Node.js server that gets scaffolded just by running the `json-server`. In `npmjs.com`, `json-server` is described as getting a "full fake REST API with zero coding in less than 30 seconds." And yes, based on experience, it does its job quite well.

Let's run it to test. Add the following code to your script:

```
"backend": "json-server --watch db.json --port 5000 --delay=1000"
```

In the terminal, run $ npm run backend.

You'll see the following resource endpoints.

```
Resources
http://localhost:5000/posts
http://localhost:5000/comments
http://localhost:5000/profile

Home
http://localhost:5000
```

Figure 6-2. *Default endpoints*

Let's check the http://localhost:5000/posts. It's formatted that way because of the JSONView Chrome extension that was installed. It reformats JSON response in the browser instead of one long line of string, much like Prettier in our editor. This extension is also available in the Firefox browser.

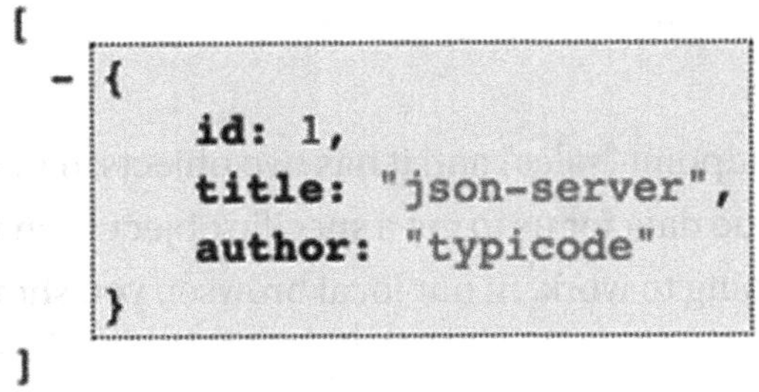

```
[
  - {
      id: 1,
      title: "json-server",
      author: "typicode"
    }
]
```

Figure 6-3. *Rendering the localhost:5000/posts*

Now, let's go back to our project; you'll notice that a new file called db.json has been auto-generated for us in the root directory. Open it, and you'll see the sample endpoints.

Now that we've seen that it is working, let's replace the auto-generated endpoints with our own fake data. Copy the following data.

Listing 6-2. db.json Server Fake Data

```json
{
  "sales": [
    {
      "id": "sgacus86fov",
      "name": "This week",
      "data": [30, 40, 25, 50, 49, 21, 70, 51]
    },
    {
      "id": "saftyaf56",
      "name": "Last week",
      "data": [23, 12, 54, 61, 32, 56, 81, 19]
    }
  ]
}
```

Listing 6-2 has the endpoint "sales", and it has two objects, namely, "This week" and "Last week". It has unique data for us to get a specific object from the array. Let's try if localhost:5000/sales is going to work. In our local browser, you should see the response like in Figure 6-4.

```
[
  - {
      id: "sgacus86fov",
      name: "This week",
    - data: [
        30,
        40,
        25,
        50,
        49,
        21,
        70,
        51
      ]
    },
  - {
      id: "saftyaf56",
      name: "Last week",
    - data: [
        23,
        12,
        54,
        61,
        32,
        56,
        81,
        19
      ]
    }
]
```

Figure 6-4. *Rendering data*

Sending HTTP Requests Using Axios

Creating an instance of axios is extremely useful when building complex or large applications, especially when we need to integrate with multiple APIs. Implementing the default Axios instance can be cumbersome at times or would mean duplicating code throughout our app.

Some examples of when you might implement instances:

- Building a full URL from a path

- Assigning default headers

- Caching

- Global handling of network errors

- Setting the Authorization header on requests automatically

- Normalizing and managing error responses

- Converting the request and response body

- Refreshing access tokens and retrying requests

- Setting a custom instance

Now that we have that, let's create our axios configuration. Create a new file called axios.ts. The file path is src/api/axios.ts.

Listing 6-3. axios.ts

```
import axios from 'axios';

/*create an instance of axios with a default base URI when sending HTTP
requests*/
/*JSON Server has CORS Policy by default*/

const api = axios.create({ baseURL: 'http://localhost:5000/', });

 export default api;

 export const EndPoints = { sales: 'sales', };
```

We import axios from axios, and we're using the create function of axios, which will create an instance of axios and put in our variable called api.

Within the instance api, there's an option to pass an object of our configuration.

Currently, our default configuration is the localhost:5000/. The localhost:5000 as the baseURL is the default URL for any HTTP request within axios. Basically, it is the consistent or permanent part of the web address.

Creating a baseURL in one location offers us the ability to edit it easily as needed and be DRY in our app development. We don't need to type repeatedly the baseURL of our API every time we create an HTTP request.

We just need to pass the endpoint (i.e., sales) of the api. See the sample in Figure 6-5. This will also help us avoid committing typo errors when typing our endpoints.

```
api.get(Endpoints.sales);
```

Figure 6-5. *How to use the api endpoints*

There are a lot of options you can use inside our axios object. We get this built-in IntelliSense because axios was built using TypeScript.

```
const api = axios.create({
  baseURL: 'http://localhost:5000/',
} (property) AxiosRequestConfig.ad ×      ⊘ auth?
  apter?: AxiosAdapter                    ⊘ cancelToken?
                                          ⊘ data?
                                          ⊘ decompress?
export const EndPoints = {               ⊘ headers?
  sales: 'sales',                         ⊘ httpAgent?
};                                        ⊘ httpsAgent?
                                          ⊘ maxBodyLength?
                                          ⊘ maxContentLength?
IAL   PROBLEMS  2   OUTPUT  DEBUG CONSOLE  ⊘ maxRedirects?
                                          ⊘ method?
                                          ⊘ onDownloadProgress?
)e s + enter at any time to create a snapshot
```

Figure 6-6. *Option configurations for the axios object*

Okay, we're done with that for now. We'll keep on updating our axios file as we create more endpoints.

Shaping the Object

In TypeScript, we pass data through *object types,* whereas in JavaScript, we group and represent data through *objects*. Simply put, *types* let us know what an item looks like: **string, number, boolean, array, function**, etc.

Recall the two approaches to shaping our object in TypeScript: **interface** and **type alias**. They are more or less the same; it is just a matter of preference what you choose.

Since we're using TypeScript, we need to define the shape or type of our object. First, create a new file and name it `sale-type.ts.`

Listing 6-4. Creating the Shape or Model of Our Object

`src/models/sale-type.ts`

Our sale object's shape or model has type string and data of type array of numbers:

```
//type alias

type SaleType = {
  name: string;
  data: number[];
}
```

Making Requests with Axios

Before we proceed, let's review a little what axios is. Axios is a promise-based HTTP client for the browser and Node.js. It allows us to intercept and cancel requests and provides a built-in feature called client-side protection against cross-site request forgery.

Let's create a new file and name it saleService.ts:

`src/services/saleService.ts`

We'll import our recently created file api/axios, the endpoints from TypeScript configuration, and the model sale-type.

Listing 6-5. Sending Http Requests

```
import api, { EndPoints } from 'api/axios';
import { SaleType } from 'models/sale-type';

export async function getSalesAxios() {
  return await api.get<SaleType[]>(EndPoints.sales);
}

/* Other commonly-used api methods:
  api.post
  api.put
  api.delete
  api.patch
*/

/* The < > bracket here is a Generic type that Typescript adapted from OOP.
  It means that the return value of the getSalesAxios is an array of
  SaleType.
  This would likewise help us with the TypeScript intell-sense when using it.
*/
```

The async-await just means that the axios function is promise-based.

Now, let's test our api.get request.

Go to src/app/views/dashboard/dashboard-default-content.tsx.

We will do additional magic here, and for that, we'll use the lifecycle Hook useEffect from React.

Import the named component from React.

Again, useEffect is a lifecycle Hook that runs after a React component is rendered. Inside this hook, we will invoke the getSalesAxios().

Make sure to import the component from services/saleService.

Listing 6-6. Calling the getSalesAxios in DashboardDefaultContent

```
import React, {useEffect} from 'react';
import { getSalesAxios } from 'services/saleService';

const DashboardDefaultContent = () => {
  useEffect(() => {
  //code to run after render goes here

    getSalesAxios();
  }, []);  //&#xOODF; empty array means to 'run once'

  return (
    <div>
      <h1>Dashboard Default Content</h1>
    </div>
  );
};
export default DashboardDefaultContent;
```

Tips   Pass an empty array [ ] in the useEffect as a second argument to limit its run or to run the useEffect only once, after the first render.

Next, open two terminals and do the following:

```
$ npm run start
$ npm run backend
```

Refresh our browser at localhost:3000/ and open the Chrome DevTools and make sure you are at the Network tab and XHR. We're doing all these so-called baby-step processes on how I build an application.

Try to execute the low-level hanging fruit first, maybe write a lot of proof of concept, or check at the DevTools if everything is firing the way it should be.

Anyway, in your browser, click the Menu tab ➤ Dashboard.

Observe your Chrome DevTools; you should see the Response Method: Get and Status Code: `200 OK`.

Click the Response tab to see the sale object data from the `json-server`.

So now we are confident that the UI is receiving data from the `json-server`. We sent the HTTP request and received JSON response from the json-server.

BUT since we might need to wrap the getSalesAxios in an async-await, we will invoke it outside of the `useEffect`.

We'll deal with the `useEffect()` in a short while.

⚠ Don't declare async-await inside the useEffect. We cannot assign any promise based parameter inside the EffectCallback. Otherwise you will get the following error:

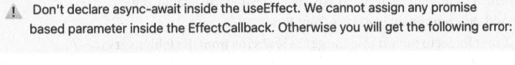

```
4    const DashboardDefaultContent = () => {
5        useEffect(( async () => {
```

ⓧ dashboard-default-content.tsx 1 of 3 problems   ⌄ ⌃ ✕

```
Argument of type 'undefined[]' is not assignable to parameter of type 'EffectCallback'.
Type 'undefined[]' provides no match for the signature '(): void | (() => void)'. ts(2
```

Figure 6-7. *Showing an error when using async inside the EffectCallback*

So let's create an awaitable function outside the useEffect and name it `fetchSales`.

Listing 6-7. Creating the fetchSales Function

```
const fetchSales = async () => {

    const data = await getSalesAxios();
    console.log(data);
}
```

We deconstructed the response to get just the data property and named it "data."

Next, make sure to call the newly created function inside the `useEffect`. This is what I meant when I said we'll be using the `useEffect()` in a short while.

Listing 6-8. Calling fetchSales in useEffect

```
const DashboardDefaultContent = () => {
  useEffect(() => {
    fetchSales();
  }, []);
```

Refresh the browser and make sure to open the Chrome DevTools again, and you should get a response from the json-server successfully.

Now that we know that we can retrieve data from the json-server, the next thing to do is create a local state using useState in the DashboardDefaultContent.

Add the component useState from React.

Don't forget to import also the getSalesAxios from the folder services/ saleService.

Listing 6-9. Creating a Local State

```
import { SaleType } from 'models/sale-type';
import React, { useEffect, useState } from 'react';
import { getSalesAxios } from 'services/saleService';

const DashboardDefaultContent = () => {

const [sales, setSales] = useState<SaleType[]>([]);
```

How do we update the value or data of the setSales?

In our fetchSales component, let's call setSales and pass the data with the same type of object in our useState.

Listing 6-10. Updating the Data of setSales

```
const fetchSales = async () => {
    const { data } = await getSalesAxios();
    console.log(data);   // ← to check in the console if we are
    successfully getting the data
    setSales(data);
  };
```

Okay, like I said before, I will often do this little proof of concept before I proceed.

Let's check if we're really passing data to the setSales. Inside our HTML, type an h2 header and render the length of the sales array.

Listing 6-11. Rendering the setSales

```
return (
    <div>
      <h1>Dashboard Default Content</h1>
      <h2>{sales.length}</h2>
    </div>
  );
};
```

When you check the browser, you should see **2** because our sales array contains two objects. Go to Chrome DevTools ➤ Network to see the objects.

Now that we know that it's working, the next plan is to improve the Dashboard Default Content.

In the components folder, let's create a template for the web page. The template page will contain the set padding, spacing, and other styling to be applied to every page in our app.

The file path is src ➤ app ➤ components ➤ pages.tsx.

Import the following components:

```
import React,{ forwardRef, HTMLProps, ReactNode }from 'react'
import { Helmet } from 'react-helmet-async';
```

Let's review some of the components here.

Forwarding Refs: This is adding a reference to the HTML. In reactjs.org, it says that it is a technique for automatically passing a ref through a component to one of its children, such as forwarding refs to DOM components or forwarding refs to higher-order components (HOCs).

Helmet: To add some tagging and allow us to build an SEO-friendly application.

Next, we'll define our typings or type definition in Listing 6-12.

Listing 6-12. Defining the Type Alias

```
type Props = {
  children?: ReactNode;
  title?: string;
} & HTMLProps<HTMLDivElement>;
```

We're making our prop children of type ReactNode and prop title of type string, both nullable by appending ?. We're also using HTMLProps of type HTMLDivElement.

And here's our Page component, which would be a reusable template for all our web pages.

Listing 6-13. Creating a Reusable Page Component

```
const Page = forwardRef<HTMLDivElement, Props>(
  ({ children, title = '', ...rest }, ref) => {
    return (
      <div ref={ref as any} {...rest}>
        <Helmet>
          <title>{title}</title>
        </Helmet>
        {children}
      </div>
    );
  },
);
export default Page;
```

That's done for now.

Let's go back to our DashboardDefaultContent component and add more styling to the Dashboard.

Add the following styling component to the DashboardDefaultContent.

The styling includes chart styling theme for charts, background colors, data tables, legends, stroke them tooltip, x-axis and y-axis, etc. You can read more about this on the Material-UI website. It's a bit long, so just bear with me:

```
const useStyles = makeStyles(() => ({
  root: {
    minHeight: '100%',
  },
}));

const getChartStyling = (theme: Theme) => ({
  chart: {
    background: theme.palette.background.paper,
    toolbar: {
      show: false,
    },
  },
  colors: ['#13affe', '#fbab49'],
  dataLabels: {
    enabled: false,
  },
  grid: {
    borderColor: theme.palette.divider,
    yaxis: {
      lines: {
        show: false,
      },
    },
  },
  legend: {
    show: true,
    labels: {
      colors: theme.palette.text.secondary,
    },
  },
  plotOptions: {
    bar: {
      columnWidth: '40%',
    },
  },
```

```
stroke: {
  show: true,
  width: 2,
  colors: ['transparent'],
},
theme: {
  mode: theme.palette.type,
},
tooltip: {
  theme: theme.palette.type,
},
xaxis: {
  axisBorder: {
    show: true,
    color: theme.palette.divider,
  },
  axisTicks: {
    show: true,
    color: theme.palette.divider,
  },
  categories: ['Sun', 'Mon', 'Tue', 'Wed', 'Thu', 'Fri', 'Sat', 'Sun'],
  labels: {
    style: {
      colors: theme.palette.text.secondary,
    },
  },
},
yaxis: {
  axisBorder: {
    show: true,
    color: theme.palette.divider,
  },
  axisTicks: {
    show: true,
    color: theme.palette.divider,
```

```
    },
    labels: {
      style: {
        colors: theme.palette.text.secondary,
      },
    },
  },
});
```

To use it in our React component, we need to import Theme and makeStyles from Material-UI:

```
import { Theme } from '@material-ui/core/styles';
import { makeStyles } from '@material-ui/styles';
```

Then, let's create two variables inside the DashboardDefaultContent – classes and theme – and assign useStyles and useTheme styles, respectively.

Listing 6-14. Adding useStyles and useTheme

```
const DashboardDefaultContent = () => {
  const classes = useStyles();
  const theme = useTheme();

  const [sales, setSales] = useState<SaleType[]>([]);

  useEffect(() => {
    fetchSales();
  }, []);

  const fetchSales = async () => {
    const { data } = await getSalesAxios();
    setSales(data);
  };
```

After setting all that up, the next thing we need to do is install ApexCharts.

Installing ApexCharts

ApexCharts is an open source and modern JS charting library for building interactive charts and visualizations using APIs. Various modern browsers support it. Let's install that:

```
npm install react-apexcharts apexcharts
```

Go back to the DashboardDefaultContent and import ApexCharts and some other style components from the Material-UI Core library.

Listing 6-15. Importing Additional Material-UI Components

```
import chart from 'react-apexcharts';
import {
  Box,
  Card,
  CardContent,
  Container,
  Grid,
  Typography,
  useTheme,
} from '@material-ui/core';
```

Now that that's done, we'll add the Page component we've created earlier:

```
import Page from 'app/components/page';
```

Use the Page component and the chart we've created. Replace the return <div> header in the Page component with the following code.

Listing 6-16. Updating the Page Component

```
<Page className={classes.root} title="Dashboard">
    <Container maxWidth={'sm'}>
      <Typography variant="h4" color="textPrimary">
        Dashboard
      </Typography>
      <Box my={5}>
```

```
<Grid container spacing={3}>
  <Grid item xs={12}>
    <Card>
      <CardContent>
<Typography variant="h5"  color="textPrimary">
        Sales
      </Typography>
      <Chart
        options={getChartStyling(theme)}
        series={sales}
        type="bar"
        height={'100%'}
      />
      </CardContent>
    </Card>
  </Grid>
</Grid>
</Box>
</Container>
```

So we're reusing the Page component and giving it the title "Dashboard."
The Container, along with other style components, sets the look and feel of the
DashboardDefaultContent page.

Run the application, and you should see these changes in the browser.

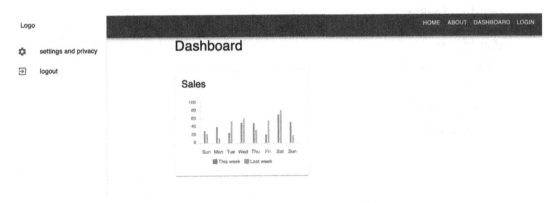

Figure 6-8. *Rendering the updated Page component*

There's still a long way to go, but we're getting there to complete our Dashboard page.

Before that, go to src ➤ index.ts, and delete the <React.StrictMode> so we don't get unnecessary warnings and errors while developing our application:

```
const ConnectedApp = ({ Component }: Props) => (
  <Provider store={store}>
    <HelmetProvider>
        <Component />
    </HelmetProvider>
  </Provider>
);
```

Next, open the file src/app/index.tsx and remove the <NavigationBar/> because we will replace it with a new layout component:

```
export function App() {
  return (
    <BrowserRouter>
      <Helmet
        titleTemplate="%s - React Boilerplate"
        defaultTitle="React Boilerplate"
      >
        <meta name="description" content="A React Boilerplate application" />
      </Helmet>

      <NavigationBar />

      <Container>
        <Routes />
      </Container>
      <GlobalStyle />
    </BrowserRouter>
  );
}
```

Creating the Main Layout

Inside the layouts directory, let's create a new folder and name it main-layout. Under the main-layout directory, create its index.tsx file. The following is the file path.

Listing 6-17. Creating a New Main-Layout Component Page

src ➤ app ➤ layouts ➤ main-layout ➤ index.tsx

Copy the following code to the index.tsx:

```tsx
import React, { ReactNode } from 'react';
import { makeStyles } from '@material-ui/core';

import NavigationBar from './navigation-bar';

type Props = {
  children?: ReactNode;
};

const MainLayout = ({ children }: Props) => {
  const classes = useStyles();

  return (

      <NavigationBar />
      <div className={classes.root}>
        <div className={classes.wrapper}>
          <div className={classes.contentContainer}>
            <div className={classes.content}>{children}</div>
          </div>
        </div>
      </div>

  );
};

const useStyles = makeStyles(theme => ({
  root: {
    backgroundColor: theme.palette.background.default,
    display: 'flex',
```

```
    height: '100%',
    overflow: 'hidden',
    width: '100%',
  },
  wrapper: {
    display: 'flex',
    flex: '1 1 auto',
    overflow: 'hidden',
    paddingTop: 64,
  },
  contentContainer: {
    display: 'flex',
    flex: '1 1 auto',
    overflow: 'hidden',
  },
  content: {
    flex: '1 1 auto',
    height: '100%',
    overflow: 'auto',
  },
}));

export default MainLayout;
```

Before we run again or check the browser if everything is still working, we will do a minor folder restructuring.

Put the navigation-bar.tsx, which is inside the components folder, under the newly created main-layout folder.

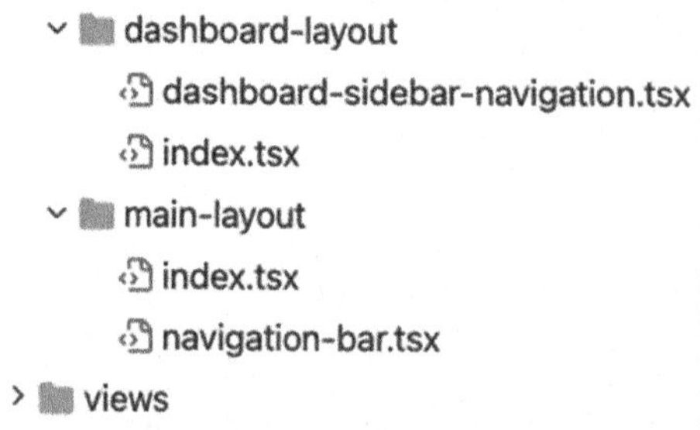

Figure 6-9. *Moving the navigation-bar.tsx inside the main-layout folder*

After doing that, go to the index.tsx of the app root folder:

Src ➤ app ➤ index.tsx

We will replace the <Container> with the <MainLayout> that we've just created. And don't forget to import the named component.

Listing 6-18. Using the MainLayout in the index.tsx of app

```
...
import MainLayout from './layouts/main-layout';
...

    <MainLayout>
      <Routes />
    </MainLayout>
```

Refresh your browser at http://localhost:3000/dashboard, and you should notice some changes in the styling and spacing.

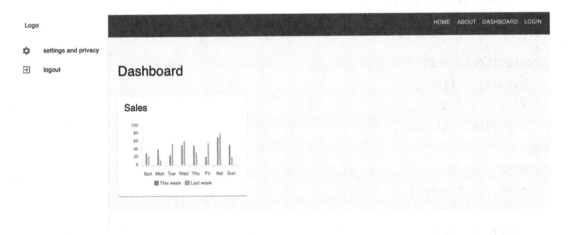

Figure 6-10. *Rendering the updated MainLayout*

Next, let's go back to the index.tsx file of the dashboard-layout folder. We will add a few styling, including the spacing and layout. Let's import the makeStyles from the Material-UI Core styles:

```
import {makeStyles} from '@material-ui/core/styles';
```

And then, add the following code for the styling.

Listing 6-19. Adding Styling to the index.tsx of dashboard-layout

```
const useStyles = makeStyles(theme => ({
  root: {
    display: 'flex',
    height: '100%',
    overflow: 'hidden',
    width: '100%',
  },
  wrapper: {
    display: 'flex',
    flex: '1 1 auto',
    overflow: 'hidden',
    paddingTop: 64,
    [theme.breakpoints.up('lg')]: {
      paddingLeft: 256,
    },
  },
  contentContainer: {
    display: 'flex',
    flex: '1 1 auto',
    overflow: 'hidden',
  },
  content: {
    flex: '1 1 auto',
    height: '100%',
    overflow: 'auto',
  },
}));
```

Next, add the useStyles and wrap the {children} in <div>.

Listing 6-20. Adding the useStyles Component to the index.tsx of the dashboard-layout

```
const classes = useStyles()

...
<DashboardSidebarNavigation />{' '}
    <div className={classes.wrapper}>
      <div className={classes.contentContainer}>
        <div className={classes.content}>{children}</div>
      </div>
    </div>
```

Check the Dashboard, and you should see a better and responsive layout.

Using React Feather Icons

Last but not least, we'll add a menu in the sidebar dashboard. We'll use the React Feather icons.

Feather - Simply beautiful open source icons

Feather is a collection of simply beautiful open source icons. Each icon is designed on a 24x24 grid with an emphasis on simplicity,

🖋 https://feathericons.com/

Install the React Feather library:

```
npm i react-feather
```

After installation, open the `dashboard-sidebar-navigation.tsx` and import the PieChart component from react-feather. We'll just rename it as `PieChartIcon`. Another thing we need to import is the `Divider` and `ListSubheader` from Material-UI Core:

```
import { PieChart as PieChartIcon } from 'react-feather';
import { Divider, ListSubheader } from '@material-ui/core';
```

Right after the Logo and before the `settings-and-privacy`, add the following code.

Listing 6-21. Updating the dashboard-sidebar-navigation.tsx

```
<Link to={`${url}`} className={classes.logoWithLink}>
            Logo
         </Link>
       </Toolbar>
       <div className={classes.drawerContainer}>
         <List>

...

<ListSubheader>Reports</ListSubheader>
            <Link className={classes.link} to={`${url}`}>
              <ListItem button>
                <ListItemIcon>
                  <PieChartIcon />
                </ListItemIcon>
                <ListItemText primary={'Dashboard'} />
              </ListItem>
            </Link>
...
<Link className={classes.link} to={`${url}/settings-and-privacy`}>
```

Refresh the browser to see changes, which should look as shown in Figure 6-11. Click the buttons to see if everything is working.

Figure 6-11. *The UI after updating the dashboard-sidebar-navigation*

Summary

We learned how to use local states, send HTTP requests while considering the DRY (Don't Repeat Yourself) principle, and use the open source charting library called ApexCharts to create interactive visualizations for our app.

In the next chapter, we'll go a little deeper into our app as we begin writing input forms using Formik and Yup validations on top of Material-UI's data tables. Hopefully, we can bring all these components together and render them to the browser to see how everything works.

CHAPTER 7

Writing Data Tables, Formik Forms, and Yup Validations

In the previous chapter, we learned how to write local states and send HTTP requests. We also installed ApexCharts to create our visual charts.

We will now move on to building our application, add new components to lay the groundwork for our data tables, and start writing forms using Formik and input validations using Yup. This chapter is the first part of a two-part series since it is a reasonably long topic. The first part would be creating data tables and other style components, which would be the foundation for the second part, the next chapter – focusing on writing forms and input validations.

The finished repository of this chapter is here:

Source: `https://github.com/webmasterdevlin/practical-enterprise-react/tree/master/chapter-7`

Component Overview

Before we proceed with our project app, let's review some of the libraries or components we will use in this chapter.

© Devlin Basilan Duldulao, Ruby Jane Leyva Cabagnot 2021
D. B. Duldulao and R. J. L. Cabagnot, *Practical Enterprise React*, https://doi.org/10.1007/978-1-4842-6975-6_7

Form Handling

Forms allow app users to directly input and submit data through our components from a profile page or login screen to a shopping checkout page and others. It is also the main reason why it is a critical part of any web application.

Based on my own experience and that of many other React developers, creating forms in a React application can be quite tedious. More importantly, forms we create from scratch may be prone to errors because of all the reactivities we need to handle ourselves.

That's why I choose to build forms using Formik. You can use many other excellent form libraries, including Redux Form, Formsy, and React Forms.

Formik

This gives us the Form, Field, and ErrorMessage components to create our forms, add form fields, and display error messages. Formik gives us three props:

- `initialValue`: For the initial values of the form fields.

- `validate`: For validation rules in the form fields.

- `onSubmit`: This takes a function when we click Submit.

More on this when we start to build forms. I think it's better to show it in code.

Yup

Yup is an object schema validator in JavaScript (Listing 7-1). With Yup, we can

- Define the object schema and its validation.

- Create a validator object with the required schema and validation.

- Verify if objects are valid (satisfy schemas and validations) using a Yup utility function. If it doesn't meet the validations, an error message is returned.

Listing 7-1. An Example of Creating the Validations with Yup

```
//define the object schema and its validation

const book = {
        published: 1951,
  author: "JD Salinger",
  title: "The Catcher in the Rye",
  pages: 234
};

//create a validator object with the required schema and validation

const yup = require("yup");

const yupObject = yup.object().shape({
  published: yup.number.required(),
  author: yup.string.required(),
  title: yup.string.required(),
  pages: yup.number()
});
```

To demonstrate how we can use all of this together, we will build a Product dashboard that will list all the products and add new products to our app.

First, we will use a data table component from Material-UI to display sets of data.

Data Tables

Product Create View

Go to views ➤ dashboard, create a new folder, and name it product. Under the product folder, create another folder and name it ProductCreateView.

And inside the ProductCreateView folder, create a new file and name it Header.tsx. Here's the file path:

views ➤ dashboard ➤ product ➤ ProductCreateView ➤ Header.tsx

Open the Header.tsx, and after typing the snippet "rafce" for VS Code or "rsc" for WebStorm, add the header <h1>Header - CreativeView Works!</h1> for the time being.

See Listing 7-2 on creating the Header component of the ProductCreateView.

Listing 7-2. Creating the Header Component of ProductCreateView

```
import React from 'react'.

const Header = () => {
  return (
    <div>
      <h1>Header - CreativeView Works!</h1>
    </div>
  )
}

export default Header;
```

Still within the ProductCreateView folder, we'll add another file and name it ProductCreateForm.tsx.

Product Create Form

Here's the file path:

views ➤ dashboard ➤ product ➤ ProductCreateView ➤ ProductCreateForm.tsx

Add an <h1> tag to the ProductCreateForm.tsx. See Listing 7-3 on creating the ProductCreateForm.tsx.

Listing 7-3. Creating the ProductCreateForm.tsx

```
import React from 'react'

const ProductCreateForm = () => {
  return (
    <div>
      <h1>ProductCreateForm Works! h1>
```

```
      </div>
    )
}
```

```
export default ProductCreateForm;
```

Next, under the `ProductCreateView` directory, add an `index.tsx` file that will import the two components that we've just created: `Header.tsx` and `ProductCreateForm.tsx`.

Listing 7-4 creates the `index.tsx` of `ProductCreateView`.

Listing 7-4. Creating the index.tsx of ProductCreateView

```
import React from 'react';
import { Container, makeStyles } from '@material-ui/core';

import Header from './Header';
import ProductCreateForm from './ProductCreateForm';

const ProductCreateView = () => {
  const classes = useStyles();

  return (

      <Container>
        <Header />
        <ProductCreateForm />
      </Container>

  );
};

const useStyles = makeStyles(theme => ({}));

export default ProductCreateView;
```

So we're done with that for now. We'll go back to those components later. The next thing we shall do is to create the product list view.

Product List View

We'll create another folder inside the product and name it `ProductListView` and, under that, add two new files and call them `Header.tsx` and `Results.tsx`, respectively:

```
views ➤ dashboard ➤ product ➤ ProductListView ➤ Header.tsx
Views ➤ dashboard ➤ product ➤ ProductListView ➤ Results.tsx
```

Open the `Header.tsx` and copy the code as follows.

Listing 7-5. Creating the Header.tsx of ProductListView

```tsx
import React from 'react';
import { makeStyles } from '@material-ui/core';

const Header = () => {
  const classes = useStyles();
  return (
    <div>
      <h1>Header - ListView - Works!</h1>
    </div>
  );
};
const useStyles = makeStyles(theme => ({
      root: {},
      action: {
        marginBottom: theme.spacing(1),
        '& + &': {
          marginLeft: theme.spacing(1),
        },
      },
    }));

export default Header;
```

You can do the same thing on your own on the `Results.tsx`. However, change the `<h1>` header to `"Results - Works!"`

After doing the `Results.tsx`, we'll add the `index.tsx` for the `ProductListView`.

Listing 7-6. Creating the index.tsx of ProductListView

```tsx
import React from 'react';
import {Container, makeStyles} from '@material-ui/core';
import Header from './Header';
import Results from './Results';

const ProductListView = () => {
  const classes = useStyles();

  return (
    <Container>
      <Header/>
      <Results/>
    </Container>
  );
};

const useStyles = makeStyles(theme =>
  createStyles({
    backdrop: {
      zIndex: theme.zIndex.drawer + 1,
      color: '#fff',
    },
    root: {
      minHeight: '100%',
      paddingTop: theme.spacing(3),
      paddingBottom: 100,
    },
  }),
);

export default ProductListView;
```

We will come back to all those components later when we need to make some
changes.

Updating the Routes

For now, we need to update our routes – one Route path for each newly created component: ProductCreateView and ProductListView.

We'll register the two indexes in the routes. Open the file

src/app/routes.tsx

Within the routes.tsx file, locate the Dashboard and settings and privacy. We will add the new Route paths between them, as shown in Listing 7-7.

Listing 7-7. Registering the Route Paths of ProductCreateView and ProductListView

```
export const Routes = () => {
  return (
    <Suspense fallback={<LinearProgress style={{ margin: '10rem' }} />}>
      <Switch>
        {/*eager loading*/}
        <Route path={'/'} component={HomePage} exact />
        {/*lazy loadings*/}
        <Route
          path={'/about'}
      component={lazy(() => import('./views/pages/AboutPage'))}
          exact
        />

        <Route
          path={'/dashboard'}
          render={({ match: { path } }) => (
            <Dashboard>
              <Switch>
                <Route
                  path={path + '/'}
                  component={lazy(
                    () => import('./views/dashboard/dashboard-default-
                    content'),
                  )}
```

```
      exact
    />
    <Route
      path={path + '/list-products'}
      component={lazy(
        () =>        import('./views/dashboard/product/
        ProductListView'),
      )}
      exact
    />

      <Route
      path={path + '/create-product'}
      component={lazy(
        () => import('./views/dashboard/product/
        ProductCreateView'),
      )}
      exact
    />
  </Switch>
</Dashboard>
```

After registering the routes, we'll update the sidebar dashboard.

Updating the Sidebar Dashboard

We will create two new menus in the sidebar dashboard, namely, **List Products** and **Create Product**.

Go to the dashboard-sidebar-navigation.tsx:

app ➤ layouts ➤ dashboard-layout ➤ dashboard-sidebar-navigation.tsx

We'll import some icons from Feather in the said file.

Listing 7-8. Updating the Named Imports for the dashboard-sidebar-navigation

```
import {PieChart as PieChartIcon,
       ShoppingCart as ShoppingCartIcon,
       ChevronUp as ChevronUpIcon,
       ChevronDown as ChevronDownIcon,
       List as ListIcon,
       FilePlus as FilePlusIcon,
       LogOut as LogOutIcon,} from 'react-feather';
```

Note that we've renamed the icons that we imported so they're more readable or other developers in the team can easily understand at a glance what they are for.

Next, we'll add a local state (useState) and create an event handler handleClick to update the local state. But first, don't forget to import the useState component from React.

Listing 7-9. Adding useState and an Event Handler to dashboard-sidebar-navigation

```
import React, { useEffect, useState } from 'react';
...
const [open, setOpen] = useState(false)

  useEffect(() => {}, []);

  const handleClick =() => {
    setOpen(!open)
  };
```

After that, we'll render a collapsible menu in the browser.

Creating a Collapsible Sidebar Menu

Let's add a collapsible menu in between the Dashboard and settings-and-privacy.

First, let's import the component Collapse from Material-UI Core:

```
import { Collapse, Divider, ListSubheader } from '@material-ui/core';
```

Then let's add the following code to our collapsible menu. We will use the local state open and the event handler handleClick and Material-UI Core's styling icon components.

Listing 7-10. Creating a Collapsible Menu (Material-UI) for dashboard-sidebar-navigation

```
<List>
          <ListSubheader>Reports</ListSubheader>
          <Link className={classes.link} to={`${url}`}>
            <ListItem button>
              <ListItemIcon>
                <PieChartIcon />
              </ListItemIcon>
              <ListItemText primary={'Dashboard'} />
            </ListItem>
          </Link>

          <ListSubheader>Management</ListSubheader>
          <ListItem button onClick={handleClick}>
            <ListItemIcon>
              <ShoppingCartIcon />
            </ListItemIcon>
            <ListItemText primary="Products" />
            {open ? <ChevronUpIcon /> : <ChevronDownIcon />}
          </ListItem>
          <Collapse in={open} timeout="auto" unmountOnExit>
            <List component="div" disablePadding>
      <Link className={classes.link} to={`${url}/list-products`}>
        <ListItem button className={classes.nested}>
              <ListItemIcon>
                <ListIcon />
              </ListItemIcon>
              <ListItemText primary="List Products" />
            </ListItem>
          </Link>
```

```
<Link className={classes.link} to={`${url}/create-product`}>
        <ListItem button className={classes.nested}>
          <ListItemIcon>
            <FilePlusIcon />
          </ListItemIcon>
          <ListItemText primary="Create Product" />
        </ListItem>
      </Link>
    </List>
  </Collapse>

  <a className={classes.link} href={'/'}>
    <ListItem button>
      <ListItemIcon>
        <LogOutIcon />
      </ListItemIcon>
      <ListItemText primary={'logout'} />
    </ListItem>
  </a>
  </List>
  </div>
  </Drawer>
</div>
```

So what's going on with our collapsible menu? We added the Management as a list subheader, and under that, we're using the `<ShoppingCartIcon />` for the collapsible Products menu to show the menus `List Products` and `Create Product`.

The `<ChevronUpIcon />` and `<ChevronDownIcon />` will open up and collapse the menu when the user clicks it.

In your editor, you may or may not notice a red squiggly line on `{classes.nested}`.

In any case, we need to do something more here. This is because we need to add it to our `useStyle` component. Just add it at the bottom.

Listing 7-11. Updating the useStyle Component of dashboard-sidebar-navigation

```
nested: {
    paddingLeft: theme.spacing(4),
  },
```

Now run the application to check if everything is still working. You should see the updated sidebar navigation like the following.

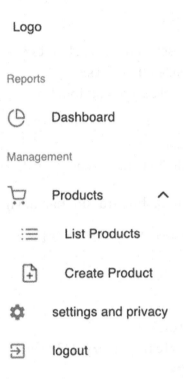

Figure 7-1. *Updated UI of dashboard-sidebar-navigation*

Click List Products and Create Product to check if you can successfully navigate between pages. You should be able to see the h1 header we've written:

(Shown when clicking the List Products tab)

```
Header - ListView Works!
Results - Works!
```

(Showing when clicking the Create Product tab)

```
Header - CreativeView Works!
ProductCreateForm Works!
```

So now that we're done with that proof of concept that we can navigate to the new pages, I think it's time to do some cleanup and remove the settings and privacy tab. We don't need it anymore; we'll add some more menus later on.

Cleaning Up a Bit...

Delete the `settings-and-privacy` from the `routes.tsx`.

Delete the file `settings-and-privacy.tsx`.

Next, go the `dashboard-sidebar-navigation.tsx`.

We will make two edits here:

1. Remove the settings and privacy.
2. Then replace the default `<ExitToAppIcon />` with our own `<LogoutIcon />`.

Listing 7-12. Logout Icon in dashboard-sidebar-navigation

```
        <a className={classes.link} href={'/'}>
            <ListItem button>
              <ListItemIcon>

<LogOutIcon/>

              </ListItemIcon>
              <ListItemText primary={'logout'} />
            </ListItem>
          </a>
```

I might have forgotten to use the `<Divider />` from Material-UI, so we'll put it now. Put it right after the `</Toolbar>`.

Listing 7-13. Adding the Divider Component in dashboard-sidebar-navigation

```
<<Toolbar
        style={{ width: '6rem', height: 'auto' }}
        className={classes.toolbar}
      >
```

```
<Link to={`${url}`} className={classes.logoWithLink}>
  Logo
</Link>
</Toolbar>
<Divider />
```

Now run or refresh the browser if the settings and privacy has been removed, and see if everything is still working.

Defining Type Alias of ProductType

After this, we'll proceed with implementing the products in a data table. Since we're using TypeScript, we'll start building first our model types or interfaces. In this case, I prefer to use types.

In the models directory, create a new file and name it product-type.ts. The shape of our ProductType object is shown in the following.

/* this is like an enum string. The pipe | here is basically a union that allows us o choose either of the three options. */

Listing 7-14. Creating the Shape of the ProductType Object

```
export type InventoryType = 'in_stock' | 'limited' | 'out_of_stock';

export type ProductType = {
  id: string;
  attributes: string[];
  category: string;
  //union means can be string or number
  createdAt: string | number;
  currency: string;
  // the ? means nullable
  image?: string;
  inventoryType: InventoryType;
  isAvailable: boolean;
  isShippable: boolean;
  name: string;
  price: number;
```

```
  quantity: number;
  updatedAt: string | number;
  variants: number;
  description: string;
  images: string[];
  includesTaxes: boolean;
  isTaxable: boolean;
  productCode: string;
  productSku: string;
  salePrice: string;
};
```

The shape or type is pretty much self-explanatory here. We need to make this extra effort now for code maintainability and for us to get IntelliSense in our editor. Doing this now saves us a lot of pain in the long run.

Creating the Products Endpoint

Before we go to the services, let's update the endpoints in the axios configuration. Open the axios.ts and add the products endpoint.

Listing 7-15. Adding the Products Endpoint in axios.ts

```
export const EndPoints = {
  sales: 'sales',
  products: 'products'
};
```

Now that we have set up the endpoints for our sales and products, it's time to set up their HTTP services.

Creating the Products Service

We'll use that endpoint in a new file called productService.ts, which we will create under the services directory:

services ➤ productService.ts

Open the new file and add the functions to create the products service, as shown in Listing 7-16.

Listing 7-16. Creating productService.ts

```
import api, {EndPoints} from '../api/axios';
import {ProductType} from '../models/product-type';

export async function getProductAxios() {
  return await api.get<ProductType[]>(EndPoints.products);
}
export async function postProductAxios(product: ProductType) {
  return await api.post<ProductType>(EndPoints.products, product);
}
```

In Listing 7-16, we created two functions:

getProductAxios and postProductAxios

Both use Axios to send a request to the JSON server, and the return type is an array of ProductType: <ProductType[ ]> and <ProductType>, respectively.

Both functions are async-await types.

After this, let's update our db.json with a sample of products or an array of four objects.

Updating the db.json Data

Head off to your db.json file and add the following data, as shown in Listing 7-17.

Listing 7-17. Adding the db.json Data with Product Objects

```
"products": [
    {
      "id": "5ece2c077e39da27658aa8a9",
      "attributes": ["Cotton"],
      "category": "dress",
      "currency": "$",
      "createdAt": "2021-01-01T12:00:27.87+00:20",
      "image": null,
      "inventoryType": "in_stock",
```

```
    "isAvailable": true,
    "isShippable": false,
    "name": "Charlie Tulip Dress",
    "price": 23.99,
    "quantity": 85,
    "updatedAt": "2021-01-01T12:00:27.87+00:20",
    "variants": 2
  },
  {
    "id": "5ece2c0d16f70bff2cf86cd8",
    "attributes": ["Cotton"],
    "category": "dress",
    "currency": "$",
    "createdAt": "2021-01-01T12:00:27.87+00:20",
    "image": null,
    "inventoryType": "out_of_stock",
    "isAvailable": false,
    "isShippable": true,
    "name": "Kate Leopard Dress",
    "price": 95,
    "quantity": 0,
    "updatedAt": "2021-01-01T12:00:27.87+00:20",
    "variants": 1
  },
  {
    "id": "5ece2c123fad30cbbff8d060",
    "attributes": ["Variety of styles"],
    "category": "jewelry",
    "currency": "$",
    "createdAt": 345354345,
    "image": null,
    "inventoryType": "in_stock",
    "isAvailable": true,
    "isShippable": false,
    "name": "Layering Bracelets Collection",
```

```
      "price": 155,
      "quantity": 48,
      "updatedAt": "2021-01-01T12:00:27.87+00:20",
      "variants": 5
    },
    {
      "id": "5ece2c1be7996d1549d94e34",
      "attributes": ["Polyester and Spandex"],
      "category": "blouse",
      "currency": "$",
      "createdAt": "2021-01-01T12:00:27.87+00:20",
      "image": null,
      "inventoryType": "limited",
      "isAvailable": false,
      "isShippable": true,
      "name": "Flared Sleeve Floral Blouse",
      "price": 17.99,
      "quantity": 5,
      "updatedAt": "2021-01-01T12:00:27.87+00:20",
      "variants": 1
    }
  ]
```

You'll notice that we've created four product objects. And just for simplicity here, the names of the objects are as follows:

```
"name": "Charlie Tulip Dress",
 "name": "Kate Leopard Dress",
 "name": "Layering Bracelets Collection",
 "name": "Flared Sleeve Floral Blouse",
```

Now that we've added the productService in our axios and updated our db.json, let's test it out by sending an HTTP request.

Sending an HTTP Request

Head off to the index.tsx file of the ProductListView.

We'll need the useEffect from React. Inside the useEffect, we'll call the getProductAxios, which is imported from services/productService.

Listing 7-18. Using the getProductAxios in ProductListView.tsx

```
...
import { getProductsAxios } from 'services/productService';

const ProductListView = () => {
  const classes = useStyles();

  useEffect(() => {
    getProductAxios();
  }, []);
```

Go to the Chrome DevTools and click the Network tab and choose the XHR. Make sure that your JSON server is running at localhost:5000/products.

Click List Products in the browser, and in the headers, you should see Status **Code: 200 OK** to indicate a successful get response from the JSON server.

Next, click the Response tab to check the JSON objects. You should be able to see the array of products that we've added in our db.json.

Refactoring the ProductListView

Okay, now that we know that it is working, we will do some code refactoring in the ProductListView to reflect the best practices.

Go to the index.tsx of ProductListView and do the following:

- Create a local state (useState) for updating the array of products' data.

- Add an async-await function to be named fetchProducts where we can call the getProductAxios().

- Put the fetchProducts() inside a try-catch block as best practice.

- Add a backdrop component from Material-UI that works much like a loader spinner.

/* local state uses Generics Type of type array, so we'll know at a glance its shape. Hover your mouse over the <ProductType[]>, and you'll see its model types. If you take out the Generics here, you'll lose the ability to see the object's model shape during hover. You'll get the type 'any' */

```
const [products, setProducts] = useState<ProductType[]>([])
```

/* No need to declare the type boolean here because we can already see its type. Usually primitives - no need to explicitly declare the types. TS can infer it. */

Listing 7-19. Updating the index.tsx of ProductListView.tsx

```
const [open, setOpen] = useState(false);

useEffect(() => {
fetchProduct()
}, []);

const fetchProduct = async () => {
  handleToggle();
  try {
    const { data } = await getProductAxios();
    setProducts(data);
  } catch (e) {
    alert('Something is wrong.');
  }
  handleClose();
};

const handleClose = () => {
  setOpen(false);
};
const handleToggle = () => {
  setOpen(!open);
}
```

We'll use the local state [open] for the backdrop. We will use that in a bit, but we need to create first some additional UI styling.

Creating Additional UI Styling

First, let's render the table in the UI, and to do that, we'll be creating a new file under the components folder and name it label.tsx.

Listing 7-20 creates the label.tsx for the aesthetic design or styling of the table.

Listing 7-20. Creating the label.tsx

```
import React, { ReactNode } from 'react';
import clsx from 'clsx';
import { fade, makeStyles } from '@material-ui/core';

//defining the shape or type of our label model

type Props = {
  className?: string;
  color?: 'primary' | 'secondary' | 'error' | 'warning' | 'success';
  children?: ReactNode;
  style?: {};
};

const Label = ({
                  className = '',
                  color = 'secondary',
                  children,
                  style,
                  ...rest
                }: Props) => {
  const classes = useStyles();

  return (
    <span
      className={clsx(
        classes.root,
        {
          [classes[color]]: color,
        },
        className,
```

```
    )}
    {...rest}
  >
    {children}
  </span>
);
};

const useStyles = makeStyles(theme => ({
  root: {
    fontFamily: theme.typography.fontFamily,
    alignItems: 'center',
    borderRadius: 2,
    display: 'inline-flex',
    flexGrow: 0,
    whiteSpace: 'nowrap',
    cursor: 'default',
    flexShrink: 0,
    fontSize: theme.typography.pxToRem(12),
    fontWeight: theme.typography.fontWeightMedium,
    height: 20,
    justifyContent: 'center',
    letterSpacing: 0.5,
    minWidth: 20,
    padding: theme.spacing(0.5, 1),
    textTransform: 'uppercase',
  },
  primary: {
    color: theme.palette.primary.main,
    backgroundColor: fade(theme.palette.primary.main, 0.08),
  },
  secondary: {
    color: theme.palette.secondary.main,
    backgroundColor: fade(theme.palette.secondary.main, 0.08),
  },
```

```
    error: {
      color: theme.palette.error.main,
      backgroundColor: fade(theme.palette.error.main, 0.08),
    },
    success: {
      color: theme.palette.success.main,
      backgroundColor: fade(theme.palette.success.main, 0.08),
    },
    warning: {
      color: theme.palette.warning.main,
      backgroundColor: fade(theme.palette.warning.main, 0.08),
    },
}));

export default Label;
```

Next, we need another component that will help us render the data table. Go to the folder ProductListView and create a new file and name it TableResultsHelpers.tsx.

Let's import the named component and define the type alias of the object, as shown in Listing 7-21.

Listing 7-21. Importing the component and adding the type alias for TableResultsHelpers

```
import React from 'react';
import { InventoryType, ProductType } from 'models/product-type';
import Label from 'app/components/label';

export type TableResultsHelpers = {
  availability?: 'available' | 'unavailable';
  category?: string;
  inStock?: boolean;
  isShippable?: boolean;
};
```

Next, let's apply the filter conditions for rendering the products to the user; see Listing 7-22.

Listing 7-22. Creating the TableResultsHelpers

```
export const applyFilters = (
  products: ProductType[],
  query: string,
  filters: TableResultsHelpers,
): ProductType[] => {
  return products.filter(product => {
    let matches = true;

    /* the product here comes from the parent component.  */

if (query && !product.name.toLowerCase().includes(query.toLowerCase())) {
    matches = false;
    }
if (filters.category && product.category !== filters.category) {
    matches = false;
    }
if (filters.availability) {
    if (filters.availability === 'available' && !product.isAvailable) {
      matches = false;
    }
    if (filters.availability === 'unavailable' && product.isAvailable) {
      matches = false;
    }}
    if (
      filters.inStock &&
      !['in_stock', 'limited'].includes(product.inventoryType)
    ) {
      matches = false;
    }
    if (filters.isShippable && !product.isShippable) {
      matches = false;
    }
```

```
    return matches;
  });
};

/* to limit the products or the number of search results shown*/

export const applyPagination = (
  products: ProductType[],
  page: number,
  limit: number,
): ProductType[] => {
  return products.slice(page * limit, page * limit + limit);
};

export const getInventoryLabel = (
  inventoryType: InventoryType,
): JSX.Element => {
  const map = {
    in_stock: {
      text: 'In Stock',
      color: 'success',
    },
    limited: {
      text: 'Limited',
      color: 'warning',
    },
    out_of_stock: {
      text: 'Out of Stock',
      color: 'error',
    },
  };

  const { text, color }: any = map[inventoryType];
  return <Label color={color}>{text}</Label>;
};
```

The TableResultsHelpers is using the label component that we just created. We're also importing InventoryType and ProductType from models/product-type.

The table helpers are for the UI, so we can query or type in the filter box and see the list of results.

After that, create a new folder under src and name it helpers. Under the helpers folder, add a new file and name it inputProductOptions.ts. This file is just for labeling the table, and it's better to put it in a separate file rather than bunching it together with the component itself.

Listing 7-23. Creating the Helpers for inputProductOptions

```
export const categoryOptions = [
  {
    id: 'all',
    name: 'All',
  },
  {
    id: 'dress',
    name: 'Dress',
  },
  {
    id: 'jewelry',
    name: 'Jewelry',
  },
  {
    id: 'blouse',
    name: 'Blouse',
  },
  {
    id: 'beauty',
    name: 'Beauty',
  },
];

export const availabilityOptions = [
  {
    id: 'all',
    name: 'All',
  },
```

147

```
  {
    id: 'available',
    name: 'Available',
  },
  {
    id: 'unavailable',
    name: 'Unavailable',
  },
];

export const sortOptions = [
  {
    value: 'updatedAt|desc',
    label: 'Last update (newest first)',
  },
  {
    value: 'updatedAt|asc',
    label: 'Last update (oldest first)',
  },
  {
    value: 'createdAt|desc',
    label: 'Creation date (newest first)',
  },
  {
    value: 'createdAt|asc',
    label: 'Creation date (oldest first)',
  },
];
```

That's done for now. Now, we'll install three NPM libraries:

```
$ npm i numeral
$ npm i @types/numeral
$ npm i react-perfect-scrollbar
```

1. numeral.js: A JavaScript library for formatting and manipulating numbers.

2. @types/numeral: numeral.js is built using JavaScript, so we need to add typings for this library.

3. react-perfect-scrollbar: This allows us to make a scrollbar easily for our data table.

After successfully installing the libraries, open the file results.tsx to make some edits. I've mentioned earlier that we will go back to this file to build it up.

Let's add the following named import components as shown in Listing 7-24. Aside from the several styling components from Material-UI Core that we will install, we're importing components from inputProductOptions, TableResultsHelpers, and the product-type from the models folder.

Listing 7-24. Adding the Named Import Components to results.tsx

```
import React, { useState, ChangeEvent } from 'react';
import clsx from 'clsx';
import numeral from 'numeral';
import PerfectScrollbar from 'react-perfect-scrollbar';
import {
  Image as ImageIcon,
  Edit as EditIcon,
  ArrowRight as ArrowRightIcon,
  Search as SearchIcon,
} from 'react-feather';
import {
  Box,
  Button,
  Card,
  Checkbox,
  InputAdornment,
  FormControlLabel,
  IconButton,
```

```
  SvgIcon,
  Table,
  TableBody,
  TableCell,
  TableHead,
  TablePagination,
  TableRow,
  TextField,
  makeStyles,
} from '@material-ui/core';

import {
  availabilityOptions,
  categoryOptions,
  sortOptions,
} from 'helpers/inputProductOptions';
import {
  applyFilters,
  applyPagination,
  TableResultsHelpers,
  getInventoryLabel,
} from './tableResultsHelpers';
import { ProductType } from 'models/product-type';
```

Next, we'll define the type or shape of the object in Listing 7-25.

Listing 7-25. Creating the Shape or Type of the Object in results.tsx

```
type Props = {
  className?: string;
  products?: ProductType[];
};
```

Following the definition of the type, we'll create some local states, as shown in Listing 7-26.

Listing 7-26. Creating the results.tsx Component

```
const Results = ({ className, products, ...rest }: Props) => {
  const classes = useStyles();

  //Explicitly stating that selectedProducts is an array of type string

const [selectedProducts, setSelectedProducts] = useState<string[]>([]);

  const [page, setPage] = useState(0);
  const [limit, setLimit] = useState(10);
  const [query, setQuery] = useState('');

  /* Explicitly stating that sort is an array of type string so we'll know
  on mouser hover that value is of type string. */

  const [sort, setSort] = useState<string>(sortOptions[0].value);
  const [filters, setFilters] = useState<TableResultsHelpers | any>({
    category: null,
    availability: null,
    inStock: null,
    isShippable: null,
  });
```

Next, we'll create the following event handlers, as shown in Listing 7-27.

Listing 7-27. Creating Event Handlers in results.tsx

```
/*Updates the query every time the user types on the keyboard  */

const handleQueryChange = (event: ChangeEvent<HTMLInputElement>): void => {
    event.persist();
    setQuery(event.target.value);
  };

  const handleCategoryChange = (event: ChangeEvent<HTMLInputElement>):
  void => {
    event.persist();

    let value: any = null;
```

```
  if (event.target.value !== 'all') {
    value = event.target.value;
  }

  setFilters(prevFilters => ({
    ...prevFilters,
    category: value,
  }));
};

const handleAvailabilityChange = (
  event: ChangeEvent<HTMLInputElement>,
): void => {
  event.persist();

  let value: any = null;

  if (event.target.value !== 'all') {
    value = event.target.value;
  }

  setFilters(prevFilters => ({
    ...prevFilters,
    availability: value,
  }));
};

const handleStockChange = (event: ChangeEvent<HTMLInputElement>): void =>
{
  event.persist();

  let value: any = null;

  if (event.target.checked) {
    value = true;
  }
```

```
    setFilters(prevFilters => ({
      ...prevFilters,
      inStock: value,
    }));
  };

  const handleShippableChange = (
    event: ChangeEvent<HTMLInputElement>,
  ): void => {
    event.persist();

    let value: any = null;

    if (event.target.checked) {
      value = true;
    }

    setFilters(prevFilters => ({
      ...prevFilters,
      isShippable: value,
    }));
  };

  const handleSortChange = (event: ChangeEvent<HTMLInputElement>): void =>
{
    event.persist();
    setSort(event.target.value);
  };
 /*Updating all selected products */
  const handleSelectAllProducts = (
    event: ChangeEvent<HTMLInputElement>,
  ): void => {
    setSelectedProducts(
      event.target.checked ? products.map(product => product.id) : [],
    );
  };
```

```
/*Updating one selected product */

  const handleSelectOneProduct = (
    event: ChangeEvent<HTMLInputElement>,
    productId: string,
  ): void => {
    if (!selectedProducts.includes(productId)) {
      setSelectedProducts(prevSelected => [...prevSelected, productId]);
    } else {
      setSelectedProducts(prevSelected =>
        prevSelected.filter(id => id !== productId),
      );
    }
  };

/*This is for the pagination*/

  const handlePageChange = (event: any, newPage: number): void => {
    setPage(newPage);
  };

  const handleLimitChange = (event: ChangeEvent<HTMLInputElement>): void => {
    setLimit(parseInt(event.target.value));
  };

  /* Usually query is done on the backend with indexing solutions, but
  we're doing it  here just to simulate it */

  const filteredProducts = applyFilters(products, query, filters);
  const paginatedProducts = applyPagination(filteredProducts, page, limit);
  const enableBulkOperations = selectedProducts.length > 0;
  const selectedSomeProducts =
    selectedProducts.length > 0 && selectedProducts.length < products.
    length;
  const selectedAllProducts = selectedProducts.length === products.length;
```

Continuing to the HTML, we're wrapping everything in Card from Material-UI Core. We're also adding Box, TextField, Checkbox, and various Table styles, as shown in Listing 7-28.

Keep in mind that all these stylings are something that you need not create from scratch. You can just go to the Material-UI website and, let's say, search for "table," and you can use anything there according to your app's requirements. All the APIs we're using here are available in Material-UI.

I'm just showing you again the possibilities of using a well-written and supported library to make your coding development a bit easier. Of course, as I've mentioned before, there are many UI component libraries that you can use, and Material-UI is just one of them.

If you are coding along, copy-paste the Card component from Material UI, as shown in Listing 7-28. We will refactor or make some changes when necessary.

Listing 7-28. Creating Event Handlers in results.tsx

```
return (
    <Card className={clsx(classes.root, className)} {...rest}>
      <Box p={2}>
        <Box display="flex" alignItems="center">
          <TextField
            className={classes.queryField}
            InputProps={{
              startAdornment: (
                <InputAdornment position="start">
                  <SvgIcon fontSize="small" color="action">
                    <SearchIcon />
                  </SvgIcon>
                </InputAdornment>
              ),
            }}
            onChange={handleQueryChange}
            placeholder="Search products"
            value={query}
            variant="outlined"
          />
```

```
      <Box flexGrow={1} />
      <TextField
        label="Sort By"
        name="sort"
        onChange={handleSortChange}
        select
        SelectProps={{ native: true }}
        value={sort}
        variant="outlined"
      >
        {sortOptions.map(option => (
          <option key={option.value} value={option.value}>
            {option.label}
          </option>
        ))}
      </TextField>
    </Box>

    <Box mt={3} display="flex" alignItems="center">
      <TextField
        className={classes.categoryField}
        label="Category"
        name="category"
        onChange={handleCategoryChange}
        select
        SelectProps={{ native: true }}
        value={filters.category || 'all'}
        variant="outlined"
      >
        {categoryOptions.map(categoryOption => (
          <option key={categoryOption.id} value={categoryOption.id}>
            {categoryOption.name}
          </option>
        ))}
      </TextField>
      <TextField
```

```
    className={classes.availabilityField}
    label="Availability"
    name="availability"
    onChange={handleAvailabilityChange}
    select
    SelectProps={{ native: true }}
    value={filters.availability || 'all'}
    variant="outlined"
  >
    {availabilityOptions.map(avalabilityOption => (
      <option key={avalabilityOption.id} value={avalabilityOption.id}>
        {avalabilityOption.name}
      </option>
    ))}
</TextField>

<FormControlLabel
  className={classes.stockField}
  control={
    <Checkbox
      checked={!!filters.inStock}
      onChange={handleStockChange}
      name="inStock"
    />
  }
  label="In Stock"
/>
<FormControlLabel
  className={classes.shippableField}
  control={
    <Checkbox
      checked={!!filters.isShippable}
      onChange={handleShippableChange}
      name="Shippable"
    />
  }
```

```
        label="Shippable"
      />
    </Box>
  </Box>

  {enableBulkOperations && (
    <div className={classes.bulkOperations}>
      <div className={classes.bulkActions}>
        <Checkbox
          checked={selectedAllProducts}
          indeterminate={selectedSomeProducts}
          onChange={handleSelectAllProducts}
        />
        <Button variant="outlined" className={classes.bulkAction}>
          Delete
        </Button>
        <Button variant="outlined" className={classes.bulkAction}>
          Edit
        </Button>
      </div>
    </div>
  )}
  <PerfectScrollbar>
    <Box minWidth={1200}>
      <Table>
        <TableHead>
          <TableRow>
            <TableCell padding="checkbox">
              <Checkbox
                checked={selectedAllProducts}
                indeterminate={selectedSomeProducts}
                onChange={handleSelectAllProducts}
              />
            </TableCell>
            <TableCell />
            <TableCell>Name</TableCell>
```

```
    <TableCell>Inventory</TableCell>
    <TableCell>Details</TableCell>
    <TableCell>Attributes</TableCell>
    <TableCell>Price</TableCell>
    <TableCell align="right">Actions</TableCell>
  </TableRow>
</TableHead>
<TableBody>
  {paginatedProducts.map(product => {
    const isProductSelected = selectedProducts.
    includes(product.id);

    return (
      <TableRow hover key={product.id}
      selected={isProductSelected}>
        <TableCell padding="checkbox">
          <Checkbox
            checked={isProductSelected}
            onChange={event =>
              handleSelectOneProduct(event, product.id)
            }
            value={isProductSelected}
          />
        </TableCell>
        <TableCell className={classes.imageCell}>
          {product.image ? (
            <img
              alt="Product"
              src={product.image}
              className={classes.image}
            />
          ) : (
            <Box p={2} bgcolor="background.dark">
              <SvgIcon>
                <ImageIcon />
```

```
              </SvgIcon>
            </Box>
          )}
        </TableCell>
        <TableCell>{product.name}</TableCell>
        <TableCell>
          {getInventoryLabel(product.inventoryType)}
        </TableCell>

        <TableCell>
          {product.quantity} in stock
          {product.variants > 1 &&
          ` in ${product.variants} variants`}
        </TableCell>
        <TableCell>
          {product.attributes.map(attr => attr)}
        </TableCell>
        <TableCell>
          {numeral(product.price).format(
            `${product.currency}0,0.00`,
          )}
        </TableCell>
        <TableCell align="right">
          <IconButton>
            <SvgIcon fontSize="small">
              <EditIcon />
            </SvgIcon>
          </IconButton>
          <IconButton>
            <SvgIcon fontSize="small">
              <ArrowRightIcon />
            </SvgIcon>
          </IconButton>
        </TableCell>
      </TableRow>
```

```
            );
          })}
        </TableBody>
      </Table>
      <TablePagination
        component="div"
        count={filteredProducts.length}
        onChangePage={handlePageChange}
        onChangeRowsPerPage={handleLimitChange}
        page={page}
        rowsPerPage={limit}
        rowsPerPageOptions={[5, 10, 25]}
      />
    </Box>
  </PerfectScrollbar>
</Card>
  );
};
```

After that, we'll just need to put the useStyles from makeStyles to the results.tsx.

Listing 7-29. Adding the useStyles to results.tsx

```
const useStyles = makeStyles(theme => ({
  availabilityField: {
    marginLeft: theme.spacing(2),
    flexBasis: 200,
  },
  bulkOperations: {
    position: 'relative',
  },
  bulkActions: {
    paddingLeft: 4,
    paddingRight: 4,
    marginTop: 6,
    position: 'absolute',
    width: '100%',
```

```
    zIndex: 2,
    backgroundColor: theme.palette.background.default,
  },
  bulkAction: {
    marginLeft: theme.spacing(2),
  },
  categoryField: {
    flexBasis: 200,
  },
  imageCell: {
    fontSize: 0,
    width: 68,
    flexBasis: 68,
    flexGrow: 0,
    flexShrink: 0,
  },

  image: {
    height: 68,
    width: 68,
  },
  root: {},
  queryField: {
    width: 500,
  },
  stockField: {
    marginLeft: theme.spacing(2),
  },
  shippableField: {
    marginLeft: theme.spacing(2),
  },
}));

export default Results;
```

We are done for now with the results.tsx. Let's make some updates to the index.tsx of the ProductListView.

We'll import a few components from Material-UI Core, including the Page template component, as shown in Listing 7-30.

Listing 7-30. Adding Named Components to the index.tsx of ProductListView

```
import {
  Backdrop,
  Box,
  CircularProgress,
  Container,
  makeStyles,
} from '@material-ui/core';

import Page from 'app/components/page';
```

And then let's add the useStyles from the makeStyles component, as shown in Listing 7-31.

Listing 7-31. Adding useStyles to the index.tsx of ProductListView

```
import { createStyles } from '@material-ui/core/styles';

...

const useStyles = makeStyles(theme =>
  createStyles({
    backdrop: {
      zIndex: theme.zIndex.drawer + 1,
      color: '#fff',
    },
    root: {
      minHeight: '100%',
      paddingTop: theme.spacing(3),
      paddingBottom: 100,
    },
  }),
);
```

Okay, now that we've got those laid down on the ProductListView, we will use the Page template, Container , and Backdrop in the JSX, as shown in Listing 7-32.

Listing 7-32. Adding Material-UI Components to the index.tsx of ProductListView

```
return (
    <Page className={classes.root} title="Product List">
      <Container maxWidth={false}>
        <Header />
        {products && (
          <Box mt={3}>
            <Results products={products} />
          </Box>
        )}
        <Backdrop
          className={classes.backdrop}
          open={open}
          onClick={handleClose}
        >
          <CircularProgress color="inherit" />
        </Backdrop>
      </Container>
    </Page>
  );
};
```

Ensure that your JSON server runs at localhost:5000/products and then refresh your UI by clicking List Products in the sidebar dashboard.

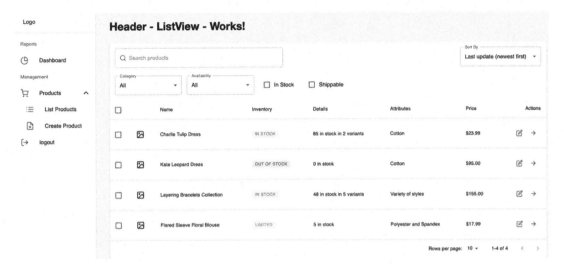

Figure 7-2. *Rendering the UI for List Products*

Play around with the search box **(Search products), Category,** and **Availability** to check if you can successfully search and get the correct results based on your typed keywords. Click the refresh button also to check if the backdrop with the spinner is working.

Summary

We saw that the Products menu is working so far, at least half of it – the List Products – but we have still a long way to go to complete the Products sidebar menu. You can say that we have just laid down the skeletal foundation before we can get to the nitty-gritty of things.

In the second part, the next chapter, we will put a few finishing touches on the ProductListView and then jump straight away to using Formik and Yup validation forms.

CHAPTER 8

Writing Data Tables, Formik Forms, and Yup Validations: Part 2

In the first part of this two-part chapter series, we started setting up the Products menu, including the ProductListView, using data tables and other styling components. This second part will continue building up the Products menu using Formik and Yup input validations.

Now that we have our proof of concept that we can render List Products in our UI, as we see in Listing 8-1, we can now update the Header component of the ProductListView.

First, import the following named components.

Listing 8-1. Adding Import Components to Header.tsx of ProductListView

```
import { Link as RouterLink } from 'react-router-dom';
import clsx from 'clsx';
import NavigateNextIcon from '@material-ui/icons/NavigateNext';
import {
  Box,
  Breadcrumbs,
  Button,
  Grid,
  Link,
  SvgIcon,
  Typography,
  makeStyles,
```

© Devlin Basilan Duldulao, Ruby Jane Leyva Cabagnot 2021
D. B. Duldulao and R. J. L. Cabagnot, *Practical Enterprise React*, https://doi.org/10.1007/978-1-4842-6975-6_8

```
} from '@material-ui/core';
import {
  PlusCircle as PlusCircleIcon,
  Download as DownloadIcon,
  Upload as UploadIcon,
} from 'react-feather';
```

Following that, we'll create the type definition and the additional changes on the Header component itself.

We're wrapping everything inside a <Grid/>, and we also made three buttons: **Import**, **Export,** and **New Product.** Copy-paste the Header component of the ProductListView; see Listing 8-2.

Listing 8-2. Updating the Header Component of ProductListView

```
/*types definition */

type Props = {
  className?: string;
};

const Header = ({ className, ...rest }: Props) => {
  const classes = useStyles();

  return (
    <Grid
      container
      spacing={3}
      justify="space-between"
      className={clsx(classes.root, className)}
      {...rest}
    >
      <Grid item>
        <Breadcrumbs
          separator={<NavigateNextIcon fontSize="small" />}
          aria-label="breadcrumb"
        >
```

```
<Link
  variant="body1"
  color="inherit"
  to="/dashboard"
  component={RouterLink}
>
  Dashboard
</Link>

<Box>
  <Typography variant="body1" color="inherit">
    List Products
  </Typography>
</Box>
</Breadcrumbs>
<Typography variant="h4" color="textPrimary">
  All Products
</Typography>
<Box mt={2}>
  <Button
    className={classes.action}
    startIcon={
      <SvgIcon fontSize="small">
        <UploadIcon />
      </SvgIcon>
    }
  >
    Import
  </Button>
  <Button
    className={classes.action}
    startIcon={
      <SvgIcon fontSize="small">
        <DownloadIcon />
      </SvgIcon>
    }
  >
```

```
              Export
            </Button>
          </Box>
        </Grid>

        <Grid item>

          <Button
            color="primary"
            variant="contained"
            className={classes.action}
            component={RouterLink}
            to="/dashboard/create-product"
            startIcon={
              <SvgIcon fontSize="small">
                <PlusCircleIcon />
              </SvgIcon>
            }
          >
            New Product
          </Button>
        </Grid>
      </Grid>
    );
  };
```

Lastly, add the styling margin to the Header component of `ProductListView`.

Listing 8-3. Adding the Styling Component to the Header Component

```
const useStyles = makeStyles(theme => ({
  root: {},
  action: {
    marginBottom: theme.spacing(1),
    '& + &': {
```

```
        marginLeft: theme.spacing(1),
    },
  },
}));
```

```
export default Header;
```

We are done now with the ProductListView; let's start building the ProductCreateView.

Updating the ProductCreateView

The ProductCreateView is where we will add the input form for our app.

Open the Header.tsx of the ProductCreateView:

```
ProductCreateView ➤ Header.tsx.
```

We will start with the named import components, as shown in Listing 8-4.

Listing 8-4. Adding Named Components to the Header.tsx of ProductCreateView

```
import { Link as RouterLink } from 'react-router-dom';
import clsx from 'clsx';
import NavigateNextIcon from '@material-ui/icons/NavigateNext';
import {
  Breadcrumbs,
  Button,
  Grid,
  Link,
  Typography,
  makeStyles,
  Box,
} from '@material-ui/core';
```

Create also the type definition, which is just a nullable className of type string:

```
type Props = {
  className?: string;
};
```

And then copy the following update to the Header component of our
ProductCreateView, as shown in Listing 8-5.

Listing 8-5. Updating the Header.tsx of ProductCreateView

```
const Header = ({ className, ...rest }: Props) => {
  const classes = useStyles();

  return (
    <Grid
      className={clsx(classes.root, className)}
      container
      justify="space-between"
      spacing={3}
      {...rest}
    >
      <Grid item>
        <Breadcrumbs
          separator={<NavigateNextIcon fontSize="small" />}
          aria-label="breadcrumb"
        >
          <Link
            variant="body1"
            color="inherit"
            to="/dashboard"
            component={RouterLink}
          >
            Dashboard
          </Link>
          <Box mb={3}>
            <Typography variant="body1" color="inherit">
              Create Product
            </Typography>
          </Box>
        </Breadcrumbs>
        <Typography variant="h4" color="textPrimary">
          Create a new product
```

```
      </Typography>
    </Grid>
    <Grid item>
      <Button component={RouterLink} to="/dashboard/list-products">
        Cancel
      </Button>
    </Grid>
  </Grid>
);
};
```

Lastly, let's add the useStyle component.

Listing 8-6. Adding the Style Component to the Header.tsx of ProductCreateView

```
const useStyles = makeStyles(() => ({
  root: {},
}));
```

We can now use this Header component in the index.tsx of the ProductCreateView.

Listing 8-7. Updating the index.tsx of ProductCreateView

```
import React from 'react';
import { Container, makeStyles } from '@material-ui/core';

import Header from './Header';
import ProductCreateForm from './ProductCreateForm';
import Page from 'app/components/page';

const ProductCreateView = () => {
  const classes = useStyles();

  return (
    <Page className={classes.root} title="Product Create">
      <Container>
        <Header />
        <ProductCreateForm />
```

```
        </Container>
      </Page>
  );
};

const useStyles = makeStyles(theme => ({
  root: {
    minHeight: '100%',
    paddingTop: theme.spacing(3),
    paddingBottom: 100,
  },
}));

export default ProductCreateView;
```

So that's good for now. We head off to update the ProductCreateForm.

Updating the ProductCreateForm

First, we need to add some additional TypeScript files.

Under the folder ProductCreateView, create a folder called schema. And under the schema, we're going to add a new file for our Yup product validation.

The file path is

ProductCreateView ➤ schema ➤ yupProductValidation.ts

Listing 8-8 shows the Yup product validation schema.

Listing 8-8. Creating the yupProductValidation Schema

```
// the * means all

import * as Yup from 'yup';

export const yupProductValidation = Yup.object().shape({
  category: Yup.string().max(255),
  description: Yup.string().max(5000),
  images: Yup.array(),
  includesTaxes: Yup.bool().required(),
```

```
  isTaxable: Yup.bool().required(),
  name: Yup.string().max(255).required(),
  price: Yup.number().min(0).required(),
  productCode: Yup.string().max(255),
  productSku: Yup.string().max(255),
  salePrice: Yup.number().min(0),
});
```

After this, we need to create the product default values or initial values for Formik. It's better to define it in a separate file, so it's a bit cleaner.

Create a new file under schema and name it productDefaultValue.ts, as shown in Listing 8-9.

The file path is

ProductCreateView ➤ schema ➤ productDefaultValue.ts

Note that we imported the ProductType component from the models folder.

Listing 8-9. Creating Initial Values in the productDefaultValue.tsx

```
import { ProductType } from 'models/product-type';

export const productDefaultValue: ProductType = {
  attributes: [],
  category: '',
  createdAt: '',
  currency: '',
  id: '',
  image: '',
  inventoryType: 'in_stock',
  isAvailable: false,
  isShippable: false,
  name: '',
  quantity: 0,
  updatedAt: '',
  variants: 0,
  description: '',
  images: [],
```

```
  includesTaxes: false,
  isTaxable: false,
  productCode: '',
  productSku: '',
  salePrice: '',
  price: 0,
};
```

Okay, we're done with the `ProductDefaultValue.tsx`. Let's now install a rich-text editor library called Quill.

Installing React Quill

Let's install the React version named `react-quill`. Recall that Quill is an open source WYSIWYG editor for the modern Web. React-quill is a React component that wraps Quill.js:

```
npm install react-quill
```

After installing it, we need to import the component in the `index.tsx` of the `src` directory.

Listing 8-10. Adding react-quill to the index.tsx of the src Directory

```
import 'react-app-polyfill/ie11';
import 'react-app-polyfill/stable';
import 'react-quill/dist/quill.snow.css';
import * as React from 'react';
import * as ReactDOM from 'react-dom';
import { Provider } from 'react-redux';
import * as serviceWorker from 'serviceWorker';
import 'sanitize.css/sanitize.css';
```

Under the components folder, create a separate new file and name it `quill-editor.tsx`. The file path is as follows:

`app ➤ components ➤ quill-editor.tsx`

Open the newly created file and import all the necessary named components.

Listing 8-11. Importing Named Components to quill-editor.tsx

```
import React from 'react';
import clsx from 'clsx';
import ReactQuill from 'react-quill';
import { makeStyles } from '@material-ui/core';
```

And then, we need the type definition and the QuillEditor component.

Listing 8-12. Adding the QuillEditor Component

```
type Props = {
  className?: string;
  [key: string]: any;
};

const QuillEditor = ({ className, ...rest }: Props) => {
  const classes = useStyles();

  return <ReactQuill className={clsx(classes.root, className)} {...rest}
/>;
};
```

In Listing 8-12, we're also returning Quill and using the rest/spread operator, which means that we pass to ReactQuill anything that the QuillEditor has.

Next, we will add the makeStyles from Material-UI Core, as shown in Listing 8-13.

Listing 8-13. Adding the Styling Components to the QuillEditor Component

```
const useStyles = makeStyles(theme => ({
  root: {
    '& .ql-toolbar': {
      borderLeft: 'none',
      borderTop: 'none',
      borderRight: 'none',
      borderBottom: `1px solid ${theme.palette.divider}`,
      '& .ql-picker-label:hover': {
        color: theme.palette.secondary.main,
      },
```

```
'& .ql-picker-label.ql-active': {
  color: theme.palette.secondary.main,
},
'& .ql-picker-item:hover': {
  color: theme.palette.secondary.main,
},
'& .ql-picker-item.ql-selected': {
  color: theme.palette.secondary.main,
},
'& button:hover': {
  color: theme.palette.secondary.main,
  '& .ql-stroke': {
    stroke: theme.palette.secondary.main,
  },
},

'& button:focus': {
  color: theme.palette.secondary.main,
  '& .ql-stroke': {
    stroke: theme.palette.secondary.main,
  },
},
'& button.ql-active': {
  '& .ql-stroke': {
    stroke: theme.palette.secondary.main,
  },
},
'& .ql-stroke': {
  stroke: theme.palette.text.primary,
},
'& .ql-picker': {
  color: theme.palette.text.primary,
},
'& .ql-picker-options': {
  padding: theme.spacing(2),
  backgroundColor: theme.palette.background.default,
  border: 'none',
```

```
      boxShadow: theme.shadows[10],
      borderRadius: theme.shape.borderRadius,
    },
  },
  '& .ql-container': {
    border: 'none',
    '& .ql-editor': {
      fontFamily: theme.typography.fontFamily,
      fontSize: 16,
      color: theme.palette.text.primary,
      '&.ql-blank::before': {
        color: theme.palette.text.secondary,
      },
    },
  },
},
}));
```

```
export default QuillEditor;
```

So that's it for the Quill editor. We need to create a component that will convert the byte's value into a human-readable string.

Under the folder utils, create a new file and name it bytes-to-size.ts; see Listing 8-14.

Listing 8-14. Creating the bytes-to-size.tsx

```
const bytesToSize = (bytes: number, decimals: number = 2) => {
  if (bytes === 0) return '0 Bytes';

  const k = 1024;
  const dm = decimals < 0 ? 0 : decimals;
  const sizes = ['Bytes', 'KB', 'MB', 'GB', 'TB', 'PB', 'EB', 'ZB', 'YB'];
  const i = Math.floor(Math.log(bytes) / Math.log(k));

  return `${parseFloat((bytes / Math.pow(k, i)).toFixed(dm))} ${sizes[i]}`;
};
```

```
export default bytesToSize;
```

The bytes-to-size component checks the byte's value and converts it into a string that users can easily understand (i.e., KB, MB, GB, TB) when uploading a file.

The next task is to create a folder named images.

Under the folder `public`, create the subfolders images ➤ `products`; and under the `products` folder, add an .svg file named `add_file.svg`.

The file path is as follows:

`public` ➤ `images` ➤ `products` ➤ `add_file.svg`

You can find the image (see Figure 8-1) in the same file path of Chapter 7 in my GitHub link in the following. Download the image and copy or drag it in the newly created .svg file.

Figure 8-1. *Screenshot of the add_file.svg*

Go to `github.com/webmasterdevlin/practical-enterprise-react/blob/master/chapter-7/public/images/products/add_file.svg`.

With this, let's import another library for a drag-and-drop capability.

Installing React Dropzone

`npm i react-dropzone`

Then let's create another file in the folder components and name it `files-dropzone.tsx`.
The file path is as follows:

`app` ➤ `components` ➤ `files-dropzone.tsx`

Let's add the named import components first, as shown in Listing 8-15.

Listing 8-15. Adding the Named Import Components to FilesDropzone

```
import React, { useState, useCallback } from 'react';
import clsx from 'clsx';
import { useDropzone } from 'react-dropzone';
import PerfectScrollbar from 'react-perfect-scrollbar';
import FileCopyIcon from '@material-ui/icons/FileCopy';
import MoreIcon from '@material-ui/icons/MoreVert';
import {
  Box,
  Button,
  IconButton,
  Link,
  List,
  ListItem,
  ListItemIcon,
  ListItemText,
  Tooltip,
  Typography,
  makeStyles,
} from '@material-ui/core';

import bytesToSize from 'utils/bytes-to-size';
```

Listing 8-15 imported the `useDropzone` from `React Dropzone` and the `PerfectScrollbar` from the `React Perfect Scrollbar` library.

We also included additional icons from Material-UI Icons. Lastly, we imported the `bytesToSize` file.

Next, let's define the type of the component and create some local states.

Listing 8-16. Creating the FilesDropzone Component

```
type Props = {
  className?: string;
};

const FilesDropzone = ({ className, ...rest }: Props) => {
  const classes = useStyles();
  const [files, setFiles] = useState<any[]>([]);
```

```
//this will be triggered when we drop a file in our component

const handleDrop = useCallback(acceptedFiles => {
  setFiles(prevFiles => [...prevFiles].concat(acceptedFiles));
}, []);

const handleRemoveAll = () => {
  setFiles([]);
};

//useDropzone - we're deconstructing it to get the properties of the
  object it returns
//we're assigning handleDrop on onDrop

const { getRootProps, getInputProps, isDragActive } = useDropzone({
  onDrop: handleDrop,
});

return (
  <div className={clsx(classes.root, className)} {...rest}>
    <div
      className={clsx({
        [classes.dropZone]: true,
        [classes.dragActive]: isDragActive,
      })}
      {...getRootProps()}
    >
      <input {...getInputProps()} />
      <div>
        <img
          alt="Select file"
          className={classes.image}
          src="/images/products/add_file.svg"        ---> here we added
          the svg file
        />
      </div>
```

```
      <div>
        <Typography gutterBottom variant="h5">
          Select files
        </Typography>
        <Box mt={2}>
          <Typography color="textPrimary" variant="body1">
            Drop files here or click <Link underline="always">browse
            </Link>{' '}
            thorough your machine
          </Typography>
        </Box>
      </div>
    </div>

    {files.length > 0 && (

      <PerfectScrollbar options={{ suppressScrollX: true }}>
        <List className={classes.list}>
          {files.map((file, i) => (
            <ListItem divider={i < files.length - 1} key={i}>
              <ListItemIcon>
                <FileCopyIcon />
              </ListItemIcon>
              <ListItemText
                primary={file.name}
                primaryTypographyProps={{ variant: 'h5' }}
                secondary={bytesToSize(file.size)}
              />
              <Tooltip title="More options">
                <IconButton edge="end">
                  <MoreIcon />
                </IconButton>
              </Tooltip>
            </ListItem>
          ))}
        </List>
```

```
      </PerfectScrollbar>
      <div className={classes.actions}>
        <Button onClick={handleRemoveAll} size="small">
          Remove all
        </Button>
        <Button color="secondary" size="small" variant="contained">
          Upload files
        </Button>
      </div>

    )}
  </div>
  );
};
```

Following this, we add the styling components for the FilesDropzone, as shown in Listing 8-17.

Listing 8-17. Adding the Styling Components for the FilesDropzone

```
const useStyles = makeStyles(theme => ({
  root: {},
  dropZone: {
    border: `1px dashed ${theme.palette.divider}`,
    padding: theme.spacing(6),
    outline: 'none',
    display: 'flex',
    justifyContent: 'center',
    flexWrap: 'wrap',
    alignItems: 'center',
    '&:hover': {
      backgroundColor: theme.palette.action.hover,
      opacity: 0.5,
      cursor: 'pointer',
    },
  },
```

```
dragActive: {
  backgroundColor: theme.palette.action.active,
  opacity: 0.5,
},
image: {
  width: 130,
},
info: {
  marginTop: theme.spacing(1),
},
list: {
  maxHeight: 320,
},
actions: {
  marginTop: theme.spacing(2),
  display: 'flex',
  justifyContent: 'flex-end',
  '& > * + *': {
    marginLeft: theme.spacing(2),
  },
},
}));

export default FilesDropzone;
```

Rerun the browser, navigate to the Create Product menu, and scroll down to Upload Images. You should see the same as what is shown in Figure 8-2.

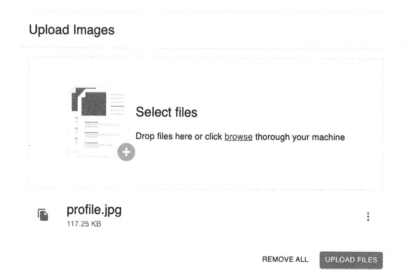

Figure 8-2. *UI of the app to upload images*

Next, we'll import a notification library to display notification messages.

Installing a Notification Library

Notistack is a React notification library that makes it easy to display notifications. It also allows users to stack snackbars and toasts on top of each other:

npm i notistack

We're going to need a notistack provider in the index.tsx of the app folder or root component.

Add the snackbar provider and import the named component, as shown in Listing 8-18.

Listing 8-18. Wrapping the App Component with SnackbarProvider

```
import * as React from 'react';
import { Helmet } from 'react-helmet-async';
import { BrowserRouter } from 'react-router-dom';
import { SnackbarProvider } from 'notistack';
import { GlobalStyle } from 'styles/global-styles';
import MainLayout from './layouts/main-layout';
```

```
import { Routes } from './routes';

export function App() {
  return (
    <BrowserRouter>
      <SnackbarProvider dense maxSnack={3}>
        <Helmet
          titleTemplate="%s - React Boilerplate"
          defaultTitle="React Boilerplate"
        >
          <meta name="description" content="A React Boilerplate
          application" />
        </Helmet>
        <MainLayout>
          <Routes />
        </MainLayout>
        <GlobalStyle />
      </SnackbarProvider>
    </BrowserRouter>
  );
}
```

After doing that, let's build up the ProductCreateForm.

Updating Product Create Form

Let's start updating the ProductCreateForm by adding the named import components, as shown in Listing 8-19.

Listing 8-19. Adding the Named Import Components to ProductCreateForm

```
import React, { useState } from 'react';
import { useHistory } from 'react-router-dom';
import clsx from 'clsx';
import { Formik } from 'formik';
import { useSnackbar } from 'notistack';
import {
```

```
  Box,
  Button,
  Card,
  CardContent,
  CardHeader,
  Checkbox,
  Divider,
  FormControlLabel,
  FormHelperText,
  Grid,
  Paper,
  TextField,
  Typography,
  makeStyles,
} from '@material-ui/core';

import FilesDropzone from 'app/components/files-dropzone';
import QuillEditor from 'app/components/quill-editor';
import { postProductAxios } from 'services/productService';
import { yupProductValidation } from'./schema/yupProductValidation';
import { productDefaultValue } from './schema/productDefaultValue';
```

You'll notice that we've added useHistory from react-router-dom. We're going to need the useHistory to allow the user to navigate the product list after creating a new product. We need Formik and the snackbar from notistack.

Aside from that, we've imported the FilesDropzone and the QuillEditor and the services {postProductAxios}, which allows us to create or add new products in the database.

We'll be using productDefaultValue, which is composed of our product objects' initial values, and the yupProductValidation to validate requirements in creating new products.

Next, let's create the type definition and some local states; see Listing 8-20.

Listing 8-20. Creating the Type Alias and Local States of ProductCreateForm

```
const categories = [
  {
    id: 'shirts',
    name: 'Shirts',
  },
  {
    id: 'phones',
    name: 'Phones',
  },
  {
    id: 'cars',
    name: 'Cars',
  },
];

type Props = {
  className?: string;
};

const ProductCreateForm = ({ className, ...rest }: Props) => {
  const classes = useStyles();
  const history = useHistory();

  //we've deconstructed the snackbar to get just the enqueueSnackbar

  const { enqueueSnackbar } = useSnackbar();
  const [error, setError] = useState('');
```

Next, let's use the Formik properties, namely, initialValues, validationSchema, and the onSubmit event handler, as shown in Listing 8-21.

Listing 8-21. Adding the Return Component of the ProductCreateForm

```
return (

    /*the required attributes or properties of Formik need to be
    initialized.
    initialValues, validationSchema, onSubmit.
    */
    <Formik
      initialValues={productDefaultValue}
      validationSchema={yupProductValidation}

      /*   The onSubmit, you can just initially write a function without
          anything inside.
Usually, I'd write an alert message first to trigger it as a proof of
concept. */

      onSubmit={async (values, formikHelpers) => {
        try {
          await postProductAxios(values);

          formikHelpers.setStatus({ success: true });
          formikHelpers.setSubmitting(false);
          enqueueSnackbar('Product Created', {
            variant: 'success',
          });
          history.push('/dashboard/list-products');
        } catch (err) {
          alert('Something happened. Please try again.');
          setError(err.message);
          formikHelpers.setStatus({ success: false });
          formikHelpers.setSubmitting(false);
        }
      }}
    >
```

```
{formikProps => (
  <form
    onSubmit={formikProps.handleSubmit}
    className={clsx(classes.root, className)}
    {...rest}
  >
    <Grid container spacing={3}>
      <Grid item xs={12} lg={8}>
        <Card>
          <CardContent>
            <TextField
              error={Boolean(
                formikProps.touched.name && formikProps.errors.name,
              )}
              fullWidth
              helperText={
                formikProps.touched.name && formikProps.errors.name
              }
              label="Product Name"
              name="name"
              onBlur={formikProps.handleBlur}
              onChange={formikProps.handleChange}
              value={formikProps.values.name}
              variant="outlined"
            />
            <Box mt={3} mb={1}>
              <Typography variant="subtitle2" color="textSecondary">
                Description
              </Typography>
            </Box>
            <Paper variant="outlined">
              <QuillEditor
                className={classes.editor}
                value={formikProps.values.description}
```

```
                    onChange={(value: string) =>
                      formikProps.setFieldValue('description', value)
                    }
                  />
                </Paper>

                {formikProps.touched.description &&
                  formikProps.errors.description && (
                    <Box mt={2}>
                      <FormHelperText error>
                        {formikProps.errors.description}
                      </FormHelperText>
                    </Box>
                  )}
            </CardContent>
          </Card>
          <Box mt={3}>
            <Card>
              <CardHeader title="Upload Images" />
              <Divider />
              <CardContent>
                <FilesDropzone />
              </CardContent>
            </Card>
          </Box>
          <Box mt={3}>
            <Card>
              <CardHeader title="Prices" />
              <Divider />

              <CardContent>
                <Grid container spacing={3}>
                  <Grid item xs={12} md={6}>
                    <TextField
```

```
          error={Boolean(
            formikProps.touched.price &&
              formikProps.errors.price,
          )}
          fullWidth
          helperText={
            formikProps.touched.price &&
            formikProps.errors.price
              ? formikProps.errors.price
              : 'If you have a sale price this will be
                shown as old price'
          }
          label="Price"
          name="price"
          type="number"
          onBlur={formikProps.handleBlur}
          onChange={formikProps.handleChange}
          value={formikProps.values.price}
          variant="outlined"
        />
      </Grid>

      <Grid item xs={12} md={6}>
        <TextField
          error={Boolean(
            formikProps.touched.salePrice &&
              formikProps.errors.salePrice,
          )}
          fullWidth
          helperText={
            formikProps.touched.salePrice &&
            formikProps.errors.salePrice
          }
          label="Sale price"
          name="salePrice"
          type="number"
```

```
                    onBlur={formikProps.handleBlur}
                    onChange={formikProps.handleChange}
                    value={formikProps.values.salePrice}
                    variant="outlined"
                  />
                </Grid>
              </Grid>
              <Box mt={2}>
                <FormControlLabel
                  control={
                    <Checkbox
                      checked={formikProps.values.isTaxable}
                      onChange={formikProps.handleChange}
                      value={formikProps.values.isTaxable}
                      name="isTaxable"
                    />
                  }
                  label="Product is taxable"
                />
              </Box>

              <Box mt={2}>
                <FormControlLabel
                  control={
                    <Checkbox
                      checked={formikProps.values.includesTaxes}
                      onChange={formikProps.handleChange}
                      value={formikProps.values.includesTaxes}
                      name="includesTaxes"
                    />
                  }
                  label="Price includes taxes"
                />
              </Box>
            </CardContent>
          </Card>
```

```
      </Box>
   </Grid>
   <Grid item xs={12} lg={4}>
      <Card>
         <CardHeader title="Organize" />
         <Divider />
         <CardContent>
            <TextField
               fullWidth
               label="Category"
               name="category"
               onChange={formikProps.handleChange}
               select
               SelectProps={{ native: true }}
               value={formikProps.values.category}
               variant="outlined"
            >
               {categories.map(category => (
                  <option key={category.id} value={category.id}>
                     {category.name}
                  </option>
               ))}
            </TextField>

            <Box mt={2}>
               <TextField
                  error={Boolean(
                     formikProps.touched.productCode &&
                        formikProps.errors.productCode,
                  )}
                  fullWidth
                  helperText={
                     formikProps.touched.productCode &&.
                     formikProps.errors.productCode
                  }
```

```
                  label="Product Code"
                  name="productCode"
                  onBlur={formikProps.handleBlur}
                  onChange={formikProps.handleChange}
                  value={formikProps.values.productCode}
                  variant="outlined"
                />
            </Box>
            <Box mt={2}>
              <TextField
                error={Boolean(
                  formikProps.touched.productSku &&
                    formikProps.errors.productSku,
                )}
                fullWidth
                helperText={
                  formikProps.touched.productSku &&
                  formikProps.errors.productSku
                }
                label="Product Sku"
                name="productSku"
                onBlur={formikProps.handleBlur}
                onChange={formikProps.handleChange}
                value={formikProps.values.productSku}
                variant="outlined"
              />
            </Box>
        </CardContent>
      </Card>
    </Grid>
  </Grid>

  {error && (
    <Box mt={3}>
      <FormHelperText error>{error}</FormHelperText>
```

```
          </Box>
        )}
        <Box mt={2}>
          <Button
            color="primary"
            variant="contained"
            type="submit"
            disabled={formikProps.isSubmitting}
          >
            Create product
          </Button>
        </Box>
      </form>
    )}
  </Formik>
  );
};
```

Okay, so what's going on in Listing 8-21? We've wrapped everything under `Formik`.
And since we did that, we're required to use its default attributes, namely:

`initialValues`: And we are passing the `productDefaultValues`.

`validationSchema`: We are passing the `yupProductValidation`.

`onSubmit`: At the start, I'd just write a function without anything inside. I'd just put an
alert to trigger it and check if it's firing.

`Formik`: This component emits the `formikProps` (you can name it whatever you
want, but I prefer to name it that way, so it is clear where it's coming from).

Inside the `formikProps`, we find `Form` and the `onSubmit` of the HTML form, which
will trigger the `onSubmit` of `Formik`.

`TextField`: Here, we're binding the name of our object. The `TextField` is coming
from Material-UI Core.

Let's briefly explain the essential parts inside the `TextField`. If you review it again, you'll see the following properties:

```
formikProps.touched.name && formikProps.errors.name,

label="Product Name"
name="name"
onBlur={formikProps.handleBlur}
onChange={formikProps.handleChange}
value={formikProps.values.name}
```

`formikProps.touched.name`: This is when you click the `TextField` of name.

`formikProps.errors.name`: This is when there's an error, for example, you exceeded the number of characters allowed or left it blank.

`formikProps.handleBlur`: This is triggered when you leave the `TextField`, for example, after clicking it, you leave it to go to another field.

`formikProps.handleChange`: This will update the value of the **name** whenever you hit or type something on the keyboard. And this will override the existing **value** in the `formikProps.values.name`. The **value** will be the data that we will see in the field.

It all looks complicated here, but really, it's more complex if we do it on our own. There's a reason why the call to action of Formik on its website `formik.org` is "build forms in React without the tears."

If you've already experienced writing forms with validation and bindings – in which you've seen changes in the input – then you know that it is quite a pain and not fun to do it from scratch. It is because what we essentially need to do is create a two-way binding.

However, the main issue with React is that it is designed with a one-way data flow. React is unlike other frameworks such as Svelte, Vue.js, and Angular, wherein two-way data binding is readily available.

In a nutshell, in two-way data binding, when you bind your model to the view, you'll know that it will be reflected in the model when you change something in the view. So basically, there's a two-way data flow that is happening between the model and the view.

One fair use case is when the user is updating or editing their profile, we know that there's already data input from the web service.

While the user is typing in the profile input form, the object model's value is also being edited. In React, it is hard to do this without writing a lot of code.

That's why there are available React libraries out there for creating forms such as React Forms, Formsy, and Redux Form, but the most popular is Formik because it's so easy to use and understand.

I highly recommend that you use Formik or any of these form libraries. As much as possible, try not to implement or write it from scratch.

Another drawback in doing this on your own is it is hard to maintain it in the long run, including when you have to pass on the project to new developers.

Most of the time, it's better to use popular libraries because it's possible that developers already know how to use or are familiar with these libraries or it's easy to understand it from the docs or get help from the online community groups.

Okay, so much for that monologue. Let's go back to the onChange in the TextField because I want to point out another thing that is going on here.

You'll notice that we're just dropping the formikProps.handleChange on the onChange and the change will be triggered. It is because the formikProps.handleChange signature matches the function that the onChange is expecting.

In this case, the onChange here emits an event. Hover your mouse over it, and you'll see it.

BUT look for the onChange under the QuillEditor. It emits a string. So it's different, and that's why the handleChange will not work here:

```
<QuillEditor
        className={classes.editor}
        value={formikProps.values.description}
        onChange={(value: string) =>
     formikProps.setFieldValue('description', value)
        }
    />
```

The question now is, How we would know it's not going to work? We'll know when we try it out, expect it to work, and get an error. *Yeah, I know. But that's my experience, meaning the* handleChange*, in this case, does not work.*

But if you encounter this kind of issue, the onChange you're using is likely emitting a different type. What you need to do is use the **formikProps.setFieldValue.** There are two arguments that we need to pass here:

string: Which is the **name** of your property

primitive type: The **value** for your description

You can check in your models ➤ product-type.ts.

📌 Whenever you encounter onChange, do a console log first to see what type or object it is emitting, especially when using JavaScript. For TypeScript, you may just hover your mouse to see.

💡 One more thing to note in the TextField is that there is a pattern in how we're writing it, and we can create an abstraction out of TextField and put it in a separate file to declutter our ProductCreateForm.

Run or refresh your application. Create or add a new product and check if it shows on the All Products page.

For Your Activity

1. Create a new function that deletes one or more products.

2. Use the handleSelectOneProduct function that stores the id of one or more products in the selectedProducts.

3. Update the postService.ts by creating a deleteProductAxios that takes an id of type string.

4. The new function should loop using an array.map while sending a delete request to the json-server. Make sure you're deleting it not just in the server but also in the UI.

Summary

We're done with this chapter, and we covered a lot of ground here, especially in learning how to build input forms in React using Formik and the Yup validations on our forms. Lastly, we touched on how to create complicated data tables the smart way with the help of Material-UI components and other libraries such as the Quill editor.

In the next chapter, we will learn an important skill: state management, or how to manage our state with the use of Redux Toolkit.

CHAPTER 9

Managing State Using Redux with Redux Toolkit

In the previous chapter, we built a Product dashboard and used Formik for our input forms and the Yup library to validate the user's input. Creating and validating forms are essential and common skills for any front-end developer to have, but now, we will move on to a more complex developer skill of managing the global state of an application using Redux with Redux Toolkit.

React and Redux are an excellent combo for state management, especially in building enterprise-level applications. But the complex process of configuring Redux has become a stumbling block for many developers. Many developers hate the complexity of setting up Redux in a React application.

Thus, Redux Toolkit was created.

As defined on its website, redux-toolkit.js.org, Redux Toolkit is the "official, opinionated, batteries-included toolset for efficient Redux development." Previously called as Redux Starter Kit, Redux Toolkit comes with it useful libraries to make life easier for React developers.

In short, Redux Toolkit is now the recommended way to use Redux.

Before we proceed with the basic concepts needed to learn how to use Redux Toolkit, let's first talk about Redux. We'll also look at some important Redux terminologies required to get going with Redux Toolkit quickly. Lastly, we'll complete the chapter with a quick Redux implementation using CodeSandbox.

© Devlin Basilan Duldulao, Ruby Jane Leyva Cabagnot 2021
D. B. Duldulao and R. J. L. Cabagnot, *Practical Enterprise React*, https://doi.org/10.1007/978-1-4842-6975-6_9

Redux Overview

According to its official website, Redux is "a predictable state container for JavaScript apps." It is used mainly for managing the state of an entire application in a single immutable state tree (object). Any change in the state creates a new object (using actions and reducers). We will discuss in detail the core concepts later in this chapter.

The Redux website at `https://redux.js.org/` is shown in Figure 9-1.

Figure 9-1. *Redux website at* `https://redux.js.org/`

We'd typically use Redux if we're building a big React project. For smaller applications, I don't think you would need Redux. Now let's discuss why we would use Redux in our application.

Why Use Redux?

For one thing, our application will have a single store for its state. Imagine the store as having all the data or state that our components need to reach. This is quite convenient, especially for large applications, because we can keep most – not necessarily all – of our data in one location and not worry about having to send props multiple levels deep in the component tree.

This process of passing data from one component to another in the React component tree that is typically multiple layers deep is called prop drilling. Yes, it can be quite a headache for many developers.

This is a common problem or issue wherein you need to pass data from one React component to another component, but you have to go through a lot of other components that do not need the data just to reach your intended destination or component.

Yes, there's a lot of passing around of data to various components that don't really need to render the data but only to pass it to the next component and onto the next until the data gets to the component that needs it.

Let's say you have this web application and you have a big <div> or component.

This component is the parent of a lot of components, which are child components. This is illustrated in Figure 9-2, where we have the Container as the parent component and two components (Dashboard and Top bar) that are one level below.

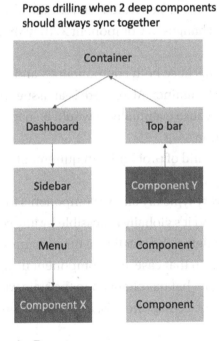

Figure 9-2. *Prop drilling in React*

Under the Dashboard, we have the following components:

Sidebar ➤ Menu ➤ Component X.

And under the Top bar, we have the following components in order of level depth:

Component Y ➤ Component ➤ Component

Synching the Dashboard and the Top bar components can be quickly done – you just need to pass or emit an event, for example, from the Dashboard to the Container and then from the Container down the Top bar and vice versa.

Figure 9-2 is an illustration of prop drilling in React.

To be fair, prop drilling is not all that bad if we are just passing data two or even three levels down. It is manageable to trace the flow of data. But problems could arise if we are already drilling too often and up to ten or more levels deep.

Case scenario:

What if you have a four-level-deep component, and you need to share or pass data to another element that is also three or four more levels deep?

Problem to solve: You need to render or pass the same type of data to Component X and Component Y. In other words, generated data should always be the same or synchronized. If there are changes in Component X, they should also reflect in Component Y.

This is a bit complicated because both components X and Y are levels apart from their parent component, the Container. Also, there is an issue with the maintainability of the application as it grows because eventually, it would be harder to keep track of what's happening with our application.

There is a solution to this kind of problem or requirement in our application. Usually, this is the job of state management.

A state management library typically allows components to access a store. A store is in-memory storage of state, and it's globally accessible by any component.

The Store also allows the data to be reactive to other components. Suppose there were any changes in the state. In that case, any component using ***that*** state will re-render the DOM difference, or what has changed in the state will be reflected in the UI no matter how deep the level of a component is, as illustrated in Figure 9-3, a Reactive State Management Store.

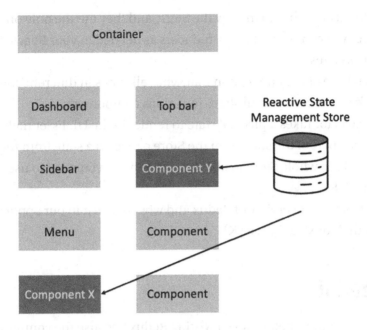

Figure 9-3. *Reactive State Management Store*

Every component *can* directly access the Store; no need to worry about passing or going back up to the parent and drilling down again to assign a data or state to another level-deep component.

Think of the Store as in-memory local storage that you can use to access a state.

State management, which is essentially a big JavaScript object store, is a popular solution for big enterprise and modern JavaScript applications like Angular, Vue.js, React, and other JavaScript frameworks to render state in different components quickly.

To get a better understanding of state management in Redux, let's look at the terminologies used in Redux.

Core parts of Redux:

Dispatch: Is the one that triggers the actions. For the receiver to receive an action, you can't just use a normal function and then send the action to the reducer.

You'll need a dispatcher function to send the action to the reducer. Imagine the dispatcher as your friendly UPS or FedEx delivery person bringing your package. Another way to think of the dispatcher is being the gun, while the action is the bullet. The gun needs to be fired before the bullet can be released to its target, which is the reducer.

Reducers: Reducers' job is to modify the Store, and they are the only ones that can modify the Store. You can have as many reducers as needed in your React-Redux app to update the Store's states.

Store: Global state of the application that syncs all states in different components. It is reactive; that's why it can sync all states in various components.

Selectors: A selector takes a piece of state to render in the UI. Essentially, selectors are functions that get a part of the state from the Store or access a state from the Store. You cannot just import the whole Store inside the component; you need to use a selector to get a state from the Store.

Now that we have an overview of Redux and why we use it in our application here, let's proceed with Redux Toolkit (RTK).

Redux Toolkit

Redux Toolkit is an opinionated way of writing Redux because the community realized that developers have each their implementation of a React-Redux app.

Before the creation of Redux Toolkit, or RTK for short, there's no standard guideline for implementing or configuring Redux in a React application. It already comes preinstalled with the useful libraries such as Redux, Immer, Redux Thunk, and Reselect.

Here's a short description of each library:

Immer: Handles immutability in stores.

Redux: For state management.

Redux Thunk: A middleware that handles async actions. Default option available with RTK, but you can also use Redux-Saga if you want to.

Reselect: Simplifies reducer functions. Allows us to get just a slice out of the global store.

Figure 9-4 is the website of Redux Toolkit if you want to learn more about RTK in detail.

Figure 9-4. *Redux Toolkit website*

Action types: To avoid typo errors for our action names.

Actions: Carry the instructions on how to modify the Store. An action brings the instructions to the reducer about what to do with the states inside the Store.

Two types of actions:

- *Non-asynchronous actions, synchronous actions, or actions without side effects*: A good example of this is if you want to save in the Store an array of selected items using checkboxes. This action does not require an HTTP request because the data you're going to hold in the Store comes from the checkboxes' details.

- *Asynchronous actions or actions with side effects*: This action usually requires an axios function to send HTTP requests, for example, saving the web service's response in the Store and then rendering it in the UI.

- *Side effects*: It is the process that CAN happen or may NOT happen in response to a Redux action. Think of it as an action where you're not quite sure what will happen next until you get a response to your action.

For example, when you're sending a request to the web server, you don't know yet if you're going to get a 200 OK or a 404 or an error 500. This process of "going out" to the world and awaiting the response to the action is called a side effect because it is essentially something we are not in "control" of or don't know until we get it.

To get a better or a bigger picture of how the Redux State Management works, let's look at Figure 9-5 – the flow of Redux State Management inside a React application.

The Flow of Redux State Management

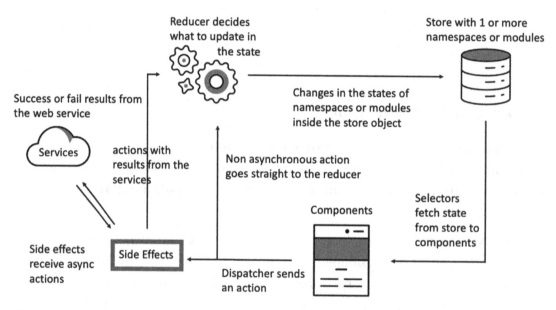

Figure 9-5. *Flow of Redux State Management inside a React app*

We have the components that are getting data from the Store. The Store has some default props upon initial setup, and every value must be initialized so as not to get an undefined return.

Selectors: You'll notice that the Selectors are fetching or selecting a piece of state from the Store. It doesn't matter whether it's an empty initial value or not because once the Store gets loaded with data or state, our Component gets re-rendered, and we'll see the new value in our UI.

Dispatcher – asynchronous and synchronous actions: The component can then send an action through the dispatcher. An action can be either an asynchronous or synchronous action.

Synchronous: Also sometimes called "***non-async or non-asynchronous***," meaning happening simultaneously.

Asynchronous: Is not happening at the same time. In simpler terms, the main difference between the two is the ***wait time.*** In the synchronous (non-async) code process, there is a step-by-step operation.

Meanwhile, asynchronous code is usually operations we don't handle ourselves, such as making an API request. We make a request; we wait for the response. But while waiting for the reply, we can do another code. When we finally get the API response, that's when we handle it.

Reducers: Synchronous or "non-async" actions will go straight to the reducers. The reducers will then modify or make changes to the Store based on the their actions.

The changes or modifications can mean changes in the state(s) of namespaces or modules inside the Store object.

So what are namespaces or modules? These are logical separations or groupings of states from each other. For example, you have a state for the profile, a state for payment, a state for another set of objects, etc. We'll go through this later in the application itself when we start implementing Redux.

Asynchronous: So what if the dispatcher sends an asynchronous action? Then this async action goes straight to the **side effects**. The side effects will send a request to the services.

The side effects either get a success (e.g., 200 OK) or fail response (e.g., 4xx or 5xx) from the web service. Whatever the response or actions we get from services, the side effects then send it to the reducers. The reducers will decide again what to do with the action they have received.

Another thing to note is that the side effects' action can be changed depending on the services' response. In the action is where we need to use the try-catch block. For example, in the try, if it's 200, do this, and if 400, do this, etc.

Using RTK in CodeSandbox

If you want to get a feel for RTK and play around a bit before implementing it in your application, visit this fantastic website `https://codesandbox.io/s/redux-toolkit-matchers-example-e765q` to see a quick implementation of Redux.

Figure 9-6 is a screenshot of the Redux Toolkit Matchers Example at the CodeSandbox website.

Figure 9-6. *Screenshot of codesandbox.io/redux-toolkit-matchers-example-e765q*

In the sidebar menu, take note of the two folders: app and features. These are Redux implementations, and according to the creators of Redux Toolkit, this is how we should structure our React-Redux application.

For example, create the folder features where you would put your namespaces, and in the app folder, you would set up your Store. The Store is different from the reducers, but it's in the Store where you'd find all the reducers.

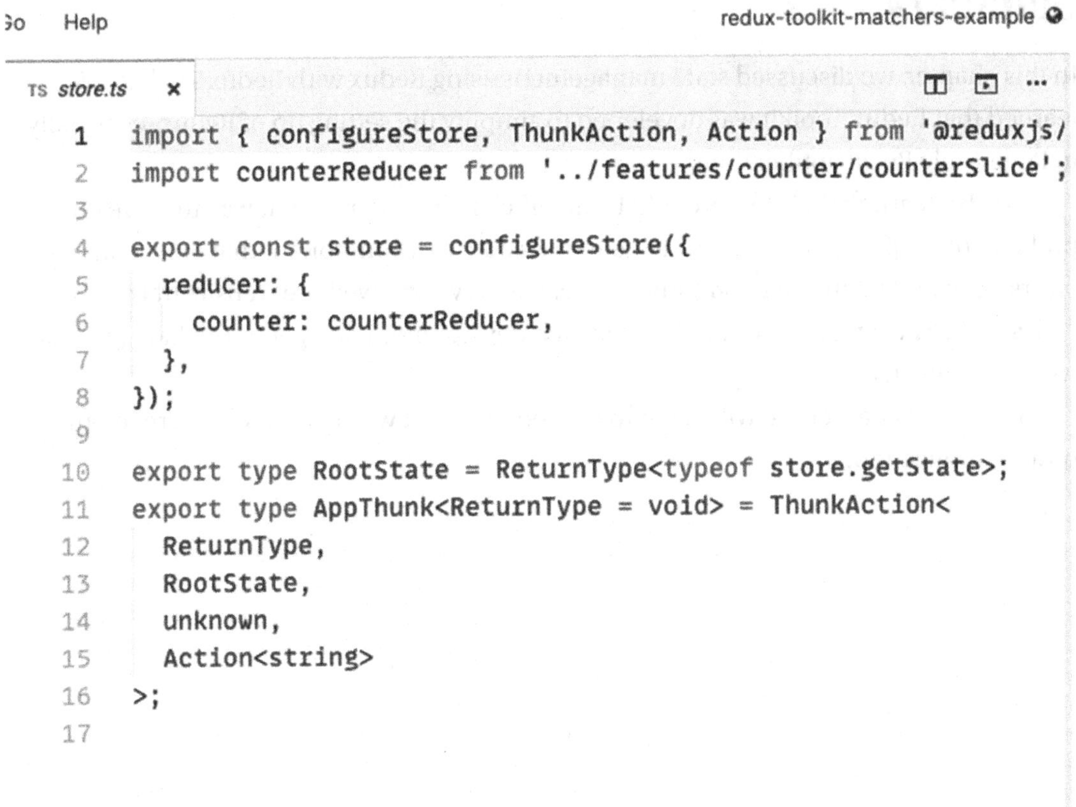

```
TS store.ts    ✕                                                    ⊓ ⊡ ⋯

 1   import { configureStore, ThunkAction, Action } from '@reduxjs/
 2   import counterReducer from '../features/counter/counterSlice';
 3
 4   export const store = configureStore({
 5     reducer: {
 6       counter: counterReducer,
 7     },
 8   });
 9
10   export type RootState = ReturnType<typeof store.getState>;
11   export type AppThunk<ReturnType = void> = ThunkAction<
12     ReturnType,
13     RootState,
14     unknown,
15     Action<string>
16   >;
17
```

Figure 9-7. *Screenshot of Store and reducers at codesandbox.io*

Every namespace or module will have its reducer. And at the end of the flow, which is the Store, is where you'd combine all the reducers.

In the next chapter, we will use the Redux DevTools. You'll see some of the reasons why React as well as Angular developers love Redux:

- time-travel debugging tool

- The state being predictable, so it is easy to test

- Centralized state and logic

- Flexible UI adaptability

As a sidenote, there's also a Redux implementation in Angular, called NgRx. It's Redux plus RxJS. There are some other state management libraries for Angular apps, but I believe NgRx is currently the most popular one.

Summary

In this chapter, we discussed state management using Redux with Redux Toolkit. We learned that Redux Toolkit was developed to simplify the setting up of Redux, especially in large-scale React applications.

We also learned that Redux could be an efficient and convenient way to solve our problem of prop drilling when we need to pass data to a component that is several layers deep and in another component tree. Lastly, we showed the website `https://codesandbox.io/` where we can do rapid web development and get immediate feedback when learning RTK.

In the next chapter, we will begin to implement what we've discussed here in our project application.

CHAPTER 10

Setting Up Redux Toolkit and Dispatching an Asynchronous Action

In the previous chapter, we learned the concept of managing the state using Redux Toolkit. We discussed prop drilling in a React app and showed the pattern when writing Redux in React.

Now, as promised, in this chapter, we are here to get down and dirty:

- Setting up Redux Toolkit

- Dispatching an asynchronous action to the reducer

- Rendering the state from the Store to our UI – specifically, a calendar view

Creating the Calendar View Component

On that note, we'll now create our calendar view component.

Open the dashboard directory, and we'll create two folders, calendar and CalendarView, and the index.tsx file:

dashboard ➤ calendar ➤ CalendarView ➤ index.tsx

Open the index.tsx file and just add for now an h1 tag <Calendar Works!>, as shown in Listing 10-1.

© Devlin Basilan Duldulao, Ruby Jane Leyva Cabagnot 2021
D. B. Duldulao and R. J. L. Cabagnot, *Practical Enterprise React*, https://doi.org/10.1007/978-1-4842-6975-6_10

Listing 10-1. Creating index.tsx of CalendarView

```
import React from 'react';

const Index = () => {
  return (
    <div>
      <h1>Calendar Works!</h1>
    </div>
  );
};

export default Index;
```

Our next drill is updating the routes as we need to register the Calendar component in our routes.tsx.

Updating the Routes

Go to `routes.tsx`, and register the `CalendarView`. We can put it after the `ProductCreateView`, as shown in Listing 10-2.

Listing 10-2. Registering the CalendarView in routes.tsx

```
<Route exact path={path + '/calendar'}
              component={lazy(
              () => import('./views/dashboard/calendar/CalendarView'),
              )} />
```

Updating the Dashboard Sidebar Nav

After registering the calendar in the routes folder, we will add a calendar icon to the dashboard sidebar navigation.

Go to the `dashboard-sidebar-navigation` to update it. First, add the calendar icon from React Feather. Again, we'll rename it as `CalendarIcon`.

Listing 10-3. Importing the Calendar Component to the dashboard-sidebar-navigation

```
import { PieChart as PieChartIcon,
        ShoppingCart as ShoppingCartIcon,
        ChevronUp as ChevronUpIcon,
        ChevronDown as ChevronDownIcon,
        Calendar as CalendarIcon,
        List as ListIcon,
        FilePlus as FilePlusIcon,
        LogOut as LogOutIcon,
} from 'react-feather';
```

Now that we've added that in the DashboardSidebarNavigation component, let's put another menu below Create Product, as shown in Listing 10-4.

Listing 10-4. Creating a Calendar Icon Menu in the dashboard-sidebar-navigation

```
<ListSubheader>Applications</ListSubheader>
            <Link className={classes.link} to={`${url}/calendar`}>
            <ListItem button>
              <ListItemIcon>
                <CalendarIcon/>
              </ListItemIcon>
              <ListItemText primary={'Calendar'} />
            </ListItem>
            </Link>
```

Refresh the browser to see the Calendar menu as shown in Figure 10-1.

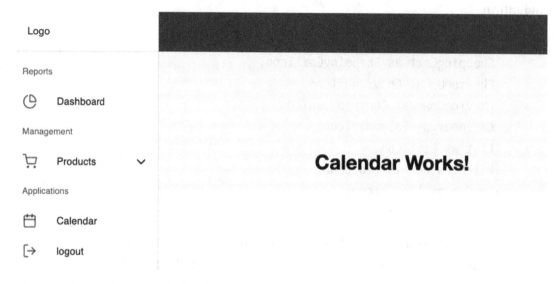

Figure 10-1. *Showing Calendar in the UI*

Now that we've seen it is working, let's build the model for our calendar. In the models folder, add a file and name it `calendar-type.ts`. We'll create the shape or model type of the CalendarView, as shown in Listing 10-5.

Listing 10-5. Creating the Shape or Model Type of the CalendarView

```
export type EventType = {
  id: string;
  allDay: boolean;
  color?: string;
  description: string;
  end: Date;
  start: Date;
  title: string;
};

//union type
export type ViewType =
  | 'dayGridMonth'
  | 'timeGridWeek'
```

```
| 'timeGridDay'
| 'listWeek';
```

Okay, it's time for the reducers to go inside the Store. Remember that reducers in Redux are what we use to manage the state in our application.

Reducers

We're going to do some refactoring first, but we'll make sure we won't lose any core functionality of Redux.

Open the reducers.tsx and replace it with the code as shown in Listing 10-6. The inserted comments are a brief explanation of each.

Listing 10-6. Refactoring the reducers.ts

```
/* Combine all reducers in this file and export the combined reducers.
combineReducers - turns an object whose values are different reducer
functions into a single reducer function. */

import { combineReducers } from '@reduxjs/toolkit';

/*  injectedReducers - an easier way of registering a reducer */

const injectedReducers = {
  //reducers here to be added one by one.
};

/* combineReducers requires an object.we're using the spread operator (...
injectedReducers) to spread out all the Reducers */

const rootReducer = combineReducers({
  ...injectedReducers,
});

/* RooState is the type or shape of the combinedReducer easier way of
getting all the types from this rootReduder instead of mapping it one
by one. RootState - we can use the Selector to give us intelli-sense in
building our components. */

export type RootState = ReturnType<typeof rootReducer>;
export const createReducer = () => rootReducer;
```

Next, we'll also need to update the Store and simplify it. There's currently Saga implementation there, but we don't need it. We'll use a more uncomplicated side effect – the Thunk.

Open configureStore.ts and refactor with the following code, as shown in Listing 10-7.

Listing 10-7. Refactoring the configureStore.ts

```
/*Create the store with dynamic reducers */

import { configureStore, getDefaultMiddleware } from '@reduxjs/toolkit';
import { forceReducerReload } from 'redux-injectors';

import { createReducer } from './reducers';

export function configureAppStore() {
  const store = configureStore({

    /*reducer is required. middleware, devTools, and the rest are optional */
    reducer: createReducer(),
    middleware: [
      ...getDefaultMiddleware({
        serializableCheck: false,
      }),
    ],
    devTools: process.env.NODE_ENV !== 'production',
  });

  /* Make reducers hot reloadable, see http://mxs.is/googmo istanbul ignore
    next */

  if (module.hot) {
    module.hot.accept('./reducers', () => {
      forceReducerReload(store);
    });
  }

  return store;
}
```

Let's further inspect what is going on in Listing 10-8.

In the Store setup, we are using the `configureStore` and `getDefaultMiddleware` from `Redux Toolkit`.

If you hover the cursor over the getDefaultMiddleware, you'll see this message: "It returns an array containing the default middleware installed by ConfigureStore(). Useful if you want to configure your store with a custom middleware array but still keep the default setting."

forceReduceReload from redux-injectors is for our hot reloading.

createReducer from the rootReducer is the function to return the combinedReducers.

middleware is an array of plugins or middleware.

store: We'll need to inject this in our components through a provider.

And after that, let's head off to the

src ➤ index.tsx

In React, if you see a component that a name provider is suffixing, this means that it is something you have to wrap in your root component.

A Provider component gives access to the whole application. In Listing 10-8, we are wrapping the root component (index.tsx) inside the Provider component.

Listing 10-8. Wrapping the Root Component (index.tsx) Inside a Provider Component

```
/*wrapping the root component inside a provider gives all the component an
   access to the provider component or the whole application */

const ConnectedApp = ({ Component }: Props) => (
  <Provider store={store}>
    <HelmetProvider>
      <Component />
    </HelmetProvider>
  </Provider>
);
```

The provider is being derived from React-Redux. This has been set up for us by the boilerplate.

Note that the provider has a required props store, and we're passing into that the store that we created inside the configureStore.ts. That's why we imported the configureAppStore from store/configureStore.

This makes the store the single source of truth – available to all components in our application.

Next, we need to update the index.tsx of the root component as shown in Listing 10-9. Keep in mind that this index.tsx is the entry file for the application – only for the setup and boilerplate code.

Listing 10-9. Updating the index.tsx of the Root Component

```
import 'react-app-polyfill/ie11';
import 'react-app-polyfill/stable';
import 'react-quill/dist/quill.snow.css';
import * as React from 'react';
import * as ReactDOM from 'react-dom';
import { Provider } from 'react-redux';
import * as serviceWorker from 'serviceWorker';
import 'sanitize.css/sanitize.css';

// Import root app
import { App } from 'app';
import { HelmetProvider } from 'react-helmet-async';
import { configureAppStore } from 'store/configureStore';

// Initialize languages
import './locales/i18n';

const store = configureAppStore();
const MOUNT_NODE = document.getElementById('root') as HTMLElement;

interface Props {
  Component: typeof App;
}

/*wrapping the root component inside a provider gives all the component an
  access to the provider component or the whole application */
```

```
const ConnectedApp = ({ Component }: Props) => (
  <Provider store={store}>
    <HelmetProvider>
      <Component />
    </HelmetProvider>
  </Provider>
);
const render = (Component: typeof App) => {
  ReactDOM.render(<ConnectedApp Component={Component} />, MOUNT_NODE);
};

if (module.hot) {

  // Hot reloadable translation json files and app
  // modules.hot.accept does not accept dynamic dependencies,
  // have to be constants at compile-time

  module.hot.accept(['./app', './locales/i18n'], () => {
    ReactDOM.unmountComponentAtNode(MOUNT_NODE);
    const App = require('./app').App;
    render(App);
  });
}

render(App);


// If you want your app to work offline and load faster, you can change
// unregister() to register() below. Note this comes with some pitfalls.
// Learn more about service workers: https://bit.ly/CRA-PWA
serviceWorker.unregister();
```

After this, let's just do a bit of cleanup.

Cleanup Time

Delete the folder _tests_ inside the store folder. We'll also take out the types folder because we already have a RootState.

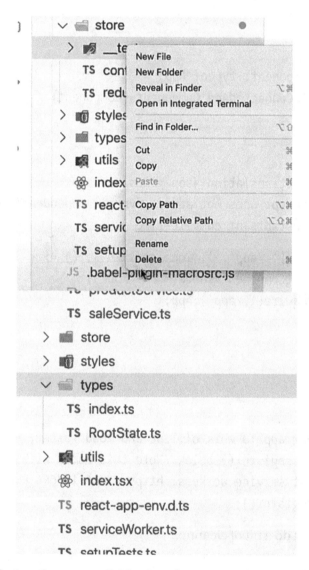

Figure 10-2. *Deleting the _tests_ folder inside store and types folder*

Next, locate the utils folder and DELETE everything EXCEPT the bytes-to-size.ts file.

Figure 10-3. *Deleting the utils folder*

Updating Axios

That's done. We are off to axios now to update the endpoints as shown in Listing 10-10.

Listing 10-10. Updating the Endpoints in axios.ts

```
Open src ➤ api ➤ axios.ts

export default api;

export const EndPoints = {
  sales: 'sales',
  products: 'products',
  events: 'event',
};
```

Then let's add another set of fake data in the db.json. Add the following Events data after products. The events array contains seven event objects.

Copy the code in Listing 10-11 and add it to the db.json file.

Listing 10-11. Adding the Events Object in db.json

```
"events": [
    {
      "id": "5e8882e440f6322fa399eeb8",
      "allDay": false,
      "color": "green",
```

```
    "description": "Inform about new contract",
    "end": "2021-01-01T12:00:27.87+00:20",
    "start": "2021-01-01T12:00:27.87+00:20",
    "title": "Call Samantha"
  },
  {
    "id": "5e8882eb5f8ec686220ff131",
    "allDay": false,
    "color": null,
    "description": "Discuss about new partnership",
    "end": "2021-01-01T12:00:27.87+00:20",
    "start": "2021-01-01T12:00:27.87+00:20",
    "title": "Meet with IBM"
  },
  {
    "id": "5e8882f1f0c9216396e05a9b",
    "allDay": false,
    "color": null,
    "description": "Prepare docs",
    "end": "2021-01-01T12:00:27.87+00:20",
    "start": "2021-01-01T12:00:27.87+00:20",
    "title": "SCRUM Planning"
  },
  {
    "id": "5e8882f6daf81eccfa40dee2",
    "allDay": true,
    "color": null,
    "description": "Meet with team to discuss",
    "end": "2020-12-12T12:30:00-05:00",
    "start": "2020-11-11T12:00:27.87+00:20",
    "title": "Begin SEM"
  },
  {
    "id": "5e8882fcd525e076b3c1542c",
    "allDay": false,
```

```
      "color": "green",
      "description": "Sorry, John!",
      "end": "2021-01-01T12:00:27.87+00:20",
      "start": "2021-01-01T12:00:27.87+00:20",
      "title": "Fire John"
   },
   {
      "id": "5e888302e62149e4b49aa609",
      "allDay": false,
      "color": null,
      "description": "Discuss about the new project",
      "end": "2021-01-01T12:00:27.87+00:20",
      "start": "2021-01-01T12:00:27.87+00:20",
      "title": "Call Alex"
   },
   {
      "id": "5e88830672d089c53c46ece3",
      "allDay": false,
      "color": "green",
      "description": "Get a new quote for the payment processor",
      "end": "2021-01-01T12:00:27.87+00:20",
      "start": "2021-01-01T12:00:27.87+00:20",
      "title": "Visit Samantha"
   }
]
```

Implementing Redux Toolkit

Okay, now let's do the fun part of implementing our Redux Toolkit.

We will be using two kinds of implementations in this application so you'll understand how both work and it would be easier for you to onboard to an existing React–Redux Toolkit project.

The implementations are pretty much the same in many different projects you'll soon encounter; sometimes, it's just a matter of folder structuring and the number of files created.

Here we're going to write all the actions and reducers in one file, and we will name it calendarSlice.ts.

Inside the src directory, create a new folder and name it features; this is where we will implement our Redux.

Inside the features, create a new folder and name it calendar. Inside the calendar, create a new file called calendarSlice.ts.

Redux Toolkit recommends adding the suffix Slice to your namespace.

```
src > features > calendar > calendarSlice.ts
```

Open the calendarSlice file, and let's add some named imports (Listing 10-12).

Listing 10-12. Adding the Named Import Components in calendarSlice

```
/*PayloadAction is for typings   */
import {
  createSlice,
  ThunkAction,
  Action,
  PayloadAction,
} from '@reduxjs/toolkit';

import { RootState } from 'store/reducers';
import { EventType } from 'models/calendar-type';
import axios, { EndPoints } from 'api/axios';
```

Next, let's do the typings in calendarSlice as shown in Listing 10-13.

Listing 10-13. Creating the Typings/Shapes in calendarSlice

```
/*typings for the Thunk actions to give us intlelli-sense */
export type AppThunk = ThunkAction<void, RootState, null, Action<string>>;

/*Shape or types of our CalendarState   */

interface CalendarState {
  events: EventType[];
  isModalOpen: boolean;
```

```
selectedEventId?: string;      //nullable
selectedRange?: {                        //nullable
  start: number;
  end: number;
};

loading: boolean;   //useful for showing spinner or loading screen

error: string;
}
```

And still in our calendarSlice file, we will initialize some values in our initialState, as shown in Listing 10-14.

Listing 10-14. Adding the Default Values of the initialState

```
/*initialState is type-safe, and it must be of a calendar state type.
  It also means that you can't add any other types here that are not part
  of the calendar state we've already defined.   */

const initialState: CalendarState = {
  events: [],
  isModalOpen: false,
  selectedEventId: null,
  selectedRange: null,
  loading: false,
  error: '',
};
```

And then, we move on to the creation of the namespace and the createSlice, as shown in Listing 10-15. We are adding the namespace and createSlice to the calendarSlice.

Listing 10-15. Adding the Namespace and createSlice

```
const calendarNamespace = 'calendar';

/*Single-File implementation of Redux-Toolkit*/

const slice = createSlice({

  /*namespace for separating related states. Namespaces are like modules*/
  name: calendarNamespace,
```

```
  /*initialState is the default value of this namespace/module and it is
  required.*/

  initialState, // same as initialState: initialState

  /*reducers --   for non asynchronous actions. It does not require Axios.*/
  /* the state here refers to the CalendarState */

  reducers: {
    setLoading(state, action: PayloadAction<boolean>) {
      state.loading = action.payload;
    },
    setError(state, action: PayloadAction<string>) {
      state.error = action.payload;
    },
    getEvents(state, action: PayloadAction<EventType[]>) {
      state.events = action.payload;
    },
  },
});

/* Asynchronous actions. Actions that require Axios (HTTP client)
 or any APIs of a library or function that returns a promise. */

export const getEvents = (): AppThunk => async dispatch => {
  dispatch(slice.actions.setLoading(true));
  dispatch(slice.actions.setError(''));
  try {
    const response = await axios.get<EventType[]>(EndPoints.events);
    dispatch(slice.actions.getEvents(response.data));
  } catch (error) {
    console.log(error.message);
    dispatch(slice.actions.setError(error.message));
  } finally {
    dispatch(slice.actions.setLoading(false));
  }
};

export default slice.reducer;
```

The createSlice is a big object that requires us to put something in the name, the initialState, and the reducers.

The reducers here are an object of non-asynchronous actions (also known as synchronous actions) that do not require axios or are not promise-based.

Non-asynchronous Actions/Synchronous Actions

Let's inspect what we have written in the non-async actions or synchronous actions inside our calendarSlice:

setLoading in reducers: There are two parameters (state and action), but you're only required to pass the PayloadAction, a boolean.

setError in reducers: The same thing with the first parameter state; no need to pass anything because Thunk will take care of it under the hood. We just need to pass something or update the PayloadAction, which is a string.

getEvents in reducers: The PayloadAction is an array of EventType.

Asynchronous Actions

And here are our asynchronous actions:

getEvents: A function that returns AppThunk and a dispatch function.

dispatch(slice.actions.setLoading(true)): Updating the loading from default false to true.

dispatch(slice.actions.setError(' ')): We're passing just an empty string, so basically, we're resetting the error here back to empty every time we have a successful request.

Inside the try-catch block, we're using an axios.get, and it's returning an array of EventType from the Endpoints.events.

The response.data that we get will be dispatched to the Store so the state can be updated.

After creating the calendarSlice, we'll now update the root reducers.

Updating the Root Reducer

Open the reducers.ts file again, and update the injectedReducers.

First, we need to import the calendarReducer from features/calendar/calendarSlice, as shown in Listing 10-16.

Listing 10-16. Adding the Named Component in reducers.ts

```
import { combineReducers } from '@reduxjs/toolkit';
import calendarReducer from 'features/calendar/calendarSlice'
```

And then, in the same file, inject our first reducer, as shown in Listing 10-17.

Listing 10-17. Injecting the calendarReducer in injectedReducers

```
const injectedReducers = {
  calendar: calendarReducer,
};
```

We can now use this namespace calendar to get the needed state from this calendar. But we will do that in our components later on.

Now, we're ready to write our selectors and dispatchers in the UI component of our calendar view or page.

Updating the CalendarView

But first, let's test the dispatch by going to the calendar view component. Open the index.tsx of the CalendarView.

First, we'll update the index.tsx of CalendarView, as shown in Listing 10-18.

Listing 10-18. Updating index.tsx of CalendarView

```
import React, { useEffect } from 'react';
import { getEvents } from 'features/calendar/calendarSlice';
import { useDispatch, useSelector } from 'react-redux';
import { RootState } from 'store/reducers';

const CalendarView = () => {
  const dispatch = useDispatch();
```

```
useEffect(() => {
  dispatch(getEvents());
}, []);
```

For now, we will check in the console the getEvents and useDispatch to see if we are successfully getting the data.

Make sure your server is running *http://localhost:5000/events* and click the refresh button in the browser *http://localhost:3000/dashboard/calendar*.

Open the Chrome DevTools ➤ Network ➤ Response to see the Events data, as shown in Figure 10-4.

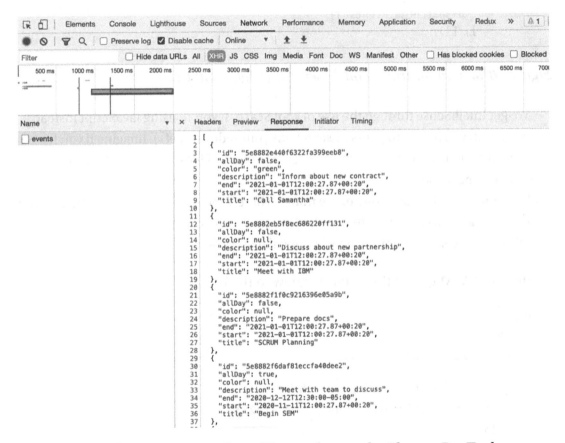

Figure 10-4. *Showing a screenshot of Events data at the Chrome DevTools*

Our proof of concept that our Redux is working! The state is in the browser, and we can use it. Let's go back to our CalendarView component, and we'll add the useSelector.

useSelector needs a function with a signature emitting and returning the RootState, and now we can access the reducer. For now, we can only access or get the calendar because this is what we've added so far, as shown in Figure 10-5.

```
const CalendarView = () => {
  const dispatch = useDispatch();
  const { events, loading, error } = useSelector(
    (state: RootState) => state.
                              (property) calendar: CalendarState
dux/index
  useEffect(() => {
    dispatch(getEvents());
  }, []);
```

Figure 10-5. *Demonstrating IntelliSense through RootState*

We get IntelliSense through the use of RootState. If you're using JavaScript instead of TypeScript, you'd have to guess or search for your reducer file(s). Imagine if you have an extensive application with dozens or even hundreds of files. Searching for it can quickly become tiresome.

This intelligent feature is one of the things where TypeScript shines. You can just type dot (.), and then it will show all the available reducers you can use.

Okay, let's do some mapping now at our CalendarView.

Listing 10-19. Mapping the CalendarView in the UI

```
return (
   <div>
     <h1>Calendar Works!</h1>

     {loading && <h2>Loading... </h2>}
     {error && <h2>Something happened </h2>}
     <ul>

             /*conditional nullable chain */

       {events?.map(e => (
         <li key={e.id}>{e.title} </li>
       ))}
```

```
      </ul>
    </div>
  );
};

export default CalendarView;
```

Okay, let's inspect what we are doing in Listing 10-19.

`loading &&`: If the condition is true, the element right after && gets run; otherwise, if the state is false, ignore it. The same logic applies to the `error &&`.

Refresh the browser to check if you can see the loading before the data is rendered.

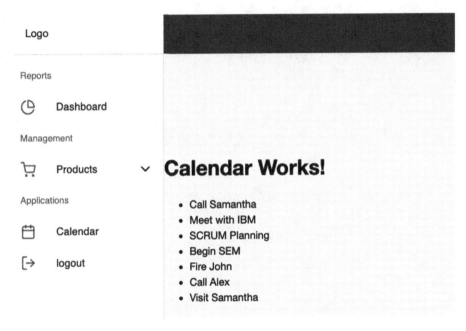

Figure 10-6. *Rendering the CalendarView in the UI*

Summary

In this chapter, I hope you've gained a better understanding of the Redux implementation flow in a React app, including how to dispatch an async action to the reducer and render the state from the Store to the UI.

We also used the state management library Redux Toolkit and implemented its helper function called createSlice. We also expanded our styling components to include the calendar view component from Material-UI.

In the next chapter, we will continue with our Redux lessons to create, delete, and update events using Redux.

CHAPTER 11

Creating, Deleting, and Updating Events on FullCalendar Using RTK

In the last chapter, we set up Redux Toolkit and learned how to dispatch an asynchronous action to the Store. We've also started to build our Calendar component.

We will continue where we left off – creating, deleting, and updating events on the Calendar component using Redux Toolkit. And for this, we're going to use the FullCalendar library to add user forms to create, delete, and update an event.

To give you a sneak peek at the finished look of the application, Figures 11-1 and 11-2, as well as Listing 11-1, provide the UI of our app at the end of this chapter.

Figure 11-1. *Screenshot of Full Calendar at the end of Chapter 11*

237

© Devlin Basilan Duldulao, Ruby Jane Leyva Cabagnot 2021
D. B. Duldulao and R. J. L. Cabagnot, *Practical Enterprise React*, https://doi.org/10.1007/978-1-4842-6975-6_11

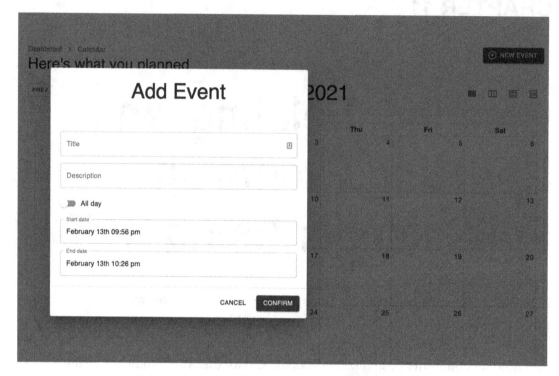

Figure 11-2. *Screenshot of Add Event at the end of Chapter 11*

Installing Moment and FullCalendar

Let's get started with installing some third-party libraries that we will need to build our Full Calendar component.

Open your terminal and install the following packages, as shown in Listing 11-1.

Listing 11-1. Importing Additional Libraries

```
npm i moment @date-io/moment@1 @fullcalendar/core
npm i @fullcalendar/daygrid @fullcalendar/interaction
npm i @fullcalendar/list @fullcalendar/react
npm i @fullcalendar/timegrid @fullcalendar/timeline
```

Let's quickly review each library that we've installed:

moment.js: A JavaScript date library for parsing, validating, manipulating, and formatting dates. A note on this famous library's project status: Even though it is now in maintenance code – meaning the creators are not planning to add more features to the

238

library – the patches and bug fixes will continue. It has over 18 million downloads and is still on the uptrend as of early 2021.

There are also a lot of JavaScript libraries that you can use for manipulating dates. But learning moment.js can likewise help you understand other React applications because many React libraries are likely using this popular date library.

If you go to *npmjs.org* and look for these libraries, you'll see their following definitions:

@date-io/moment: Part of date-io-monorepo and contains the unified interface of the moment. We'll be needing version 1.

@fullcalendar/core: Provides core functionality, including the Calendar class.

@fullcalendar/daygrid: Displays events on Month view or DayGrid view.

@fullcalendar/interaction: Offers functionality for an event drag-and-drop, resizing, dateClick, and selectable actions.

@fullcalendar/list: View your events as a bulleted list.

@fullcalendar/react: It's a connector. It tells the core FullCalendar package to begin rendering with React Virtual DOM nodes instead of the Preact nodes it uses typically, transforming FullCalendar into a "real" React component.

@fullcalendar/timegrid: Displays your events on a grid of time slots.

@fullcalendar/timeline: Displays events on a horizontal time axis (without resources).

After you've successfully imported all the libraries and modules, let's update the root component.

Updating the Root Component

First, let's add these modules in `index.tsx`, as shown in Listing 11-2.

Listing 11-2. Importing Modules in the Root Component index.tsx

```
import MomentUtils from '@date-io/moment';
import {MuiPickersUtilsProvider} from '@material-ui/pickers';
```

In the same root file, we'll use the `MuiPickersUtils` to wrap everything starting from `SnackbarProvider`, as shown in Listing 11-3.

Listing 11-3. Adding MuiPickersUtilsProvider to the Root Component

```
export function App() {
  return (
    <BrowserRouter>

            /*required props called utils and we're passing the
             MomentUtils */
      <MuiPickersUtilsProvider utils={MomentUtils}>
      <SnackbarProvider dense maxSnack={3}>
        <Helmet
          titleTemplate="%s - React Boilerplate"
          defaultTitle="React Boilerplate"
        >
          <meta name="description" content="A React Boilerplate
          application" />
        </Helmet>

        <MainLayout>
          <Routes />
        </MainLayout>

        <GlobalStyle />
      </SnackbarProvider>
      </MuiPickersUtilsProvider>
    </BrowserRouter>
  );
}
```

Updating the calendarSlice

Let's go next to the component calendarSlice. We will add new non-async or synchronous actions and also asynchronous actions.

Creating the Event Actions

We'll first create the event actions, as shown in Listing 11-4.

Listing 11-4. Creating the Event Actions in calendarSlice.ts

```
createEvent(state, action: PayloadAction<EventType>) {
    state.events.push(action.payload);
  },
  selectEvent(state, action: PayloadAction<string>) {
    state.isModalOpen = true;
    state.selectedEventId = action.payload;
  },
  updateEvent(state, action: PayloadAction<EventType>) {
    const index = state.events.findIndex(e => e.id === action.payload.id);
    state.events[index] = action.payload;
  },
  deleteEvent(state, action: PayloadAction<string>) {
    state.events = state.events.filter(e => e.id !== action.payload);
  },

  /*{start: number; end: number} - this is the shape of the model that we
  can define here right away, although we can also write it separately in
  the models' folder. */

  selectRange(state, action: PayloadAction<{ start: number; end:
  number }>) {

          /*deconstructing the payload */
    const { start, end } = action.payload;

    state.isModalOpen = true;
    state.selectedRange = {
      start,
      end,
    };
  },

  openModal(state) {
    state.isModalOpen = true;
  },
  closeModal(state) {
```

```
     state.isModalOpen = false;
     state.selectedEventId = null;
     state.selectedRange = null;
   },
```

Let's review what is happening in Listing 11-4.

createEvent: The parameter for createEvent is an object of EventType, and to produce a new event, we are just going to push it in an existing array. This would generate a new object in the array of EvenType.

selectEvent: Takes a string, and we're modifying two states here.

updateEvent: Takes an event type, and then we need to get the position (findIndex) of this EventType that we're passing. This is updating an existing object.

deleteEvent: We are passing a string, and then we're doing a filter. The filter returns a new array without the id (string) we selected.

selectRange: Takes an object with a start and end – both of type number.

openModal: Does not require any parameter; it's just updating the state to true.

closeModel: Does not require any parameter; it's just updating the state back to false, selectedEventId, and selectedRange to null.

Next, we will export some non-async actions in the same file calendarSlice.ts, as shown in Listing 11-5

Adding the Non-async Actions

Listing 11-5. Adding non-async actions in calendarSlice.ts

```
/* Export these actions so components can use them.  Non-asynchronous
actions. HTTP client is not needed. */

export const selectEvent = (id?: string): AppThunk => dispatch => {
  dispatch(slice.actions.selectEvent(id));
};

export const selectRange = (start: Date, end: Date): AppThunk => dispatch
=> {
  dispatch(
    slice.actions.selectRange({
      start: start.getTime(),
```

```
      end: end.getTime(),
    }),
  );
};

export const openModal = (): AppThunk => dispatch => {
  dispatch(slice.actions.openModal());
};

export const closeModal = (): AppThunk => dispatch => {
  dispatch(slice.actions.closeModal());
};
```

Again, let's see what is going on in Listing 11-5.

selectEvent: This is a higher-order function that takes an id and returns a dispatch for execution.

The id is coming from the selectEvent. The function selectEvent is named the same as the dispatch selectEvent to avoid confusion when importing it to the components.

selectRange: The function also has the same name as the action selectRange.

And let's continue adding our asynchronous event actions in calendarSlice.ts, as shown in Listing 11-6.

Listing 11-6. Adding Asynchronous Event Actions in calendarSlice.ts

```
export const createEvent = (event: EventType): AppThunk => async dispatch
=> {

/* data - we deconstructed the response object */

const { data } = await axios.post<EventType>(EndPoints.events, event);

  dispatch(slice.actions.createEvent(data));
};

export const updateEvent = (update: EventType): AppThunk => async dispatch
=> {

  /*updating the state in the database */
```

```
  const { data } = await axios.put<EventType>(
    `${EndPoints.events}/${update.id}`,
    update,
  );

  /*updating the state in the UI */

  dispatch(slice.actions.updateEvent(data));
};

export const deleteEvent = (id: string): AppThunk => async dispatch => {
  /*deleting from the database */

  await axios.delete(`${EndPoints.events}/${id}`);

  /*deleting it from the UI */
  dispatch(slice.actions.deleteEvent(id));
};
```

In Listing 11-6, we added three more events – createEvent, updateEvent, and deleteEvent:

createEvent: We're exporting and using the createEvent function, which takes an EventType object. We are running dispatch asynchronously as we *await* the axios. post, which takes the EventType, from the Endpoints.events. The required body parameter is an event.

We deconstructed the response object because we only need one property, the data.

We're passing the data in the createEvent action and dispatching it.

updateEvent: It also takes an update of EventType and runs the dispatch asynchronously and awaits the axios.put, and it returns an EventType.

deleteEvent: Here, we only need an id. After running the async dispatch and deleting it in the database, we're also filtering it out from the UI.

FOR YOUR ACTIVITY

If you notice, there's no try-catch block in the **createEvent**, **updateEvent**, and **deleteEvent**.

For example, in the deleteEvent, if there's no try-catch and the axios.delete fails, the dispatch will continue to run and remove the object in the UI even if the object in the database has not been erased. So now, the state in the UI and that in the database would be mismatched.

For your activity, implement a try-catch in the three async events. See what we did with the getEvents. Don't also forget to implement the setLoading and setError actions.

After doing the activity, we'll update the index.tsx of the CalendarView.

Updating the CalendarView

We will import the Page component template and the Container and makeStyles modules from Material-UI Core, as shown in Listing 11-7.

Listing 11-7. Importing Named Components in CalendarView

```
import { Container, makeStyles} from '@material-ui/core';
import Page from 'app/components/page';
```

Then let's replace the return <div> with the newly imported Page and Container. We'll add some styling, too, on the height and padding, as shown in Listing 11-8.

Listing 11-8. Updating the Styling of the CalendarView Component

```
const CalendarView = () => {
const classes = useStyles();
const dispatch = useDispatch();

/* destructuring it because we only need the events, loading, error */

const { events, loading, error } = useSelector(
  (state: RootState) => state.calendar,
);
```

```
  useEffect(() => {
    dispatch(getEvents());
  }, []);

  return (
    <Page className={classes.root} title="Calendar">
      <Container maxWidth={false}>
        <h1>Calendar Works!</h1>
        {loading && <h2>Loading... </h2>}
        {error && <h2>Something happened </h2>}
        <ul>
          {events?.map(e => (
            <li key={e.id}>{e.title} </li>
          ))}
        </ul>
      </Container>
    </Page>
  );
};

export default CalendarView;

const useStyles = makeStyles(theme => ({
  root: {
    minHeight: '100%',
    paddingTop: theme.spacing(3),
    paddingBottom: theme.spacing(3),
  },
}));
```

After this, let's add a Header component for the CalendarView. Create a new file Header.tsx:

calendar ➤ CalendarView ➤ Header.tsx

Creating the Header Component

In Listing 11-9, we are importing the named components for Header.tsx.

Listing 11-9. Importing the Named Components in Header.tsx

```
import React from 'react';
import { Link as RouterLink } from 'react-router-dom';
import clsx from 'clsx';
import { PlusCircle as PlusCircleIcon } from 'react-feather';
import NavigateNextIcon from '@material-ui/icons/NavigateNext';
import {
  Button,
  Breadcrumbs,
  Grid,
  Link,
  SvgIcon,
  Typography,
  makeStyles,
  Box,
} from '@material-ui/core';
```

We'll follow it up right away with our Header function component, as shown in Listing 11-10.

Listing 11-10. Creating the Header Component

```
/*nullable className string and nullable onAddClick function  */

type Props = {
  className?: string;
  onAddClick?: () => void;
};

/* using the Props here and ...rest operator  */

const Header = ({ className, onAddClick, ...rest }: Props) => {
  const classes = useStyles();

  return (
```

247

```
<Grid
  className={clsx(classes.root, className)}
  container
  justify="space-between"
  spacing={3}
  {...rest}
>
  <Grid item>
    <Breadcrumbs
      separator={<NavigateNextIcon fontSize="small" />}
      aria-label="breadcrumb"
    >
      <Link
        variant="body1"
        color="inherit"
        to="/app"
        component={RouterLink}
      >
        Dashboard
      </Link>
      <Box>
        <Typography variant="body1" color="inherit">
          Calendar
        </Typography>
      </Box>
    </Breadcrumbs>
    <Typography variant="h4" color="textPrimary">
      Here's what you planned
    </Typography>
  </Grid>

  <Grid item>
    <Button
      color="primary"
      variant="contained"
      onClick={onAddClick}
```

```
              className={classes.action}
              startIcon={
                <SvgIcon fontSize="small">
                  <PlusCircleIcon />
                </SvgIcon>
              }
            >
              New Event
            </Button>
          </Grid>
        </Grid>
      );
    };
```

And lastly, the useStyles from makeStyles of Material-UI Core, as shown in Listing 11-11.

Listing 11-11. Adding the Styling Margin for the Header Component

```
const useStyles = makeStyles(theme => ({
  root: {},
  action: {
    marginBottom: theme.spacing(1),
    '& + &': {
      marginLeft: theme.spacing(1),
    },
  },
}));

export default Header;
```

Next, we'll use the newly created Header component in the index.tsx of the CalendarView, as shown in Listing 11-12.

Listing 11-12. Using the Header Component in the index.tsx of the CalendarView

```
import Header from './Header';
...
return (
    <Page className={classes.root} title="Calendar">
      <Container maxWidth={false}>
        <Header />
        <h1>Calendar Works!</h1>
```

Refresh the browser, and you should see the same.

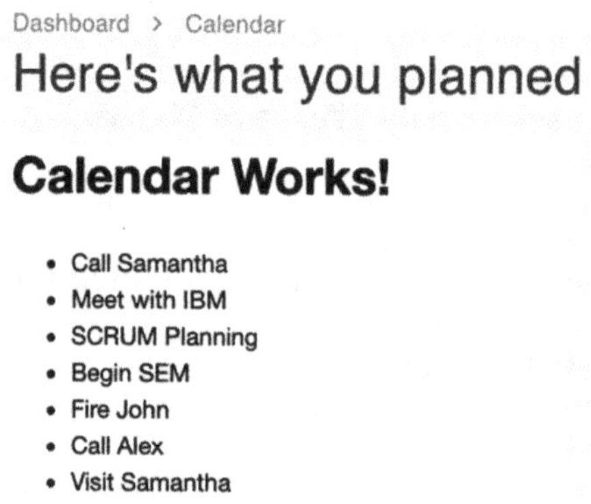

Dashboard > Calendar

Here's what you planned

Calendar Works!

- Call Samantha
- Meet with IBM
- SCRUM Planning
- Begin SEM
- Fire John
- Call Alex
- Visit Samantha

Figure 11-3. *Screenshot of the UI after using the Header component in the index.tsx*

So baby steps again. We can see that it's working. We can now proceed with the Add Edit Event form. Inside the `CalendarView` folder, create another component and name it `AddEditEventForm.tsx`.

Creating an Add Edit Event Form Using Formik

In the `AddEditEventForm,` among others, we'll be using `moment.js`, `Formik,` and `yup validation`. In this case, we don't need to do a separate file for the Yup validation.

Open the file `AddEditEventForm` and add the following named components, as shown in Listing 11-13.

Listing 11-13. Adding the Named Components in AddEditEventForm

```
import React from 'react';
import moment from 'moment';
import * as Yup from 'yup';
import { Formik } from 'formik';
import { useSnackbar } from 'notistack';
import { DateTimePicker } from '@material-ui/pickers';
import { Trash as TrashIcon } from 'react-feather';
import { useDispatch } from 'react-redux';
import {
  Box,
  Button,
  Divider,
  FormControlLabel,
  FormHelperText,
  IconButton,
  makeStyles,
  SvgIcon,
  Switch,
  TextField,
  Typography,
} from '@material-ui/core';

/*the async actions we created earlier in the calendarSlice */

import {
  createEvent,
  deleteEvent,
  updateEvent,
} from 'features/calendar/calendarSlice';
import { EventType } from 'models/calendar-type';
```

The new addition here from Material-UI is the DateTimePicker. If you check out the Material-UI website, you'll see a lot of date-time picker components you can reuse, and you don't have to create your own from scratch.

Next, let's write the type definition for our component AddEditEventForm, as shown in Listing 11-14.

Listing 11-14. Creating the Type or Shape of the AddEditEventForm

```
/* the ? indicates it is a nullable type */

type Props = {
  event?: EventType;
  onAddComplete?: () => void;
  onCancel?: () => void;
  onDeleteComplete?: () => void;
  onEditComplete?: () => void;
  range?: { start: number; end: number };
};
```

In Listing 11-14, we have the Props, and we're using it in the AddEditEventForm component, as shown in Listing 11-15.

Listing 11-15. Creating the AddEditEventForm Component

```
const AddEditEventForm = ({
  event,
  onAddComplete,
  onCancel,
  onDeleteComplete,
  onEditComplete,
  range,
}: Props) => {
  const classes = useStyles();
  const dispatch = useDispatch();
  const { enqueueSnackbar } = useSnackbar();

 /*event is coming from the parent of the AddEditEventForm */

  const isCreating = !event;

  const handleDelete = async (): Promise<void> => {
    try {
```

```
    await dispatch(deleteEvent(event?.id));
    onDeleteComplete();
  } catch (err) {
    console.error(err);
  }
};
```

As you'll notice in Listing 11-15, **AddEditEventForm** is using Props, as well as the dispatch Snackbar, while **handleDelete** is an async function that dispatches the deleteEvent action and passes the event.id.

We are not done yet, of course. Next, let's use Formik to create our form. Since we are using TypeScript, we must initialize the following three Formik props: initialValues, validationSchema, and onSubmit.

We will start first with the initialValues and the ValidationSchema using Yup as shown in Listing 11-16.

Listing 11-16. Creating the Two Formik Props: initialValues and validationSchema

```
return (
  <Formik
    initialValues={getInitialValues(event, range)}
    validationSchema={Yup.object().shape({
      allDay: Yup.bool(),
      description: Yup.string().max(5000),
      end: Yup.date().when(
        'start',
        (start: Date, schema: any) =>
          start &&
          schema.min(start, 'End date must be later than start date'),
      ),
      start: Yup.date(),
      title: Yup.string().max(255).required('Title is required'),
    })}
```

Let's see what we did in Listing 11-16:

initialValues: The getInitialValues is added in Listing 11-17.

validationSchema: Usually, the validation schema is saved in another file, especially if it's a long one, but in this instance, we're already writing it here because it's just a small validation object.

In short, it is common to put in a separate file the initialValues and the validationSchema and just use them in a component where you need them.

Okay, next, let's add another required Formik prop: onSubmit.

Listing 11-17. Creating the onSubmit on the AddEditEventForm

```
onSubmit={async (
        /* where the input values (i.e. from TextField)  are being
        combined. */

        values,

         /* Formik helper deconstructed.*/
        { resetForm, setErrors, setStatus, setSubmitting },
      ) => {
        try {
          const data = {
            allDay: values.allDay,
            description: values.description,
            end: values.end,
            start: values.start,
            title: values.title,
            id: '',
          };

          if (event) {
            data.id = event.id;
            await dispatch(updateEvent(data));
          } else {
            await dispatch(createEvent(data));
          }

          resetForm();
          setStatus({ success: true });
          setSubmitting(false);
```

```
      enqueueSnackbar('Calendar updated', {
        variant: 'success',
      });

      if (isCreating) {
        onAddComplete();
      } else {
        onEditComplete();
      }
    } catch (err) {
      console.error(err);
      setStatus({ success: false });
      setErrors({ submit: err.message });
      setSubmitting(false);
    }
  }}
>

  /*deconstructing here the Formik props   */

  {(({
    errors,
    handleBlur,
    handleChange,
    handleSubmit,
    isSubmitting,
    setFieldTouched,
    setFieldValue,
    touched,
    values,
  }) => (

    /*this will trigger the onSubmit of Formik */

    <form onSubmit={handleSubmit}>
      <Box p={3}>
        <Typography
          align="center"
```

```
        gutterBottom
        variant="h3"
        color="textPrimary"
      >
        {isCreating ? 'Add Event' : 'Edit Event'}
      </Typography>
    </Box>

  /*TextField -- make sure to map everything to title */
    <Box p={3}>
      <TextField
        error={Boolean(touched.title && errors.title)}
        fullWidth
        helperText={touched.title && errors.title}
        label="Title"
        name="title"
        onBlur={handleBlur}
        onChange={handleChange}
        value={values.title}
        variant="outlined"
      />
      <Box mt={2}>

    /*TextFields -- make sure to map everything to description */

        <TextField
          error={Boolean(touched.description && errors.description)}
          fullWidth
          helperText={touched.description && errors.description}
          label="Description"
          name="description"
          onBlur={handleBlur}
          onChange={handleChange}
          value={values.description}
          variant="outlined"
        />
```

```
</Box>

/*Form Control Label  */

<Box mt={2}>
  <FormControlLabel
    control={
      <Switch
        checked={values.allDay}
        name="allDay"
        onChange={handleChange}
      />
    }
    label="All day"
  />
</Box>

/*DateTimePicker for Start date.
onChange - we're using the setFieldValue because the onChange
emits a date, not an event.
  */

<Box mt={2}>
  <DateTimePicker
    fullWidth
    inputVariant="outlined"
    label="Start date"
    name="start"
    onClick={() => setFieldTouched('end')} // install the @
    date-io/moment@1.x
    onChange={date => setFieldValue('start', date)} // and use
    it in MuiPickersUtilsProvider
    value={values.start}
  />
</Box>

  /*DateTimePicker for End date*/
```

```
            <Box mt={2}>
              <DateTimePicker
                fullWidth
                inputVariant="outlined"
                label="End date"
                name="end"

onClick={() => setFieldTouched('end')}
onChange={date => setFieldValue('end', date)}
                value={values.end}
              />
            </Box>

          /*FormHelperText - to show an error message */

            {Boolean(touched.end && errors.end) && (
              <Box mt={2}>
                <FormHelperText error>{errors.end}</FormHelperText>
              </Box>
            )}
          </Box>
          <Divider />
          <Box p={2} display="flex" alignItems="center">
            {!isCreating && (
              <IconButton onClick={() => handleDelete()}>
                <SvgIcon>
                  <TrashIcon />
                </SvgIcon>
              </IconButton>
            )}
            <Box flexGrow={1} />
            <Button onClick={onCancel}>Cancel</Button>
            <Button
              variant="contained"
              type="submit"
```

```
            disabled={isSubmitting}      ➤   /* this is to prevent double
            clicking */

            color="primary"
            className={classes.confirmButton}

          >
            Confirm
          </Button>
        </Box>
      </form>
    )}
  </Formik>
  );
};

export default AddEditEventForm;
```

And here is Listing 11-18, the getInitialValues for the Formik prop initialValues.

Listing 11-18. Creating the getInitialValues of Formik

```
const getInitialValues = (
  event?: EventType,
  range?: { start: number; end: number },
) => {
  if (event) {
    const defaultEvent = {
      allDay: false,
      color: '',
      description: '',
      end: moment().add(30, 'minutes').toDate(),
      start: moment().toDate(),
      title: '',
      submit: null,
    };
    return { ...defaultEvent, event };
  }
```

```
  if (range) {
    const defaultEvent = {
      allDay: false,
      color: '',
      description: '',
      end: new Date(range.end),
      start: new Date(range.start),
      title: '',
      submit: null,
    };
    return { ...defaultEvent, event };
  }

  return {
    allDay: false,
    color: '',
    description: '',
    end: moment().add(30, 'minutes').toDate(),
    start: moment().toDate(),
    title: '',
    submit: null,
  };
};
```

In Listing 11-18, we have the **getInitialValues** – a function that takes the event and range of the value. This function is showing a default event or a range of events.

After creating the Formik props, we go back to the index.tsx of the CalendarView to make some updates.

Updating the CalendarView

Let's import closeModal and openModal in the calendarSlice, as shown in Listing 11-19.

Listing 11-19. Importing Modules in calendarSlice

```
import {
  getEvents,
  openModal,
  closeModal,
} from 'features/calendar/calendarSlice';
```

In the same index file of the CalendarView, we use the following: isModalOpen and selectedRange in useSelector. We will also create a handleAddClick and a handleModalClose, as shown in Listing 11-20.

Listing 11-20. Adding States and Handles in calendarSlice

```
const { events, loading, error, isModalOpen, selectedRange } = useSelector(
    (state: RootState) => state.calendar,
  );

useEffect(() => {
    dispatch(getEvents());
  }, []);

  const handleAddClick = (): void => {
    dispatch(openModal());
  };

  const handleModalClose = (): void => {
    dispatch(closeModal());
  };
```

Updating the Header

So now we can update the Header with the handleClick function, as shown in Listing 11-21.

Listing 11-21. Using the handleAddClick in the Header

```
<Page className={classes.root} title="Calendar">
    <Container maxWidth={false}>
      <Header onAddClick={handleAddClick} />
      <h1>Calendar Works!</h1>
```

Updating the CalendarView

Let's add styling components in the index.tsx of CalendarView. We will import these style components from Material-UI Core, as shown in Listing 11-22.

Listing 11-22. Adding Styling Components to the index.tsx of CalendarView

```
import {
  Container,
  makeStyles,
    Dialog,    //a modal popup
    Paper,     //in Material Design, the physical properties of paper are
                  translated to the screen.
  useMediaQuery,    // a CSS media query hook for React. Detects when its
                       media queries change
} from '@material-ui/core';
```

In the same index file, we will need a small function for selecting an event.

We will also import the EventType and ViewType components from the models/calendar-type and the AddEditEventForm, as shown in Listing 11-23.

Listing 11-23. Creating an Event Selector in the index.tsx of CalendarView

```
import Header from './Header';
import { EventType, ViewType } from 'models/calendar-type';
import AddEditEventForm from './AddEditEventForm';

...
export default CalendarView;

const selectedEventSelector = (state: RootState): EventType | null => {
  const { events, selectedEventId } = state.calendar;

  if (selectedEventId) {
    return events?.find(_event => _event.id === selectedEventId);
  } else {
```

```
    return null;
  }
};

const useStyles = makeStyles(theme => ({
...
```

In Listing 11-23, we have the **selectedEventSelector** – a function that takes a state, RootState, and the calendar, and what we're passing from the calendar are the variable events and selectedEventId.

Now we'll call the useSelector and pass selectedEventSelector, as shown in Listing 11-24

Listing 11-24. Using the useSelector in the index.tsx of CalendarView

```
const selectedEvent = useSelector(selectedEventSelector);
```

Still in the same index file, we'll do some refactoring inside the Container.

We will replace the current h1 tags with the Dialog, isModalOpen, and AddEditEventForm, as shown in Listing 11-25.

Listing 11-25. Adding Dialog and AddEditEventForm in index.tsx of CalendarView

```
<Container maxWidth={false}>
        <Header onAddClick={handleAddClick} />
        <Dialog
          maxWidth="sm"
          fullWidth
          onClose={handleModalClose}
          open={isModalOpen}
        >

          {isModalOpen && (
            <AddEditEventForm
              event={selectedEvent}
              range={selectedRange}
              onAddComplete={handleModalClose}
              onCancel={handleModalClose}
```

```
            onDeleteComplete={handleModalClose}
            onEditComplete={handleModalClose}
        />
      )}
    </Dialog>
  </Container>
```

In Listing 11-25, we have the **Dialog** – a Material-UI modal component – and we're defining the size here and using the event onClose and open dialog. And also the **isModalOpen**, if true, shows the AddEditEventForm. In the AddEditEventForm props, we are passing selectedEvent, selectedRange, and handleModalClose.

Checking the UI of CalendarView

Let's see how it works in the UI. Refresh the browser and open Chrome DevTools. Click New Event. You should see the pop-up modal dialog entitled Add Event.

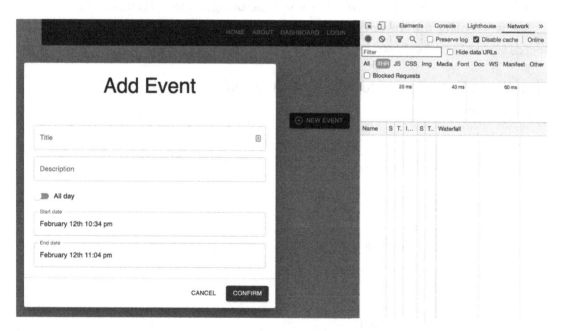

Figure 11-4. *Screenshot of the modal dialog Add Event in the browser*

Try creating an event and click the Confirm button. You'll see the data events being successfully returned in the Chrome DevTools, as shown in Figure 11-5.

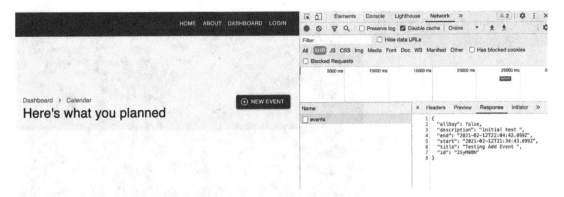

Figure 11-5. *Screenshot of event requests in Chrome DevTools*

Checking the Chrome DevTools

Note also that the modal dialog automatically closes. In the Chrome DevTools, check the Headers, and you'll see the Status Code 201 created. This means we're able to create an object and save it in the database.

Checking the Redux DevTools

Next, open the Redux DevTools. Make sure to choose Calendar – React Boilerplate on the top dropdown arrow.

The Redux DevTools records dispatched actions and the Store's state. We can inspect our application's state through its time-travel debugging feature at every point in time without the need to reload or restart the app.

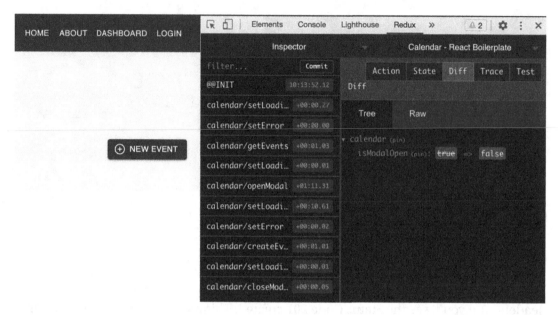

Figure 11-6. *Screenshot of event requests in Redux DevTools*

We're interested in looking at the Diff where you can see the state is changing from
setLoading to createEvents to closeModal and so on.

You can see the events or array of events you can access from the store, you can also
look for any error message, etc. All the actions are being recorded, and we can play it
back via the time-travel debugging feature of the Redux DevTools.

Creating the Toolbar

We will create a Toolbar component, Toolbar.tsx, under the CalendarView folder.

First, we import the named components, as shown in Listing 11-26.

Listing 11-26. Adding Named Components in Toolbar.tsx

```
import React, { ElementType, ReactNode } from 'react';
import clsx from 'clsx';
import moment from 'moment';
import {
  Button,
  ButtonGroup,
  Grid,
```

```
  Hidden,
  IconButton,
  Tooltip,
  Typography,
  makeStyles,
} from '@material-ui/core';
import ViewConfigIcon from '@material-ui/icons/ViewComfyOutlined';
import ViewWeekIcon from '@material-ui/icons/ViewWeekOutlined';
import ViewDayIcon from '@material-ui/icons/ViewDayOutlined';
import ViewAgendaIcon from '@material-ui/icons/ViewAgendaOutlined';

import { ViewType } from 'models/calendar-type';
```

In Listing 11-26, we imported moment and the standard style modules from
Material-UI Core. The new ones are the different icons from Material-UI icons.

We also imported the ViewType from models/calendar-type.

In the same Toolbar.tsx file, we'll create the type or schema of our model Toolbar
and type for ViewOption, as shown in Listing 11-27.

Listing 11-27. Creating the Type or Schema of Toolbar

```
type ViewOption = {
  label: string;
  value: ViewType;
  icon: ElementType;
};

type Props = {
  children?: ReactNode;
  className?: string;
  date: Date;

  /* the ? means it's a nullable void function

  onDateNext?: () => void;
  onDatePrev?: () => void;
  onDateToday?: () => void;
  onAddClick?: () => void;
```

```
/* takes a view object and returns nothing or void */

onViewChange?: (view: ViewType) => void;
view: ViewType;
};
```

In Listing 11-27, we have the type Props, and it has date and view as required type properties, while the rest are nullable types. The type ViewOption takes three required props: label, value, and icon. We will use the ViewPoint in a short while. We are just preparing it here now.

And so, we'll now use the Props that we've defined in the Toolbar component, as shown in Listing 11-28.

Listing 11-28. Using the Props in the Toolbar Component

```
const Toolbar = ({
  className,
  date,
  onDateNext,
  onDatePrev,
  onDateToday,
  onAddClick,
  onViewChange,
  view,
  ...rest        // the rest parameter
}: Props) => {
  const classes = useStyles();
```

In Listing 11-28, you will notice the **rest parameter**. This allows us to take multiple arguments in our function and get them as an array.

★ Rest parameters can be used in functions, arrow functions, or classes. But in the function definition, the rest parameter must appear last in the parameter list; otherwise, the TypeScript compiler will complain and show an error.

Next, we'll make the return statement in the same Toolbar component file.

We're wrapping everything in a Grid and adding the ButtonGroup.

We're formatting the date using the moment, and we're also mapping the four objects in the viewOptions, as shown in Listing 11-29, and returning the Tooltip key **title** and IconButton.

Listing 11-29. Adding the Return Statement of the Toolbar Component

```
return (
    <Grid
      className={clsx(classes.root, className)}
      alignItems="center"
      container
      justify="space-between"
      spacing={3}
      {...rest}
    >
      <Grid item>
        <ButtonGroup size="small">
          <Button onClick={onDatePrev}>Prev</Button>
          <Button onClick={onDateToday}>Today</Button>
          <Button onClick={onDateNext}>Next</Button>
        </ButtonGroup>
      </Grid>
      <Hidden smDown>
        <Grid item>
          <Typography variant="h3" color="textPrimary">
            {moment(date).format('MMMM YYYY')}
          </Typography>
        </Grid>

        <Grid item>
          {viewOptions.map(viewOption => {
            const Icon = viewOption.icon;

            return (
              <Tooltip key={viewOption.value} title={viewOption.label}>
                <IconButton
                  color={viewOption.value === view ? 'primary' : 'default'}
                  onClick={() => {
                    if (onViewChange) {
                      onViewChange(viewOption.value);
                    }
```

```
                    }}
                 >
                    <Icon />
                 </IconButton>
              </Tooltip>
            );
          })}
        </Grid>
      </Hidden>
    </Grid>
  );
};

export default Toolbar;
```

Next, we add the ViewOption and makeStyles components, as shown in Listing 11-30.

Listing 11-30. Creating ViewOption and makeStyles components in Toolbar.tsx

```
const viewOptions: ViewOption[] = [
  {
    label: 'Month',
    value: 'dayGridMonth',
    icon: ViewConfigIcon,
  },
  {
    label: 'Week',
    value: 'timeGridWeek',
    icon: ViewWeekIcon,
  },
  {
    label: 'Day',
    value: 'timeGridDay',
    icon: ViewDayIcon,
  },
  {
    label: 'Agenda',
    value: 'listWeek',
```

```
    icon: ViewAgendaIcon,
  },
];

const useStyles = makeStyles(() => ({
  root: {},
}));
```

It's time again to update the index.tsx of the CalendarView.

Styling the CalendarView

We will start with adding new styling components in the index.tsx of the CalendarView, as shown in Listing 11-31.

Listing 11-31. Adding Styling Components in the index.tsx of CalendarView

```
calendar: {
    marginTop: theme.spacing(3),
    padding: theme.spacing(2),
    '& .fc-unthemed .fc-head': {},
    '& .fc-unthemed .fc-body': {
      backgroundColor: theme.palette.background.default,
    },
    '& .fc-unthemed .fc-row': {
      borderColor: theme.palette.divider,
    },
    '& .fc-unthemed .fc-axis': {
      ...theme.typography.body2,
    },
    '& .fc-unthemed .fc-divider': {
      borderColor: theme.palette.divider,
    },
    '& .fc-unthemed th': {
      borderColor: theme.palette.divider,
    },
```

```
'& .fc-unthemed td': {
  borderColor: theme.palette.divider,
},
'& .fc-unthemed td.fc-today': {},
'& .fc-unthemed .fc-highlight': {},
'& .fc-unthemed .fc-event': {
  backgroundColor: theme.palette.secondary.main,
  color: theme.palette.secondary.contrastText,
  borderWidth: 2,
  opacity: 0.9,
  '& .fc-time': {
    ...theme.typography.h6,
    color: 'inherit',
  },

  '& .fc-title': {
    ...theme.typography.body1,
    color: 'inherit',
  },
},
'& .fc-unthemed .fc-day-top': {
  ...theme.typography.body2,
},
'& .fc-unthemed .fc-day-header': {
  ...theme.typography.subtitle2,
  fontWeight: theme.typography.fontWeightMedium,
  color: theme.palette.text.secondary,
  padding: theme.spacing(1),
},
'& .fc-unthemed .fc-list-view': {
  borderColor: theme.palette.divider,
},
'& .fc-unthemed .fc-list-empty': {
  ...theme.typography.subtitle1,
},
```

```
  '& .fc-unthemed .fc-list-heading td': {
    borderColor: theme.palette.divider,
  },
  '& .fc-unthemed .fc-list-heading-main': {
    ...theme.typography.h6,
  },
  '& .fc-unthemed .fc-list-heading-alt': {
    ...theme.typography.h6,
  },
  '& .fc-unthemed .fc-list-item:hover td': {},
  '& .fc-unthemed .fc-list-item-title': {
    ...theme.typography.body1,
  },
  '& .fc-unthemed .fc-list-item-time': {
    ...theme.typography.body2,
  },
},
```

The additional styling components in Listing 11-31 are just several border colors for the calendar, along with some margins and paddings.

Now in the same index file of the CalendarView, we will import the moment library and the modules from the FullCalendar library, as shown in Listing 11-32.

Listing 11-32. Importing Named Components in index.tsx of CalendarView

```
import moment from 'moment';
import FullCalendar from '@fullcalendar/react';
import dayGridPlugin from '@fullcalendar/daygrid';
import timeGridPlugin from '@fullcalendar/timegrid';
import interactionPlugin from '@fullcalendar/interaction';
import listPlugin from '@fullcalendar/list';
import timelinePlugin from '@fullcalendar/timeline';
```

Then let's add and use some modules from the calendarSlice and React Hooks, as shown in Listing 11-33.

Listing 11-33. Importing Additional Modules from calendarSlice and React Hooks

```
import React, { useEffect, useState, useRef } from 'react';

import {
  getEvents,
  openModal,
  closeModal,
  selectRange,
  selectEvent,
  updateEvent
} from 'features/calendar/calendarSlice';
```

Again, in the same index file, we'll create some local states, as shown in Listing 11-34.

Listing 11-34. Creating local states in index.tsx of CalendarView

```
const selectedEvent = useSelector(selectedEventSelector);

  const mobileDevice = useMediaQuery('(max-width:600px)');
  const [date, setDate] = useState<Date>(moment().toDate());
  const [view, setView] = useState<ViewType>(
    mobileDevice ? 'listWeek' : 'dayGridMonth',
  );

  const calendarRef = useRef<FullCalendar | null>(null);

  useEffect(() => {
    dispatch(getEvents());
  },
```

Let's have a look at what's happening in Listing 11-34. We have the **useRef** to access DOM elements and persist values or states in the succeeding or next renders. Hover your mouse over the useRef, and you'll read that it is a React.MutableRefObject<FullCalen dar>. It means that we have access to the APIs or interfaces of this FullCalendar.

useMediaQuery: We're using it for detecting small browser screens such as that of a mobile device.

After that, we will create additional handle functions below the handleModalClose, as shown in Listing 11-35.

Listing 11-35. Creating Additional Handle Events in the index.tsx of
CalendarView

```
/* calendarRef is a reference to the element FullCalendar*/

const handleDateNext = (): void => {
    const calendarEl = calendarRef.current;

/*the getApi here is part of FullCalendar. If you 'dot space'
the  'calendarEl,' you'll see the interfaces or APIs available.  */

    if (calendarEl) {
      const calendarApi = calendarEl.getApi();

      calendarApi.next();
      setDate(calendarApi.getDate());
    }
  };

  const handleDatePrev = (): void => {
    const calendarEl = calendarRef.current;

    if (calendarEl) {
      const calendarApi = calendarEl.getApi();

      calendarApi.prev();
      setDate(calendarApi.getDate());
    }
  };

  const handleDateToday = (): void => {
    const calendarEl = calendarRef.current;

    if (calendarEl) {
      const calendarApi = calendarEl.getApi();

      calendarApi.today();
      setDate(calendarApi.getDate());
    }
  };
```

```
const handleViewChange = (newView: ViewType): void => {
  const calendarEl = calendarRef.current;

  if (calendarEl) {
    const calendarApi = calendarEl.getApi();

    calendarApi.changeView(newView);
    setView(newView);
  }
};

/*the arg: any - could be a string or a number */

const handleEventSelect = (arg: any): void => {
  dispatch(selectEvent(arg.event.id));
};
/*We have here a try-catch block because handleEventDrop is an async
 function */

const handleEventDrop = async ({ event }: any): Promise<void> => {
  try {
    await dispatch(
      updateEvent({
        allDay: event.allDay,
        start: event.start,
        end: event.end,
        id: event.id,
      } as any),
    );
  } catch (err) {
    console.error(err);
  }
};

const handleEventResize = async ({ event }: any): Promise<void> => {
  try {
    await dispatch(
      updateEvent({
```

```
            allDay: event.allDay,
            start: event.start,
            end: event.end,
            id: event.id,
          } as any),
      );
  } catch (err) {
    console.error(err);
  }
};
const handleRangeSelect = (arg: any): void => {
  const calendarEl = calendarRef.current;

  if (calendarEl) {
    const calendarApi = calendarEl.getApi();

    calendarApi.unselect();
  }

  dispatch(selectRange(arg.start, arg.end));
};
```

We're still not yet done here. We need to add the paper module from Material-UI and the FullCalendar for the UI styling.

Locate the Dialog tag in the return statement; we've written that the Dialog is only visible when the isModalOpen is true. So after the Header component and before the Dialog, we will put the FullCalendar, as shown in Listing 11-36.

Listing 11-36. Rendering the FullCalendar in the UI of the index.tsx of CalendarView

```
return (
    <Page className={classes.root} title="Calendar">
      <Container maxWidth={false}>
        <Header onAddClick={handleAddClick} />
        <Toolbar
          date={date}
          onDateNext={handleDateNext}
```

```
          onDatePrev={handleDatePrev}
          onDateToday={handleDateToday}
          onViewChange={handleViewChange}
          view={view}
        />
        <Paper className={classes.calendar}>
          <FullCalendar
            allDayMaintainDuration
            droppable
            editable
            selectable
            weekends
            dayMaxEventRows
            eventResizableFromStart
            headerToolbar={false}
            select={handleRangeSelect}
            eventClick={handleEventSelect}
            eventDrop={handleEventDrop}
            eventResize={handleEventResize}
            initialDate={date}
            initialView={view}
            events={events}
            height={800}
            ref={calendarRef}
            rerenderDelay={10}
            plugins={[
              dayGridPlugin,
              timeGridPlugin,
              interactionPlugin,
              listPlugin,
              timelinePlugin,
            ]}
          />
        </Paper>
        <Dialog
```

```
maxWidth="sm"
fullWidth
onClose={handleModalClose}
open={isModalOpen}
>
```

If you notice in Listing 11-36, some of the properties (i.e., `allDayMaintainDuration`, `droppable`, `editable`, etc.) are without the equal = sign; it means they are by default set as true.

This is shorthand for writing `allDayMaintainDuration={true}`, and this also means that they are all boolean.

But for the `headerToolbar`, we had to state the false value explicitly. We're setting it to false because we have our Toolbar component that we will add shortly.

Checking the FullCalendar in the UI

Let's test everything out in our browser. Refresh it, and you should be able to see the Full Calendar and the test events we've created earlier.

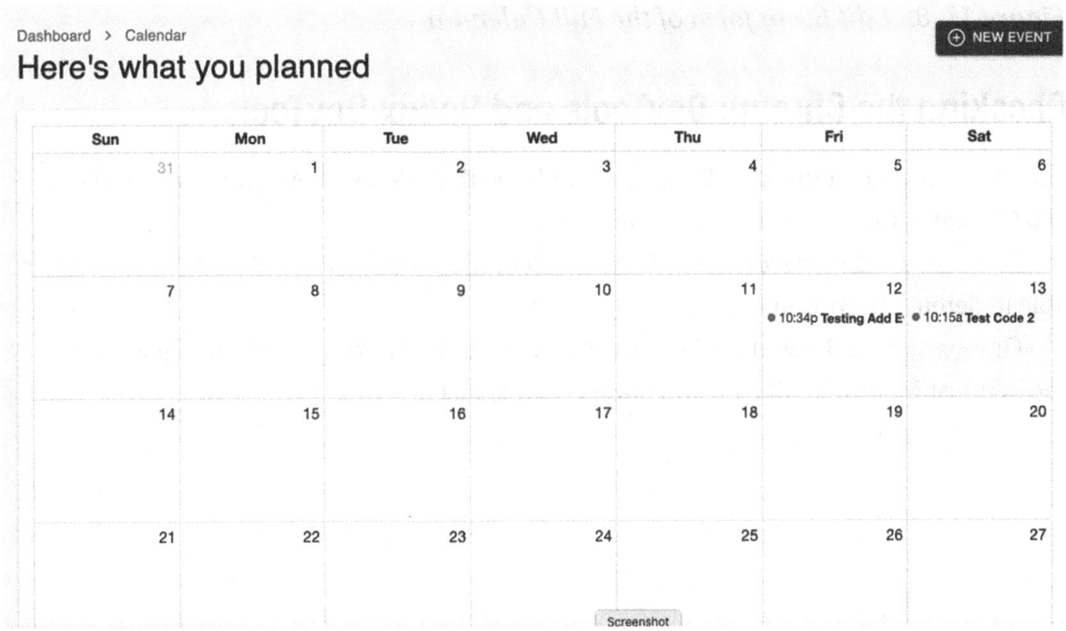

Figure 11-7. Screenshot of the Full Calendar

Click the event shown and try to edit it. You should be able to make the changes successfully, as shown in Figure 11-8.

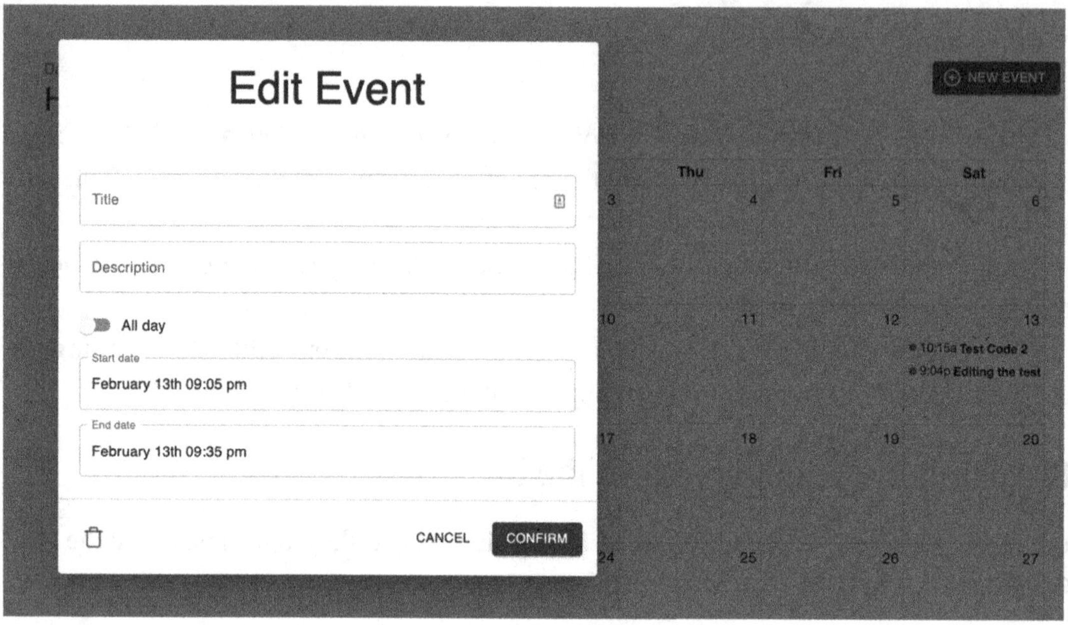

Figure 11-8. *Edit Event form of the Full Calendar*

Checking the Chrome DevTools and Redux DevTools

Take a peek at the Redux DevTools and you'll see that it's also being updated, and see the 200 OK Status Code in the Chrome DevTools.

Test also the delete icon at the bottom left of the Edit Event form, and you should be able to delete the chosen event.

Once you have deleted it, check the Network in the Chrome DevTools again to see the Request Method: DELETE and Status Code: 200 OK.

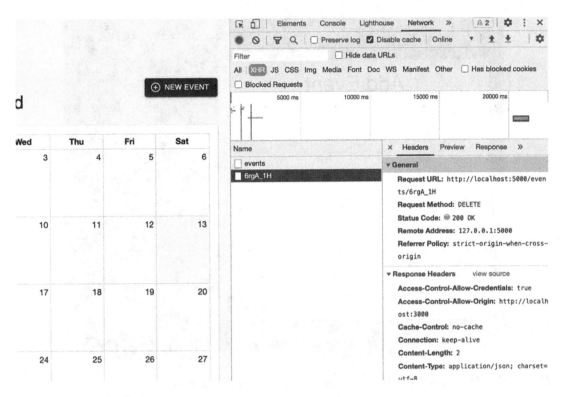

Figure 11-9. *Deleting an event*

How about creating an event that has about a two-week range in two consecutive months? In Figure 11-10, we can see that we have successfully added an event for a multi-month calendar.

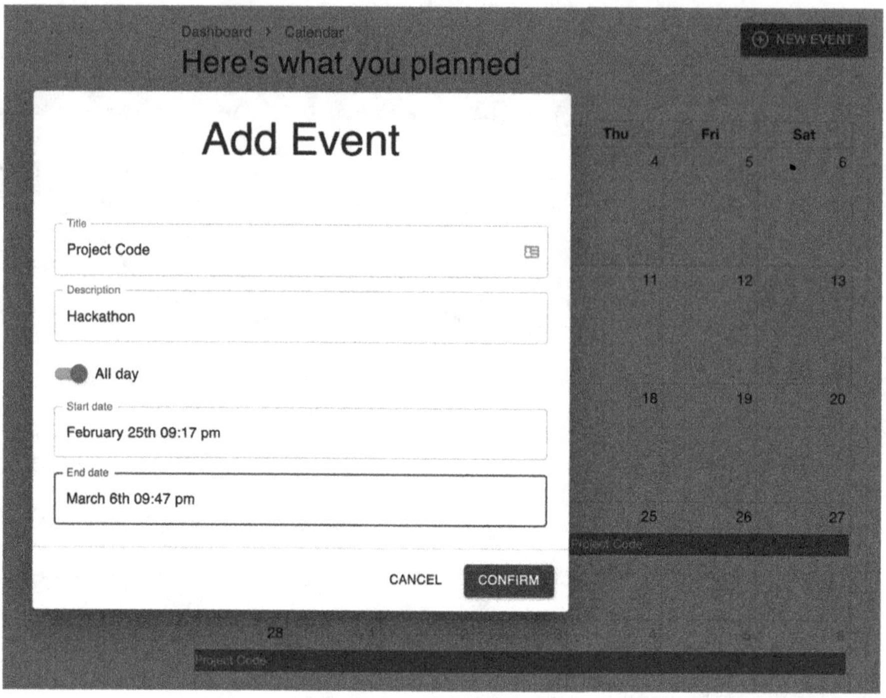

Figure 11-10. *Creating an event in a multi-month calendar*

We were able to create the multi-month event from February to March. However, you'll notice that we can't navigate to the next month.

This is because we still need to add one more thing, which is the Toolbar. So let's import it now in the `index.tsx` of `CalendarView`.

We will import the Toolbar component and use it below the Header component, as shown in Listing 11-37.

Listing 11-37. Adding the Toolbar Component in the index.tsx of CalendarView

```
import Toolbar from './Toolbar';

...

<Header onAddClick={handleAddClick} />
        <Toolbar
          date={date}
          onDateNext={handleDateNext}
          onDatePrev={handleDatePrev}
          onDateToday={handleDateToday}
```

```
        onViewChange={handleViewChange}
        view={view}
    />
```

Check the UI, and you should see the changes as shown in Figure 11-11. You should be able to navigate now to the previous or the subsequent months.

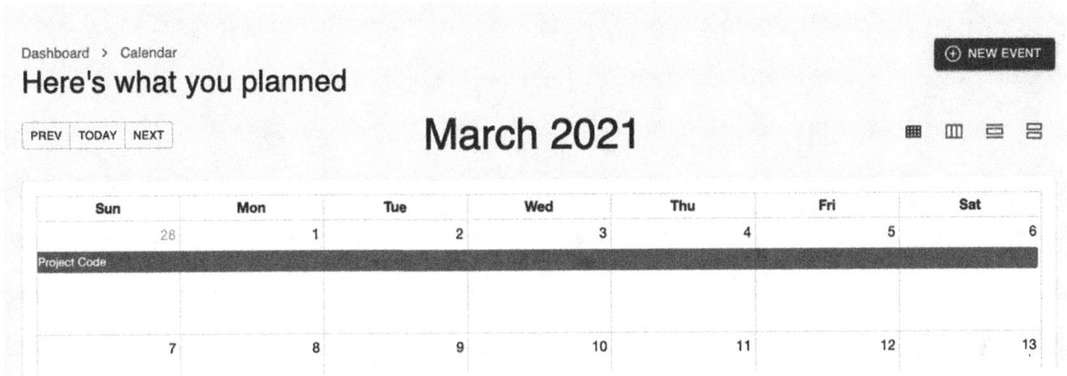

Figure 11-11. *Screenshot of the updated UI following the addition of Toolbar*

Summary

In this chapter, we've continued building our application. We installed the FullCalendar library and learned how to create, delete, and update events on our Calendar component using Redux Toolkit. Hopefully, you have a better understanding now of the implementation flow of Redux Toolkit.

In the next chapter, we will build the login and registration forms. We will need the help of our fake Node json-server and json-server-auth, along with some more styling components from the excellent Material-UI.

CHAPTER 12

Protecting Routes and Authentication in React

In the last chapter, we've shown how to create, delete, and update our app's events using Redux Toolkit. We've learned how efficient and convenient it is to do CRUD with our Store, which holds all our application's global state.

In this chapter, we are going to build a login and a registration form for our application. We will start with the fake Node json-server, which we have installed in the previous chapter. The **json-server** allows us to send HTTP methods or HTTP requests.

Setting Up the Fake Server

Setting up the fake server only takes us a few minutes, and it's a big help in building our UI; we don't need to wait for our back-end dev team to give us the API. We can just create a fake API and use it to test out the UI.

So that's what we're doing in our json-server. We will also use the `json-server-auth`, a plugin or module, to create an authentication service inside the json-server.

Aside from the `json-server-auth`, we are using `concurrently`.

`Concurrently` allows us to run two npm commands simultaneously in one run.

So we will need to modify our scripts.

Go to the `package.json`, and edit the back-end script and add a `start:fullstack` script, as shown in Listing 12-1.

Listing 12-1. Modifying the Scripts in package.json

```
"backend": "json-server --watch db.json --port 5000 --delay=1000 -m ./node_
modules/json-server-auth",
  "start:fullstack": "concurrently \"npm run backend\" \"npm run start\""
```

© Devlin Basilan Duldulao, Ruby Jane Leyva Cabagnot 2021
D. B. Duldulao and R. J. L. Cabagnot, *Practical Enterprise React*, https://doi.org/10.1007/978-1-4842-6975-6_12

Concurrently runs multiple commands together or at the same time.

Now that we have it in setup, let's give it a try. Cancel all the running applications, and then in the terminal, type the following command:

```
npm run start:fullstack
```

db.json

Once that's done, let's update the db.json. Below the events, we are going to add an array of the user object, as shown in Listing 12-2.

Listing 12-2. Adding the users Object in the db.json

```
"users": [
  {
    "id": "7fguyfte5",
    "email": "demo@acme.io",
    "password": "$2a$10$Pmk32D/fgkig8pU.r1rGrOpYYJSrnqqpLO6dRdo88i
    YxxIsl1sstC",
    "name": "Mok Kuh",
    "mobile": "+34782364823",
    "policy": true
  }
],
```

We will use it later for logging in. The user's endpoint is an array of the user's object. It has the login details, including the hashed password.

API: Login and Register

Next, in the axios.ts file, let's update the endpoints, as shown in Listing 12-3.

Listing 12-3. Updating the Endpoints in axios.ts

```
export const EndPoints = {
  sales: 'sales',
  products: 'products',
  events: 'events',
```

```
  login: 'login',
  register: 'register',
};
```

Both the "login" and "register" are part of the json-server-auth. If you go to `npmjs.`
`org` and search for json-server-auth, you'll see that we can use any of the following routes
in the authentication flow.

In this case, we went with login and register, as shown in Figure 12-1.

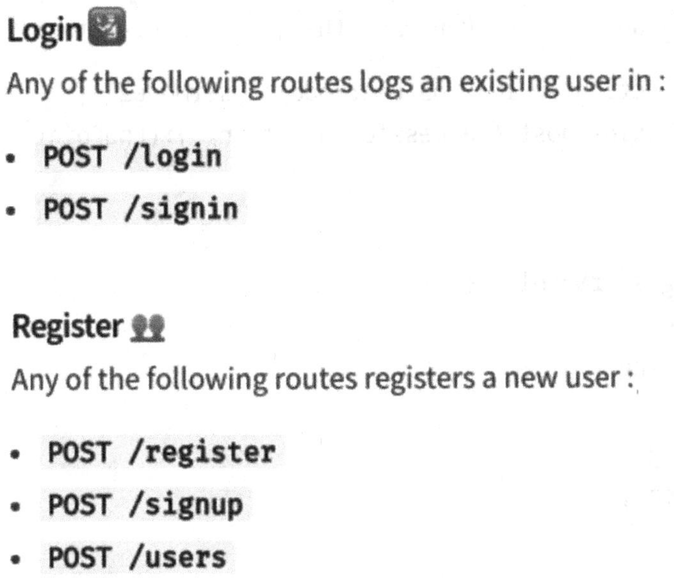

Login 🗝

Any of the following routes logs an existing user in :

- **POST /login**
- **POST /signin**

Register 👥

Any of the following routes registers a new user :

- **POST /register**
- **POST /signup**
- **POST /users**

Figure 12-1. *Authentication flow in json-server-auth*

authService

We can now update the service. In the services folder, create a new file called
`authService.ts`.

The `authService` is a file that contains our logging and registering services with the
use of axios.

Listing 12-4. Creating the authService.ts

```ts
import axios, { EndPoints } from 'api/axios';

export type UserModel = {
  email: string;
  password: string;
};

/*The return object will be an object with an access token of type string.
We're expecting an access token from the json-server-auth */

export async function loginAxios(userModel: UserModel) {
  return await axios.post<{ accessToken: string }>(EndPoints.login,
  userModel);
}

export type RegisterModel = {
  email: string;
  password: string;
  name: string;
  mobile: string;
  policy: boolean;
};

export async function registerAxios(registerModel: RegisterModel) {
  return await axios.post<{ accessToken: string }>(
    EndPoints.register,
    registerModel,
  );
}
```

In Listing 12-4, we have the **loginAxios** – requests a userModel – and we're defining it in the type UserModel, which requires an email and password of type string. We also have the **registerAxios** – requests a registerModel – and we're describing it in the RegisterModel, which requires email, password, name, mobile, and policy.

Let's move on now to the creation of the Login page.

Inside the views ➤ pages folder, create a new folder and name it auth, and inside the auth, add another folder and name it components.

In the auth folder, create a new file and name it **LoginPage.tsx**:

app ➤ views ➤ pages ➤ auth ➤ LoginPage.tsx

In the components folder, create a new file and name it **LoginForm.tsx**:

app ➤ views ➤ pages ➤ auth ➤ components ➤ LoginForm.tsx

Setting Up the Login Form

Let's build up first the LoginForm. Import the named components, as shown in Listing 12-5.

Listing 12-5. Importing Named Components of LoginForm.tsx

```
import React, { useState } from 'react';
import * as Yup from 'yup';
import { Formik } from 'formik';
import { Alert } from '@material-ui/lab';
import { useHistory } from 'react-router-dom';
import {
  Box,
  Button,
  FormHelperText,
  TextField,
  CardHeader,
  Divider,
  Card,
} from '@material-ui/core';

import { loginAxios } from 'services/authService';
```

We have the usual suspects of named imports in Listing 12-5. Let's see what else we have here that is new:

Alert: We're importing Alert from Material-UI for the first time here. Alert is used to display a short and important message to get the user's attention without interrupting the user's task.

useHistory: This is a Hook that we import from the React-Router-DOM; this allows us to access the history instance and lets us navigate back.

We also imported the loginAxios from the authService.

Then let's create the function for the LoginForm and another function to save the user's auth details. And, of course, we will name it as such, as shown in Listing 12-6.

As a best practice, we should name our functions and methods as descriptively as possible to make it easy on ourselves and other developers reading our code.

Listing 12-6. Creating the Function for LoginForm.tsx

```
const LoginForm = () => {
  const key = 'token';
  const history = useHistory();
  const [error, setError] = useState('');

  const saveUserAuthDetails = (data: { accessToken: string }) => {
    localStorage.setItem(key, data.accessToken);
  };
```

LoginForm: In here, we're defining the "token" as the key and using the useHistory and the useState for the error.

saveUserAuthDetails: A function that saves users' details in the local storage. The local storage is a native part of the browser, so we have access to it. It's a first-class citizen supported, so we don't need to import it anymore.

Next, let's add the return statement of our LoginForm, which contains Formik and its required props, as shown in Listing 12-7.

Listing 12-7. Creating Formik in the LoginForm

```
return (
  <Formik
    initialValues={{
      email: 'demo@acme.io',
      password: 'Pass123!',
    }}
    validationSchema={Yup.object().shape({
      email: Yup.string()
        .email('Must be a valid email')
```

```
      .max(255)
      .required('Email is required'),
    password: Yup.string().max(255).required('Password is required'),
  })}
  onSubmit={async (values, formikHelpers) => {
    try {
      const { data } = await loginAxios(values);
      saveUserAuthDetails(data);
      formikHelpers.resetForm();
      formikHelpers.setStatus({ success: true });
      formikHelpers.setSubmitting(false);
      history.push('dashboard');
    } catch (e) {
      setError('Failed. Please try again.');
      console.log(e.message);
      formikHelpers.setStatus({ success: false });
      formikHelpers.setSubmitting(false);
    }
  }}
>

  {/* deconstructed Formik props */}

  {(({
    errors,
    handleBlur,
    handleChange,
    handleSubmit,
    isSubmitting,
    touched,
    values,
  }) => (
    <Card>
      <form noValidate onSubmit={handleSubmit}>
        <CardHeader title="Login" />
        <Divider />
```

```
<Box m={2}>
  <TextField
    error={Boolean(touched.email && errors.email)}
    fullWidth
    autoFocus
    helperText={touched.email && errors.email}
    label="Email Address"
    margin="normal"
    name="email"
    onBlur={handleBlur}
    onChange={handleChange}
    type="email"
    value={values.email}
    variant="outlined"
  />

  <TextField
    error={Boolean(touched.password && errors.password)}
    fullWidth
    helperText={touched.password && errors.password}
    label="Password"
    margin="normal"
    name="password"
    onBlur={handleBlur}
    onChange={handleChange}
    type="password"
    value={values.password}
    variant="outlined"
  />
  <Box mt={2}>
    <Button
      color="primary"
      disabled={isSubmitting}
      fullWidth
      size="large"
      type="submit"
```

```
                   variant="contained"
                >

                   Log In
                </Button>
              </Box>
              {error && (
                <Box mt={3}>
                  <FormHelperText error>{error}</FormHelperText>
                </Box>
              )}
              <Box mt={2}
                <Alert severity="info">
                  <div>
                     Use <b>demo@acme.io</b> and password <b>Pass123!</b>
                  </div>
                </Alert>
              </Box>
            </Box>
          </form>
        </Card>
      )}
    </Formik>
  );
};

export default LoginForm;
```

Let's review some of what we have done here in Listing 12-7:

initialValues: A required prop of Formik. We are initializing it with the value of email and password.

validationSchema: A Yup validation schema. We're defining the email as a string with a valid email address with a max character of 255 and the password a string with a max character of 255.

onSubmit: An async function that takes on `values` and `formikHelpers`. Since it's an async function, we are wrapping it in a try-catch block.

Inside the try, we're using the loginAxios to see if we can log in. The result we need is just this data, which is a destructuring of a big object result. We don't need to get all the properties of this enormous object.

We then save the data to the saveUserAuthDetails, which means keeping it in our local storage.

Then we have a set of formikHelpers such as resetForm, setStatus, and setSubmitting that we are using.

For the catch, we put the setError in case of an unsuccessful login.

We're using the Card component from Material-UI to style the login UI, and we are using two TextFields, one each for the Email and the Password.

Creating a Register Form

After that, we'll need to create another component under the auth ➤ components folder. Let's name it RegisterForm.tsx.

Again, let's do the named components first, as shown in Listing 12-8.

Listing 12-8. Importing Named Components in RegisterForm.tsx

```
import React, { useState } from 'react';
import * as Yup from 'yup';
import { Formik } from 'formik';
import { Alert } from '@material-ui/lab';
import {
  Box,
  Button,
  Card,
  CardContent,
  CardHeader,
  Checkbox,
  CircularProgress,
  Divider,
  FormHelperText,
  Grid,
  Link,
  TextField,
```

```
  Typography,
} from '@material-ui/core';
import { useHistory } from 'react-router-dom';
import { registerAxios } from 'services/authService';
```

The Register Form needs the same as the Login except for a few more modules from Material-UI. We're also adding the registerAxios from authService.

Next, let's create the functions to register the user and save their auth details in the local storage, as shown in Listing 12-9.

Listing 12-9. Adding the RegisterForm Function

```
const RegisterForm = () => {
  const key = 'token';
  const history = useHistory();
  const [error, setError] = useState('');
  const [isAlertVisible, setAlertVisible] = useState(false);

  const saveUserAuthDetails = (data: { accessToken: string }) => {
    localStorage.setItem(key, data.accessToken);
  };
```

And the return statement wrapped in Formik, as shown in Listing 12-10.

Listing 12-10. Creating Formik in the RegisterForm.tsx

```
return
    <Formik
      initialValues={{
        email: 'johnnydoe@yahoo.com',
        name: 'John',
        mobile: '+34782364823',
        password: 'Pass123!',
        policy: false,
      }}
      validationSchema={Yup.object().shape({
        email: Yup.string().email().required('Required'),
        name: Yup.string().required('Required'),
```

```
    mobile: Yup.string().min(10).required('Required'),
    password: Yup.string()
      .min(7, 'Must be at least 7 characters')
      .max(255)
      .required('Required'),policy: Yup.boolean().oneOf([true], 'This
      field must be checked'),
  })}

  onSubmit={async (values, formikHelpers) => {
    try {
      const { data } = await registerAxios(values);
      saveUserAuthDetails(data);
      formikHelpers.resetForm();
      formikHelpers.setStatus({ success: true });
      formikHelpers.setSubmitting(false);
      history.push('dashboard');
    } catch (e) {
      setError(e);
      setAlertVisible(true);
      formikHelpers.setStatus({ success: false });
      formikHelpers.setSubmitting(false);
    }
  }}
>
  {(({
      errors,
      handleBlur,
      handleChange,
      handleSubmit,
      isSubmitting,
      touched,
      values,
    }) => (
    <Card>
      <CardHeader title="Register Form" />
      <Divider />
```

```
    <CardContent>
      {isAlertVisible && (
        <Box mb={3}>
<Alert onClose={() => setAlertVisible(false)} severity="info">{error}!
</Alert>
        </Box>
      )}

      {isSubmitting ? (
  <Box display="flex" justifyContent="center" my={5}>
      <CircularProgress />

    {/*for the loading spinner*/}

      </Box>
      ) : (
        <Box>
          <Grid container spacing={2}>
            <Grid item md={6} xs={12}>
              <TextField
        error={Boolean(touched.name && errors.name)}
                fullWidth
        helperText={touched.name && errors.name}
                label="Name"
                name="name"
                onBlur={handleBlur}
                onChange={handleChange}
                value={values.name}
                variant="outlined"
              />
            </Grid>
            <Grid item md={6} xs={12}>
              <TextField
      error={Boolean(touched.mobile && errors.mobile)}
                fullWidth
      helperText={touched.mobile && errors.mobile}
                label="Mobile"
```

```
                    name="mobile"
                    onBlur={handleBlur}
                    onChange={handleChange}
                    value={values.mobile}
                    variant="outlined"
                  />
                </Grid>
              </Grid>

              <Box mt={2}>
                <TextField
        error={Boolean(touched.email && errors.email)}
                  fullWidth
          helperText={touched.email && errors.email}
                  label="Email Address"
                  name="email"
                  onBlur={handleBlur}
                  onChange={handleChange}
                  type="email"
                  value={values.email}
                  variant="outlined"
                />
              </Box>
              <Box mt={2}>
                <TextField
    error={Boolean(touched.password && errors.password)}
                  fullWidth
      helperText={touched.password && errors.password}
                  label="Password"
                  name="password"
                  onBlur={handleBlur}
                  onChange={handleChange}
                  type="password"
                  value={values.password}
                  variant="outlined"
                />
              </Box>
```

```
<Box alignItems="center" display="flex" mt={2} ml={-1}>
                <Checkbox
                  checked={values.policy}
                  name="policy"
                  onChange={handleChange}
                />
      <Typography variant="body2" color="textSecondary">
                I have read the{' '}
        <Link component="a" href="#" color="secondary">
                Terms and Conditions
                </Link>
                </Typography>
              </Box>
          {Boolean(touched.policy && errors.policy) && (
                <FormHelperText error>{errors.policy}</FormHelperText>
              )}
              <form onSubmit={handleSubmit}>
                <Button
                  color="primary"
                  disabled={isSubmitting}
                  fullWidth
                  size="large"
                  type="submit"
                  variant="contained"
                >
                  Sign up
                </Button>
              </form>
            </Box>
          )}
        </CardContent>
      </Card>
      )}
```

```
    </Formik>
  );
};
```

```
export default RegisterForm;
```

In the initialValues, you can leave it an empty string or pass an example value. Note that we don't save or store the password here. We are just doing it for demo purposes.

Also, the initialValues and validationSchema are typically saved in a separate file for a cleaner code, especially a long file.

So that's it for now in the Register Form; we'll test it out later. Let's build up the Login page now.

Adding the Login Page

Let's now create the LoginPage, and we'll start with importing the named components that we need, as shown in Listing 12-11.

Listing 12-11. Importing the Named Components in LoginPage.tsx

```
import React, { useState } from 'react';
import { makeStyles } from '@material-ui/styles';
import { Box, Button, Container, Divider } from '@material-ui/core';

import LoginForm from './components/LoginForm';
import RegisterForm from './components/RegisterForm';
import Page from 'app/components/page';
```

We imported the LoginForm and RegisterForm that we've just created. We also have the Page template.

So, next, let's create the LoginPage component function, as shown in Listing 12-12.

Listing 12-12. Creating the LoginPage Function

```
const LoginPage = () => {
const classes = useStyles();
const [isLogin, setIsLogin] = useState(true);
```

isLogin: A local state, and it's a Boolean that is set to true by default because we're logging in. If this is false, we are showing the Register Form. How do we do that? By doing this: {isLogin ? <LoginForm /> : <RegisterForm />}.

So now, let's make that return statement next, as shown in Listing 12-13.

Listing 12-13. Adding the Return Statement of the LoginPage.tsx

```
return (
    <Page className={classes.root} title="Authentication">
      <Container>
        <Box
          my={5}
          display={'flex'}
          flexDirection={'column'}
          justifyContent={'center'}
          alignItems={'center'}
        >

          {/*if isLogin is true - show LoginForm, otherwise show
          RegisterForm */}

          {isLogin ? <LoginForm /> : <RegisterForm />}
          <Divider />
          <Box mt={5}>
            Go to{' '}
            {isLogin ? (
              <Button
                size={'small'}
                color={'primary'}
                variant={'text'}
                onClick={() => setIsLogin(false)}
              >
                Register Form
              </Button>
            ) : (
              <Button
                size={'small'}
```

```
                    color={'primary'}
                    variant={'text'}
                    onClick={() => setIsLogin(true)}
                  >
                    Login Form
                  </Button>
                )}
              </Box>
            </Box>
          </Container>
        </Page>
    );
};

const useStyles = makeStyles(() => ({root: {},}));

export default LoginPage;
```

Okay, that's done for now. Time to update the routes.tsx.

Updating the Routes

Below the AboutPage routes, insert the LoginPage routes, as shown in Listing 12-14.

Listing 12-14. Adding the LoginPage Routes

```
<Route
    exact
    path={'/login'}
    component={lazy(() => import('./views/pages/auth/LoginPage'))}
      />
```

Let's test it in our browser. Click the refresh button or go to your localhost:3000/login, and you should see the Login page, as shown in Figure 12-2.

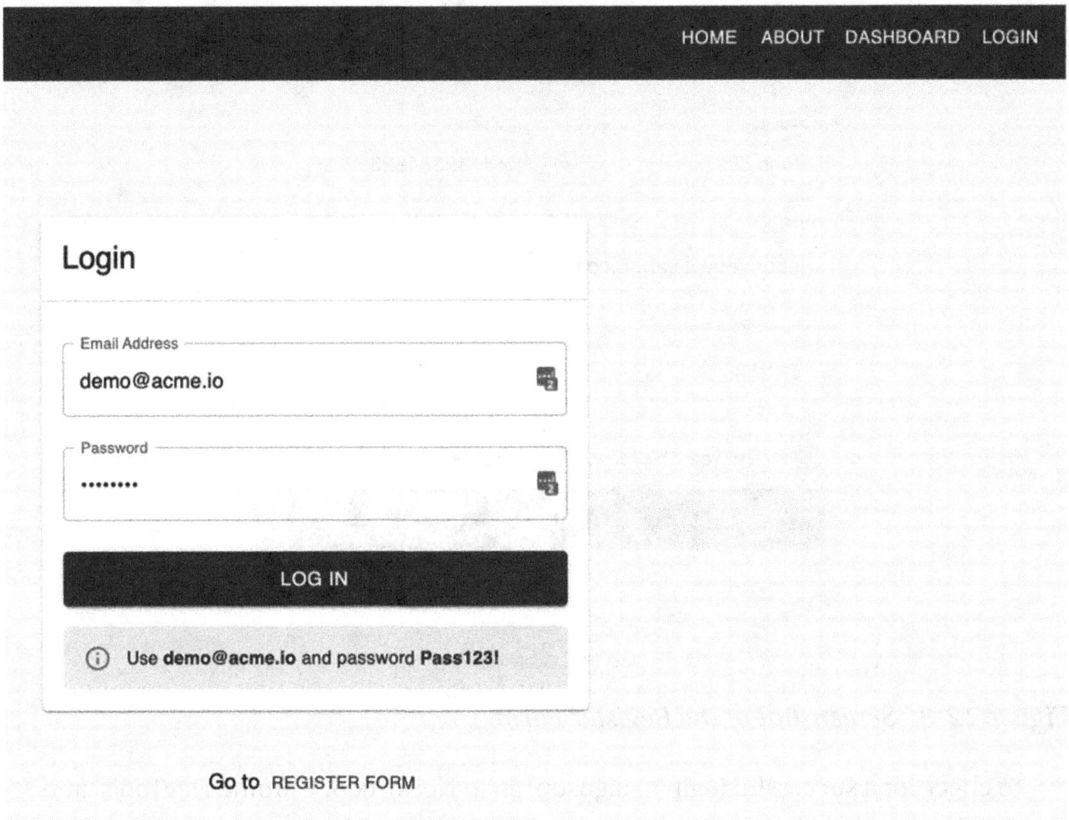

Figure 12-2. *Screenshot of the Login page*

Click the Register Form and create your account, as shown in Figure 12-3.

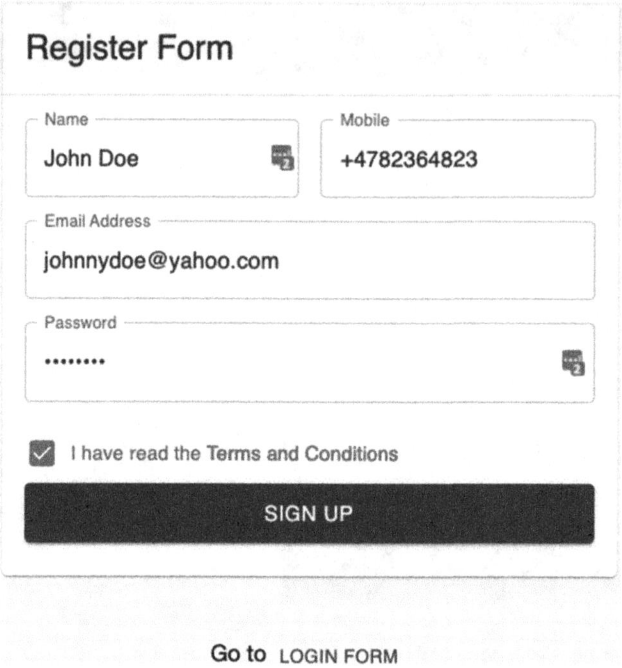

Figure 12-3. *Screenshot of the Register Form*

To check for a successful login or sign-up, go to Network of Chrome DevTools, and you should see under the Headers Status Code OK, and in the Response, you'll see the access token.

Copy the access token, and let's see what's inside. And for that, we will go to this excellent site jwt.io and paste our access token there.

JSON Web Token (JWT)

The JWT has the Header, Payload, and Signature. In the Header, you'll see the alg or algorithm and the typ or type. In the Payload, data are the decoded values of the access token or the JWT. The decoded values are what we need inside our React app in the next chapter.

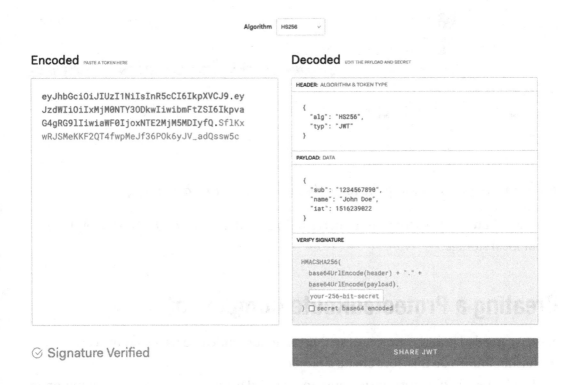

Figure 12-4. *Checking the access token response from the server*

Learn more about the JSON Web Token structure here at `jwt.io/introduction`.

Simply, JSON Web Tokens or JWTs are token-based authentications used to get access to a resource. Token-based authentication, which is stateless, is different from session-based authentication, which is stateful and requires a cookie with the session ID placed in the user's browser.

This is a vast topic, so I urge you to read more about it.

Let's go back to our app's Chrome DevTools and click Application ➤ Local Storage and the localhost.

Figure 12-5. *Screenshot of the token being stored in the local storage*

The **token** indicates that we've successfully stored the JWT or the JSON Web Token in our local storage.

Creating a ProtectedRoute Component

Next, we need to protect our routes so that an unauthenticated user cannot access or see the dashboard. To do this, let's create a protected route.

Inside the app directory, go to components, and inside that, create a new component and name it protected-route.tsx:

app ➤ components ➤ protected-route.tsx

Open the protected-route.tsx file and copy the following code, as shown in Listing 12-15.

Listing 12-15. Creating the protected-route.tsx

```
import React from 'react';
import { Redirect, Route } from 'react-router-dom';

const ProtectedRoute = props => {
  const token = localStorage.getItem('token');

  return token ? (
    <Route {...props} />
  ) : (
```

```
    <Redirect to={{ pathname: '/login' }} />
  );
};
```

```
export default ProtectedRoute;
```

In Listing 12-15, we keep it simple for now, but we will update it later as the authentication gets more complicated.

We imported the Redirect and Route from the React-Router-DOM. And we have the **ProtectedRoute** – a function that takes props and retrieves the user token from the localStorage.

In the return statement, we're checking if there's an existing **token ?** If this is true, the user is directed to a specific path inside the dashboard; otherwise, the user is redirected to the Login page.

After doing that, we can now use the ProtectedRoute component to wrap the dashboard route.

Updating the Routes.tsx

Go to routes.tsx, and we will use the ProtectedRoute component, as shown in Listing 12-16.

Listing 12-16. Adding the ProtectedRoute in the routes.tsx

```
import ProtectedRoute from './components/protected-route';
...
<ProtectedRoute
        path={'/dashboard'}
        render={({ match: { path } }) => (
          <Dashboard>
            <Switch>
              <Route
                exact
                path={path + '/'}
                component={lazy(() => import('./views/dashboard/
                dashboard-default-content'),)/>
```

Check if it's working. Open a new window and go to `localhost:3000/dashboard`. Since the token is already in our local storage, we can access the dashboard right away without being redirected to the Login page.

Updating the Dashboard Sidebar Navigation

After this, we will need to update the logout.

Go to the `dashboard-layout` ➤ `dashboard-sidebar-navigation.tsx`.

We will create a new handle event function for the logout. Put it just below the `handleClick` function, as shown in Listing 12-17.

Listing 12-17. Updating the dashboard-sidebar-navigation.tsx

```
const handleLogout = () => {
    localStorage.clear();
  };
```

handleLogout: A function that is clearing the `localStorage` by removing all the stored values

Inside the same file, go to the logout, and let's add an `onClick` event on the button so we can trigger it, as shown in Listing 12-18.

Listing 12-18. Adding an onClick Event for the handleLogout

```
<ListItem button onClick={handleLogout}>
                <ListItemIcon>
                  <LogOutIcon />
                </ListItemIcon>
                <ListItemText primary={'logout'} />
              </ListItem>
```

Let's test it.

Time to Test

Go to the dashboard and also open your Chrome DevTools and click Application.

Click the logout button, and the browser should refresh, and you'll be directed to the main page; and if you look at the Chrome DevTools, the token should get deleted.

Figure 12-6. *Screenshot of the LocalStorage after the token was deleted after logout*

So this is how we can create a simple authentication.

We will be improving on this in the coming chapters as our app gets complicated.

I want to emphasize that it's vital that we know the basics of authentication and how it works. But these days, to be honest, I would highly recommend authentication as a service or an identity provider.

Some reasons why I would recommend a third-party identity as a service:

1. Decentralizing the identity from your applications. The user's identity info will not be stored in your database.

2. Allows developers to focus on developing the application's business value instead of working for weeks building the authentication and authorization service.

3. Most third-party identity as a service companies such as Auth0, which I also personally use and recommend, are very secure and reliable. Auth0 also has good documentation, lots of open source projects that you can build on, and a strong community support.

    Other excellent identity as a service providers that I've tried are AWS Cognito, Azure AD, and Okta. Many of them offer a free tier program, which is best for small projects, so you can understand how it works.

(Full disclosure: I'm currently an Auth0 Ambassador. No, I'm not an employee of the company, nor do I get any monetary compensation. I occasionally get some swags and other excellent perks whenever I speak at a conference and mention them. BUT I became an Auth0 Ambassador precisely because I've been using it and recommending them even before.)

4. Lastly, these third-party identity providers are being developed and maintained by security engineers or those specializing in security. They are more updated on what's going on in the world of cybersecurity, including the best practice, trends, and issues.

Summary

This chapter built the Login and Registration Forms with the styling help from the Material-UI components. We used the library json-server-auth inside our pseudo Node json-server to simulate the implementation flow of authenticating and protecting our routes. We also made it easy for ourselves to run and build our app when we added concurrently in our scripts.

In the next chapter, we will be building more components and functionalities in our React application. We begin with creating a Profile Form and then syncing it to different deep layer components in our app – all with the powerful help of Redux.

Lastly, we will show that not all of our components need to be tied up to Redux. If we don't need the added complexity, then it does not make sense to use it. Some people have this mistaken notion that once we add Redux to our app, all our components must include it. Use it if you need it; otherwise, you don't have to.

CHAPTER 13

Writing a Profile Form and Syncing It to Components

Previously, we showed how we could protect parts of the application from anyone who is not authenticated or authorized. This chapter will begin to write a Profile Form and sync that profile to various components.

Since this part is rather long, we would make this a three-part chapter series. In the first part, we will focus more on creating the Profile Form, Register Form, and Login Form using Formik and JWT for authentication. Here, we will learn how to sync the Profile Form to various components in our application.

We will update the dashboard navigation and sync data between the sidebar navigation and top navigation bar in the second part. We will add more functionalities to our application with the help of Redux, Formik, and the Yup validation schema.

In the last part of the chapter series, we will continue to consolidate our learnings of Redux as we build the few remaining components we need to complete the UI of our application.

The overall goal here is to create several components from different layers of the application and pass data seamlessly from one component to another using Redux – for example, syncing the Profile data to the navigation bars, the sidebar and the top navigation bar, using Redux.

Before we proceed, let me show you the finished UI at the end of this chapter series. Figures 13-1 through 13-4 show the completed UI of our app.

© Devlin Basilan Duldulao, Ruby Jane Leyva Cabagnot 2021
D. B. Duldulao and R. J. L. Cabagnot, *Practical Enterprise React*, https://doi.org/10.1007/978-1-4842-6975-6_13

Figure 13-1 is the Settings page.

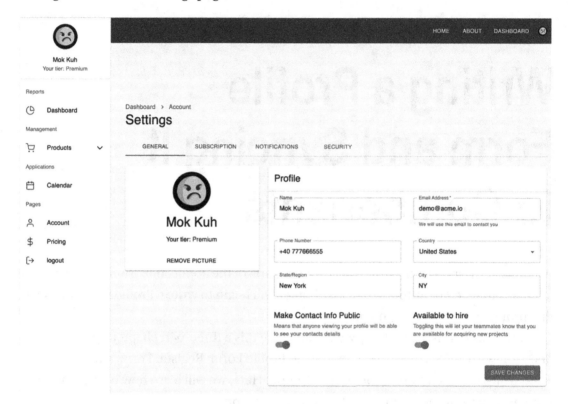

Figure 13-1. *Settings page*

Figure 13-2 is the Subscription page.

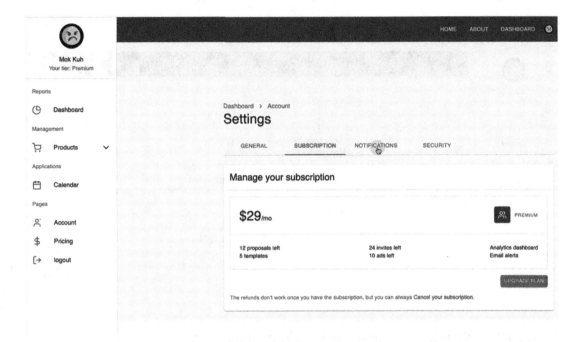

Figure 13-2. *Subscription form*

Figure 13-3 is the Notifications page.

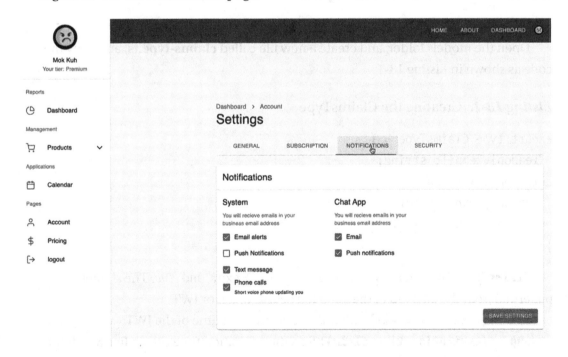

Figure 13-3. *Notifications page*

Figure 13-4 is the Security page.

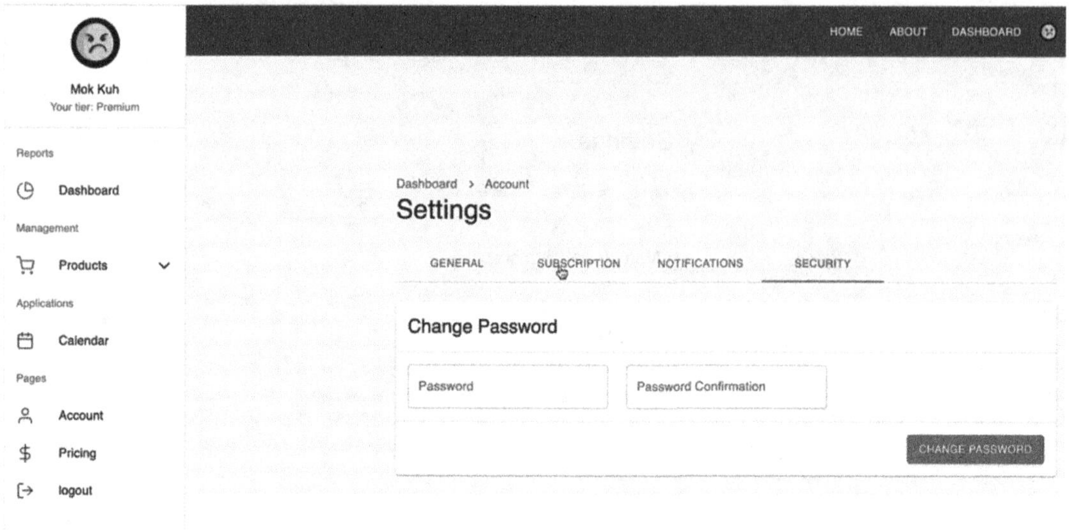

Figure 13-4. *Security page at the end of the chapter series*

Creating the Claims Type

Okay, let's start. First, let's create a model or type for claims.

Open the models folder, and create a new file called **claims-type.ts**, and copy the code as shown in Listing 13-1.

Listing 13-1. Creating the ClaimsType

```
export type ClaimsType = {
  readonly email: string;
  readonly iat: number;
  readonly exp: number;
  readonly sub: string;
};
```

ClaimsType: Contains read-only `email`, `iat`, `exp`, and `sub`. The shapes here are patterned from the payload of the decoded access token or JWT.

iat - (issued at claim): Identifies the issuance time of the JWT.

exp - (expiration time claim): Sets the expiration time on or after which the access token MUST NOT be accepted for processing.

sub - (subject claim): Identifies the subject of the access token or JWT.

There are still a lot of reserved JSON Web Token claims, and if you want to read more, you can visit sites like iana.org or `https://tools.ietf.org/`.

Next, let's add the shape of our user. In the models folder, add the user-type.ts and copy the code, as shown in Listing 13-2.

Creating the User Type

Listing 13-2. Creating the UserType

```
export type Subscription = {
  name: string;
  price: number;
  currency: string;
  proposalsLeft: number;
  templatesLeft: number;
  invitesLeft: number;
  adsLeft: number;
  hasAnalytics: boolean;
  hasEmailAlerts: boolean;
};

export type UserType = {
  id: string;
  email: string;
  password: string;
  country: string;
  isPublic: boolean;
  phone: string;
  role: string;
  state: string;
  tier: string;
  name: string;
  avatar: string;
```

```
  city: string;
  canHire: boolean;
  subscription?: Subscription;
};
```

Adding APIs: Users and UsersDb

Then we need to update our endpoints again. So go to **axios.ts** and add two more endpoints, as shown in Listing 13-3.

Listing 13-3. Updating the Endpoints for Users and UsersDb

```
export const EndPoints = {
  sales: 'sales',
  products: 'products',
  events: 'events',
  login: 'login',
  register: 'register',
  users: 'users',
  usersDb: 'users-db',
};
```

Users: This is for editing or updating the password of a user. We will allow the user to update or edit their password.

UsersDb: This is for storing the details of the UserType and the subscription type in our models folder. Ideally, this should be put in a separate database, just like in the real world when we separate the database for the users' authentication from the users' profile or subscription.

Creating the userDbService

Let's create a new service file. Go to the services folder and add a new file called userDbService.ts, as shown in Listing 13-4.

Listing 13-4.   Creating UserDbService

```
import api, { EndPoints } from 'api/axios';
import { UserType } from 'models/user-type';

export async function getUserByIdFromDbAxios(id: string) {
  return await api.get<UserType>(`${EndPoints.usersDb}/${id}`);
}

export async function putUserFromDbAxios(user: UserType) {
  return await api.put<UserType>(`${EndPoints.usersDb}/${user.id}`, user);
}
```

userDbService has two HTTP methods or functions. We imported the UserType from the models, and we're naming our first function to be as specific and descriptive as possible, getUserByIdFromDbAxios, and the return type is the UserType.

The other axios function we named as putUserFromDbAxios, and it takes the UserType, and we're making an update with the expected response of UserType.

Updating the authService

After that, we will need to update the authService. Open the authService.ts and add the following function, as shown in Listing 13-5.

Listing 13-5.   Adding changePasswordAxios in authService

```
export type ChangePasswordModel = {
  email: string;
  password: string;
  id: string;
};

export async function changePassWordAxios(
  changePasswordModel: ChangePasswordModel,
) {
  return await axios.put<void>(
    `${EndPoints.users}/${changePasswordModel.id}`,
    changePasswordModel,
  );
}
```

changePasswordAxios is an async service function that takes the type changePasswordModel to change the password. We are sending in a put request using axios to update the specific user's password with this id.

Another Way of Using Redux

Next, we will be creating a profileActionTypes, and we are going to use Redux here.

This is another way of writing Redux. In the previous chapters, we put everything in one file in the calendarSlice, but we will do separate files for the actions and the slice this time. The main reason for this is the separation of concerns and for code readability.

Here's a snapshot in Figure 13-5 of the folder structure that we are planning for the profile folder as one way to structure our React-Redux app.

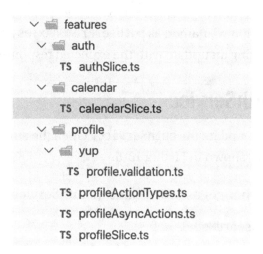

Figure 13-5. Folder structure of profile

Creating the profileActionTypes

Inside the features folder, let's create a new directory and name it profile.

Inside the profile folder, add a file and name it profileActionTypes.ts:

features ➤ profile ➤ profileActionTypes.ts

In Listing 13-6, we are creating the profileActionTypes.

Listing 13-6. Creating the profileActionTypes.ts

```
import { UserType } from 'models/user-type';

export type ProfileStateType = {
  readonly profile: UserType;
  readonly loading: boolean;
  readonly error: string;
};

export const profileNamespace = 'profile';

/* action types */

export const ProfileActionTypes = {
  FETCH_AND_SAVE_PROFILE: `${profileNamespace}/FETCH_AND_SAVE_PROFILE`,
  UPDATE_PROFILE: `${profileNamespace}/UPDATE_PROFILE`,
};
```

Creating the profileAsyncActions

Next, we need to add a new file inside the profile folder. We will name it profileAsyncActions.ts, as shown in Listing 13-7.

Listing 13-7. Creating the profileAsyncActions

```
import { createAsyncThunk } from '@reduxjs/toolkit';
import { UserType } from 'models/user-type';

import { ProfileActionTypes } from './profileActionTypes';
import {
  getUserByIdFromDbAxios,
  putUserFromDbAxios,
} from 'services/userDbService';

export const getProfileAction = createAsyncThunk(
  ProfileActionTypes.FETCH_AND_SAVE_PROFILE,
  async (id: string) => {
    return (await getUserByIdFromDbAxios(id)).data;
  },
);
```

```
export const putProfileAction = createAsyncThunk(
  ProfileActionTypes.UPDATE_PROFILE,
  async (user: UserType) => {
    return (await putUserFromDbAxios(user)).data;
  },
);
```

We import the module createAsyncThunk from Redux Toolkit for the side effects. We also have the UserType from the models, the action type profileActionTypes, and the two axios functions from the userDbService.

getProfileAction: This is our first async action. It is coming from an instance of the createAsyncThunk, and we're required to pass a string (FETCH_AND_SAVE_PROFILE) as the first argument, and the second argument is an async and await function.

The id parameter of type string is connected to the getProfileAction, so whenever we use this getProfileAction, we are required to pass an argument string.

Then we will use that id in the getUserByIdFromDbAxios, wrapping it in open-close parentheses so we can extract that object with the dot (.) notation and then data.

putProfileAction: This is for updating the profile. We also have the createAsyncThunk instance and then pass the string instructions to the reducers to update the profile. The second argument is a promise-based anonymous function or an async and await function.

This is the pattern in implementing Redux Toolkit, and you use this as a guideline even in your future Redux projects.

Creating the profileSlice

After that, we will need to create the slice. Inside the profile folder, create a new file called profileSlice.ts.

We have in the following the import named components, including the ProfileStateType profileNamespace, the profileActionTypes, and the getProfileAction and putProfileAction from the profileAsyncActions, as shown in Listing 13-8.

Listing 13-8. Creating profileSlice.ts

```
import { createSlice, PayloadAction } from '@reduxjs/toolkit';
import { UserType } from 'models/user-type';

import { profileNamespace, ProfileStateType } from './profileActionTypes';
import { getProfileAction, putProfileAction } from './profileAsyncActions';

/* profile state */
/* initial state or default state or initial values, it's up to you */
export const initialState: ProfileStateType = {
  profile: {} as UserType,
  loading: false,
  error: '',
};

/* profile store */

export const profileSlice = createSlice({

  /*
   name: is your feature or also called module, or namespace,
   or context, etc. The terminologies here can be interchangeable.
   This is required.
  */
  name: profileNamespace,

  /*initialState is the default value of this namespace/module and it is
   required.*/

  initialState,

  /*Non asynchronous actions. Does not require Axios.*/

  reducers: {},

  /*Asynchronous actions. Actions that require Axios.
    extraReducers - allows createSlice to respond not only to its own
     action type but other action types also*/
```

```
 /*state - is coming from the initialState; no need to define it because
the Redux Toolkit can already infer what particular state it is.   */

  extraReducers: builder => {
    builder.addCase(
      getProfileAction.fulfilled,
      (state, action: PayloadAction<UserType>) => {
        state.profile = action.payload;
      },
    );

    builder.addCase(
      putProfileAction.pending,
      (state, action: PayloadAction) => {
        state.loading = true;
        state.error = '';
      },
    );
    builder.addCase(
      putProfileAction.fulfilled,
      (state, action: PayloadAction<UserType>) => {
        state.loading = false;
        state.profile = action.payload;
      },
    );
    builder.addCase(
      putProfileAction.rejected,
      (state, action: PayloadAction<any>) => {
        state.loading = false;
        state.error = 'Something wrong happened';
        console.log(action?.payload);
      },
    );
  },
});

export default profileSlice.reducer;
```

extraReducers: We are not using any non-asynchronous or synchronous action here. For the async actions in Redux, we need the `extraReducers`, which is also a part of the slice.

To use the `extraReducers`, we need to set or add a function signature called the `builder`.

builder: Returns the `addCase` that we are going to build.

addCase: Requires a string, which is the action type.

If you look at the various `addCases`, you will see that it seems like just one big try-catch block function.

getProfileAction.fulfilled: For example, the preceding block of code gets run if we receive a 2xx Status Code.

putProfileAction.pending: This is run before the rejected and the fulfilled function. This is the time when we're sending a request to any web service. We use the pending to enable the spinner or loader by setting it to true. We don't need a payload in pending because we're changing the loading directly from false to true.

putProfileAction.fulfilled: In here, we're getting the Status Code 2xx and then we update the reducer.

putProfileAction.rejected: This will run whenever we get Status Code other than 2xx, for example, 4xx, which means unauthorized, or 5xx, which means problem issues with the server. If that happens, we set the loading to false and run the error message.

And at the bottom, we export the reducer: **profileSlice.reducer**.

FOR YOUR ACTIVITY

Add two more `addCases` in the `getProfileAction`. Add the pending and the rejected. Just follow the pattern in the `putProfileAction`.

Listing 13-9 is a ToDo activity: create addCase pending and addCase rejected in the getProfileAction.

Listing 13-9. Activity for Chapter 13

```
extraReducers: builder => {

  // todo activity: create addCase pending

  builder.addCase(
    getProfileAction.fulfilled,
    (state, action: PayloadAction<UserType>) => {
      state.profile = action.payload;
    },
  );

  // todo activity: create addCase rejected
```

Once you finish the activity, let's update the root reducer now. Go to store ➤ reducers.ts.

Adding profileReducer to the Reducers

We need to import the profileReducer from the profileSlice and add it inside the injectedReducers of the root reducer, as shown in Listing 13-10.

Listing 13-10. Adding the profileReducer in the reducers.ts

```
import { combineReducers } from '@reduxjs/toolkit';
import calendarReducer from 'features/calendar/calendarSlice';
import profileReducer from'features/profile/profileSlice';

/* easier way of registering a reducer */

const injectedReducers = {
  calendar: calendarReducer,
  profile: profileReducer,
};
```

We have the profileReducer in our Store; the profileReducer is now accessible in every application component.

Creating the authSlice

Next, we are going to create another slice. We need the authSlice to save the access token and the claims to the global Store.

So, in the folder features, add a new folder and name it auth and inside it create a new file called authSlice.ts:

features ➤ auth ➤ authSlice.ts

Open it and import createSlice and PayloadAction from Redux Toolkit and also the ClaimsType from the models. Import the named components first, as shown in Listing 13-11.

Listing 13-11. Importing Modules in the authSlice.ts

```
import { createSlice, PayloadAction } from '@reduxjs/toolkit';
import { ClaimsType } from 'models/claims-type';
```

Then we add the namespace, the shape of AuthStateType, and the initial state, as shown in Listing 13-12.

Listing 13-12. Adding the Namespace, Type, and initialState in authSlice.ts

```
const authNamespace = 'auth';

export type AuthStateType = {
  readonly accessToken: string;
  readonly claims: ClaimsType;
};

/*we are using the AuthStateType to type safe our initial state */

export const initialState: AuthStateType = {
  accessToken: '',
  claims: null,
};
```

Next, let's use the createSlice to take on the namespace, initialState, object full of reducer functions, and slice name we created, as shown in Listing 13-13.

Listing 13-13. Passing createSlice in our authSlice

```
export const authSlice = createSlice({

  /*namespace for separating related states. Namespaces are like modules*/

  name: authNamespace,

  /* initialState is the default value of this namespace/module and it is
  required */

  initialState,

  /*Non asynchronous actions. Does not require Axios.*/

  reducers: {
    saveTokenAction: (state, action: PayloadAction<string>) => {
      state.accessToken = action?.payload;
    },
    saveClaimsAction: (state, action: PayloadAction<ClaimsType>) => {
      state.claims = action?.payload;
    },
  },

  /*Asynchronous actions. Actions that require Axios.*/

  extraReducers: builder => {},
});

/* export all non-async actions */

export const { saveClaimsAction, saveTokenAction } = authSlice.actions;

export default authSlice.reducer;
```

In Listing 13-13, we have two non-async actions, which means they don't require the use of axios.

The two non-async actions – saveTokenAction and saveClaimsAction – will not need the help of axios.

Next, we export these non-async actions by extracting them from the authSlice. actions.

Lastly, we export the authSlice.reducer so we can call it in the root reducer.

Adding the authSlice to the Reducers

Go to the reducers.ts, and let's inject the authReducer in the injectedReducers as well as import the named component, as shown in Listing 13-14.

Listing 13-14. Adding the authReducer in the reducers.ts

```
import authReducer from '../features/auth/authSlice';

const injectedReducers = {
  calendar: calendarReducer,
  auth: authReducer,
  profile: profileReducer,
};
```

The authReducer is now part of the combined reducers and store.

Installing JWT-decode

Next, we will need to install a popular JavaScript library called jwt-decode. It decodes JWT tokens, useful for browser applications:

```
npm i jwt-decode
```

After installing the jwt-decode, let's head off to the protected route and improve it: components ➤ protected-route.tsx

Updating the ProtectedRoute

First, let's import the additional named components in the protected-route.tsx, as shown in Listing 13-15.

Listing 13-15. Adding Named Components in protected-route.tsx

```
import { useDispatch } from 'react-redux';
import jwt_decode from 'jwt-decode';

import { saveClaimsAction } from 'features/auth/authSlice';
import { ClaimsType } from 'models/claims-type';
```

Next, let's update the ProtectedRoute component, as shown in Listing 13-16.

Listing 13-16. Updating the ProtectedRoute Component

```
const ProtectedRoute = props => {
  const dispatch = useDispatch();
  const token = localStorage.getItem('token');

  /* this is cleaning up the localStorage and redirecting user to login */
  if (!token) {
    localStorage.clear();
    return <Redirect to={{ pathname: '/login' }} />;
  }

  const decoded: ClaimsType = jwt_decode(token);
  const expiresAt = decoded.exp * 1000;
  const dateNow = Date.now();
  const isValid = dateNow <= expiresAt;

  dispatch(saveClaimsAction(decoded));

  return isValid ? (
    <Route {...props} />
  ) : (
    <Redirect to={{ pathname: '/login' }} />
  );
};

export default ProtectedRoute;
```

We need the useDispatch and the token from the localStorage. We are cleaning up the localStorage and redirecting the user to the Login page if it is false or has no token.

We are passing the **token** to the jwt_decode to decode it. The decoded **token** will be compared to expiresAt or expiration date of the token with respect to the dateNow or current date.

The dateNow should be equal to or less than the expiresAt.

Next, we will pass the **decoded** token in the saveClaimsAction and then dispatch it.

In the return statement, if the token isValid, then go to where the user is navigating; otherwise, redirect the user to the Login page.

Updating the Login Form

We're now going to update the Login Form. First, we will add a few named components, as shown in Listing 13-17.

Listing 13-17. Updating the Named Components in LoginForm

```
import jwt_decode from 'jwt-decode';
import { useDispatch } from 'react-redux';

import { saveClaimsAction, saveTokenAction } from 'features/auth/
authSlice';
import { loginAxios } from 'services/authService';
import { ClaimsType } from 'models/claims-type';
```

We're adding the useDispatch from React Redux and the jwt_decode. We also need the saveClaimsAction, saveTokenAction, and ClaimsType.

Next, we need to update the LoginForm function, as shown in Listing 13-18.

Listing 13-18. Hooks in Login Form

```
const LoginForm = () => {
  const key = 'token';
  const history = useHistory();
  const dispatch = useDispatch();
  const [error, setError] = useState('');
```

We are using the useDispatch in Listing 13-18 to dispatch an action to save the access token and claims to the Store, as shown in Listing 13-19.

Listing 13-19. Updating the saveUserAuthDetails Function in the LoginForm

```
const saveUserAuthDetails = (data: { accessToken: string }) => {
    localStorage.setItem(key, data.accessToken);
    const claims: ClaimsType = jwt_decode(data.accessToken);
    console.log('Claims::', claims);    /*just to check it  */
    dispatch(saveTokenAction(data.accessToken));
    dispatch(saveClaimsAction(claims));
  };
```

Updating the Register Form

We're going to do similar updates to the Register Form. We start off importing the named components, as shown in Listing 13-20.

Listing 13-20. Updating the Named Components in the Register Form

```
import { useDispatch } from 'react-redux';

import { saveClaimsAction, saveTokenAction } from 'features/auth/
authSlice';
import jwt_decode from 'jwt-decode';

import { ClaimsType } from 'models/claims-type';
```

In Listing 13-20, we added the useDispatch, saveClaimsAction, saveTokenAction, jwt_decode, and ClaimsType.

Next, we update the RegisterForm as shown in Listing 13-21.

Listing 13-21. Hooks in the Registration Form

```
const RegisterForm = () => {
  const key = 'token';
  const history = useHistory();
  const dispatch = useDispatch();
  const [error, setError] = useState('');
  const [isAlertVisible, setAlertVisible] = useState(false);
```

In Listing 13-21, we also have the useDispatch to dispatch or send an action to save the access token and the claims to the Store, as shown in Listing 13-22.

Listing 13-22. saveUserAuthDetails Function

```
const saveUserAuthDetails = (data: { accessToken: string }) => {
  localStorage.setItem(key, data.accessToken);
  const claims: ClaimsType = jwt_decode(data.accessToken);
  console.log('Claims::', claims);
  dispatch(saveTokenAction(data.accessToken));
  dispatch(saveClaimsAction(claims));
};
```

Once saved in the Store, the access token and claims are now accessible anywhere in the application.

Let's run our application:

```
npm run start:fullstack
```

Refresh the browser and open the Redux DevTools, as shown in Figure 13-6.

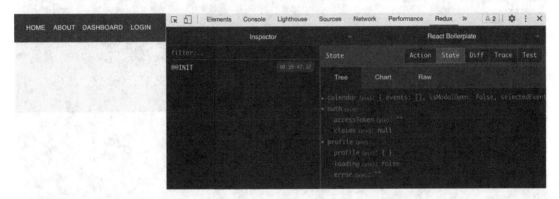

Figure 13-6. *Screenshot of Redux DevTools without the data yet in the localStorage*

Note that there's no data yet in the auth and profile states. They are all in the default value.

Next, let's go to the Login page and let's log in. When we log in, this will save the state in the Store, as shown in Figure 13-7.

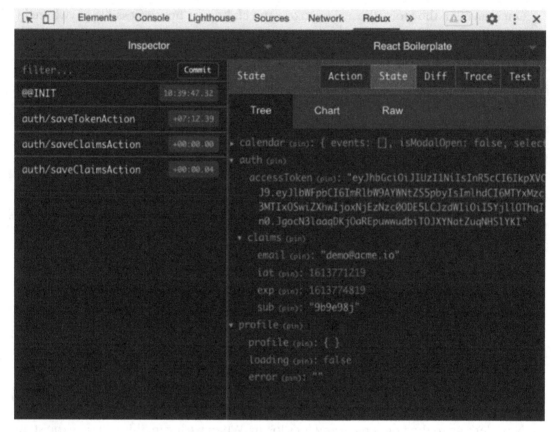

Figure 13-7. *Screenshot of Redux DevTools after logging in*

In the Redux DevTools, we can see the saveClaimsAction and the saveTokenAction. We have the data for the accessToken and the values in the claims.

We have now verified that we can receive the accessToken and the claims from the server.

The profile is still empty because we will use the claims id (sub) to fetch the data for that particular user.

Creating the Header Profile

Next, we move on to create a new React component and name it header-profile.tsx:

app ➤ components ➤ header-profile.tsx

Let's import the named components we need, as shown in Listing 13-23.

Listing 13-23. Adding the Named Components of the HeaderProfile

```
import React, { useState, MouseEvent } from 'react';
import clsx from 'clsx';
import { Theme, withStyles } from '@material-ui/core/styles';
import Menu, { MenuProps } from '@material-ui/core/Menu';
import { LogOut as LogOutIcon, Hexagon as HexagonIcon } from 'react-
feather';
import { useSelector } from 'react-redux';
import { RootState } from 'store/reducers';
import { createStyles } from '@material-ui/styles';
import {
  Avatar,
  Box,
  Divider,
  ListItemIcon,
  ListItemText,
  makeStyles,
  MenuItem,
} from '@material-ui/core';
```

Okay, what's new here? From the Material-UI Core styles, we've imported the Menu and MenuProps and the Hexagon from React Feather.

We are also using the useSelector from Redux and the RootState for typings.

Then let's add the HeaderProfile function, as shown in Listing 13-24.

Listing 13-24. Creating the HeaderProfile Function Component

```
const HeaderProfile = () => {
  const classes = useStyles();

  /*using the profile to render an avatar */
  const { profile } = useSelector((state: RootState) => state.profile);

  const [anchorEl, setAnchorEl] = useState<null | HTMLElement>(null);

  const handleClick = (event: MouseEvent<HTMLElement>) => {
    setAnchorEl(event.currentTarget);
  };
```

333

```
const handleClose = () => {
  setAnchorEl(null);
};

const handleLogout = () => {
  localStorage.clear();
};
```

In Listing 13-24, we use the useSelector to get the profile and use the profile.avatar to render the Avatar component. See Listing 13-25 for adding the return statement of the HeaderProfile React component.

Listing 13-25. Adding the Return Statement of the HeaderProfile

```
return (
    <div>
      <Box display="flex" justifyContent="center" onClick={handleClick}>
        <Avatar
          variant={'circle'}
          alt="User"
          className={clsx(classes.avatar, classes.small)}
          src={profile.avatar}
        />
      </Box>
      <StyledMenu
        id="customized-menu"
        anchorEl={anchorEl}
        keepMounted
        open={Boolean(anchorEl)}
        onClose={handleClose}
      >

        <MenuItem>
          <ListItemText primary={profile.email} />
        </MenuItem>
        <Divider />
        <MenuItem>
```

```
        <ListItemIcon>
          <HexagonIcon />
        </ListItemIcon>
        <ListItemText primary="Partners" />
      </MenuItem>
      <a className={classes.link} href={'/'}>
        <MenuItem onClick={handleLogout}>
          <ListItemIcon>
            <LogOutIcon />
          </ListItemIcon>
          <ListItemText primary="Logout" />
        </MenuItem>
      </a>
    </StyledMenu>
  </div>
 );
};

export default HeaderProfile;
```

Lastly, add the style components, as shown in Listing 13-26.

Listing 13-26. Styling Components for the HeaderProfile

```
const useStyles = makeStyles((theme: Theme) =>
  createStyles({
    avatar: {
      cursor: 'pointer',
      width: 64,
      height: 64,
    },
    link: { textDecoration: 'none', color: 'inherit' },
    small: {
      width: theme.spacing(3),
      height: theme.spacing(3),
    },
  }),
);
```

```
const StyledMenu = withStyles({
  paper: {
    border: '1px solid #d3d4d5',
  },
})((props: MenuProps) => (
  <Menu
    elevation={0}
    getContentAnchorEl={null}
    anchorOrigin={{
      vertical: 'bottom',
      horizontal: 'center',
    }}
    transformOrigin={{
      vertical: 'top',
      horizontal: 'center',
    }}
    {...props}
  />
));
```

All of the styling components we are using here are coming from Material-UI. For example, go to the website material-ui.com and search for menus.

Search for a particular menu that you need, copy the code, and tweak it to your preference. You can usually see the APIs at the bottom of the web page.

Updating the Navigation Bar

Let's head off to the navigation bar. Go to layouts ➤ main-layout ➤ navigation-bar. tsx and we will update it.

We need to hide or remove the Login button from the menu when the user is logged in.

First, we need to add the useSelector, RootState, and HeaderProfile, and the useSelector is for accessing or getting the claims, as shown in Listing 13-27.

Listing 13-27. Adding Import Components and Using useSelector

```
import {useSelector} from 'react-redux';
import {RootState} from 'store/reducers';
import HeaderProfile from 'app/components/header-profile';

export default function NavigationBar() {
  const classes = useStyles();
  const { claims } = useSelector((state: RootState) => state.auth);
```

Next, we are getting the claims from Auth and will use the claims to update the Dashboard and Login.

We will put the Dashboard button and the Login button inside some curly braces and then add the claims and add the HeaderProfile below the button Dashboard.

Listing 13-28. Using the Claims to Wrap the Dashboard and Login Buttons in the Navigation Bar

```
{claims ? (

                <Button color="inherit">
                  <Link className={classes.link} to={'/dashboard'}>
                    Dashboard
                  </Link>
                </Button>
                <HeaderProfile/>

          ) : (
            <Button color="inherit">
              <Link className={classes.link} to={'/login'}>
                Login
              </Link>
            </Button>
          )
          }
```

So what it does is that if the claims are valid, the Dashboard link is rendered. Otherwise, the Login link is rendered.

Refresh the browser, and you should see the avatar in the upper-right corner of the Login page, as shown in Figure 13-8.

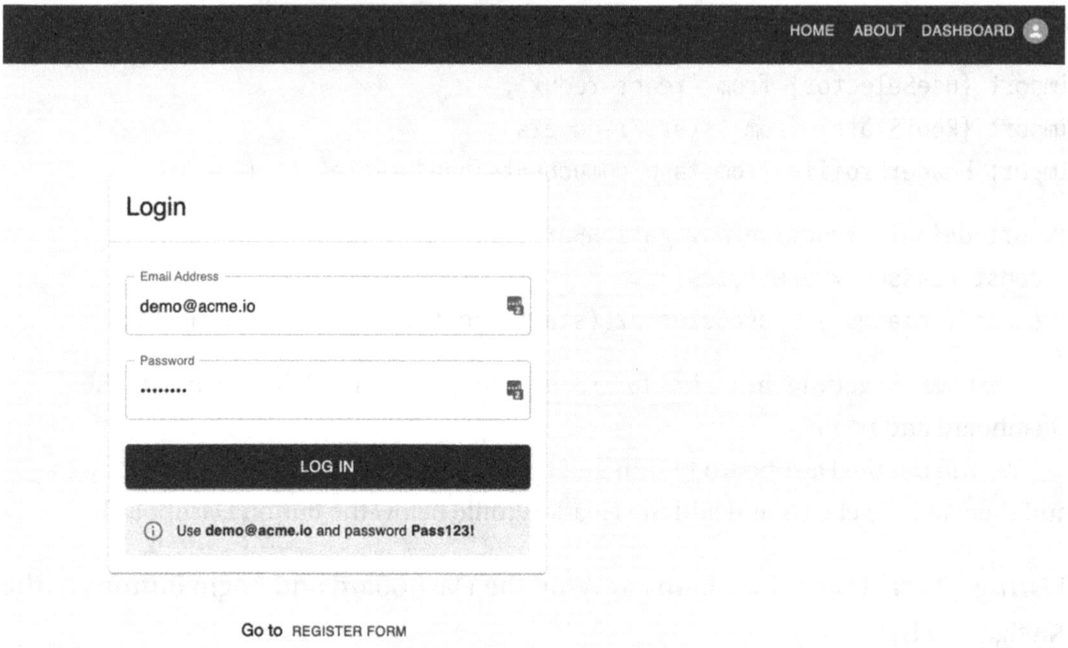

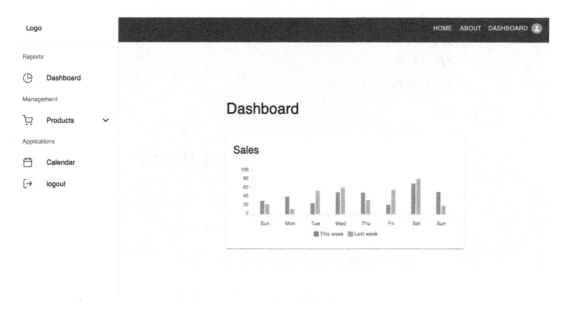

Figure 13-8. *Showing the dashboard avatar of the Login page*

And see the dashboard avatar after logging in, as shown in Figure 13-9.

Figure 13-9. *Showing the dashboard avatar after logging in*

Creating the AccountView

Now we move on to the views folder and create a new folder called account and, inside that, another folder called AccountView. Inside the AccountView, add the index.tsx:

views ➤ account ➤ AccountView ➤ index.tsx

For now, we will just add our standard Page template with the tag <h1> AccountView Page Works</h1>. See Listing 13-29.

Listing 13-29. Creating the Standard Page for the AccountView

```
import React from 'react';
import { Container, makeStyles } from '@material-ui/core';
import Page from 'app/components/page';

const AccountView = () => {
  const classes = useStyles();

  return (
    <Page className={classes.root} title="Settings">
      <Container maxWidth="lg">
        <h1>AccountView Page Works</h1>
      </Container>
    </Page>
  );
};

export default AccountView;

const useStyles = makeStyles(theme => ({
  root: {
    minHeight: '100%',
    paddingTop: theme.spacing(3),
    paddingBottom: theme.spacing(3),
  },
}));
```

For now, the Account page is just for showing that we can navigate here; we will go back to that later to update it.

Adding Images

Let's add more images to our application. Go to images ➤ products.

You can grab the images from here in my GitHub:

Source: `https://github.com/webmasterdevlin/practical-enterprise-react/tree/master/chapter-12/public/images/products`

Place these four images inside the products:

```
product_extended.svg,
product_premium.svg,
product_premium-outlined.svg,
product_standard.svg.
```

And lastly, add this avatar to the images directory:

avatar_6.png

You can grab the image from here:

`https://github.com/webmasterdevlin/practical-enterprise-react/blob/master/chapter-12/public/images/avatar_6.png`

Creating the Pricing Page

Next, let's create a new component and call it Pricing page:

`views ➤ pages ➤ pricing ➤ PricingPage.tsx`

This page is purely for aesthetics or design. And we will just be importing the standard styling components from Material-UI, as shown in Listing 13-30.

Listing 13-30. Adding the Named Components of the PricingPage

```
import React from 'react';
import clsx from 'clsx';
import {
  Box,
  Button,
  Container,
  Divider,
  Grid,
  Paper,
```

```
  Typography,
  makeStyles,
} from '@material-ui/core';
```

```
import Page from 'app/components/page';
```

Then we add the PricingPage component that we will just reuse from Material-UI. We are showing the different price offerings or pricing options that we typically see on a website, for example, the Standard option, the Premium option, and the Extended option. See Listing 13-31.

Listing 13-31. Creating the PricingPage Component

```
const PricingPage = () => {
  const classes = useStyles();

  return (
    <Page className={classes.root} title="Pricing">
      <Container maxWidth="sm">
        <Typography align="center"
         variant="h2" color="textPrimary">
          Start Selling!
        </Typography>
        <Box mt={3}>
          <Typography align="center"
         variant="subtitle1" color="textSecondary">
            Welcome to the best platform for selling products
          </Typography>
        </Box>
      </Container>
      <Box mt="160px">
        <Container maxWidth="lg">
          <Grid container spacing={4}>
            <Grid item md={4} xs={12}>
              <Paper className={classes.product}
               elevation={1}>
                <img
                  alt="Product"
```

```
      className={classes.productImage}
      src="images/products/product_standard.svg"
    />

    <Typography
      component="h4"
      gutterBottom
      variant="overline"
      color="textSecondary"
    >
      Standard
    </Typography>
    <div>
      <Typography
        component="span"
        display="inline"
        variant="h4"
        color="textPrimary"
      >
        $5
      </Typography>
      <Typography
        component="span"
        display="inline"
        variant="subtitle2"
        color="textSecondary"
      >
        /month
      </Typography>
    </div>

    <Typography variant="overline"
              color="textSecondary">
      Max 1 user
    </Typography>
    <Box my={2}>
      <Divider />
```

```
    </Box>
    <Typography variant="body2"
                color="textPrimary">
      20 proposals/month
      <br />
      10 templates
      <br />
      Analytics dashboard
      <br />
      Email alerts
    </Typography>
    <Box my={2}>
      <Divider />
    </Box>
    <Button
      variant="contained"
      fullWidth
      className={classes.chooseButton}
    >
      Choose
    </Button>
  </Paper>
</Grid>

<Grid item md={4} xs={12}>
  <Paper
    className={clsx(classes.product,
                classes.recommendedProduct)}
    elevation={1}
  >
    <img
      alt="Product"
      className={classes.productImage}
      src="images/products/product_premium--outlined.svg"
    />
```

```
<Typography
  component="h4"
  gutterBottom
  variant="overline"
  color="inherit"
>
  Premium
</Typography>
<div>
  <Typography
    component="span"
    display="inline"
    variant="h4"
    color="inherit"
  >
    $29
  </Typography>

  <Typography
    component="span"
    display="inline"
    variant="subtitle2"
    color="inherit"
  >
    /month
  </Typography>
</div>
<Typography variant="overline" color="inherit">
  Max 3 user
</Typography>
<Box my={2}>
  <Divider />
</Box>
<Typography variant="body2" color="inherit">
  20 proposals/month
  <br />
```

```
          10 templates
          <br />
          Analytics dashboard
          <br />
          Email alerts
        </Typography>

        <Box my={2}>
          <Divider />
        </Box>
        <Button
          variant="contained"
          fullWidth
          className={classes.chooseButton}
        >
          Choose
        </Button>
      </Paper>
    </Grid>
    <Grid item md={4} xs={12}>
      <Paper className={classes.product} elevation={1}>
        <img
          alt="Product"
          className={classes.productImage}
          src="images/products/product_extended.svg"
        />
        <Typography
          component="h4"
          gutterBottom
          variant="overline"
          color="textSecondary"
        >
          Extended
        </Typography>
```

```
<div>
  <Typography
    component="span"
    display="inline"
    variant="h4"
    color="textPrimary"
  >
    $259
  </Typography>
  <Typography
    component="span"
    display="inline"
    variant="subtitle2"
    color="textSecondary"
  >
    /month
  </Typography>
</div>
<Typography variant="overline" color="textSecondary">
  Unlimited
</Typography>
<Box my={2}>
  <Divider />
</Box>

<Typography variant="body2"
color="textPrimary">
    All from above
    <br />
    Unlimited 24/7 support
    <br />
    Personalised Page
    <br />
    Advertise your profile
</Typography>
```

```
            <Box my={2}>
              <Divider />
            </Box>
            <Button
              variant="contained"
              fullWidth
              className={classes.chooseButton}
            >
              Choose
            </Button>
          </Paper>
        </Grid>
      </Grid>
    </Container>
  </Box>
</Page>
  );
};
```

Next, we need to add the styling components such as padding, positioning, transition themes, etc. from Material-UI, as shown in Listing 13-32.

Listing 13-32. Adding the Styling Components to the PricingPage

```
const useStyles = makeStyles(theme => ({
  root: {
    minHeight: '100%',
    height: '100%',
    paddingTop: 120,
    paddingBottom: 120,
  },
  product: {
    position: 'relative',
    padding: theme.spacing(5, 3),
    cursor: 'pointer',
    transition: theme.transitions.create('transform', {
```

```
    easing: theme.transitions.easing.sharp,
    duration: theme.transitions.duration.leavingScreen,
  }),
  '&:hover': {
    transform: 'scale(1.1)',
  },
},
productImage: {
  borderRadius: theme.shape.borderRadius,
  position: 'absolute',
  top: -24,
  left: theme.spacing(3),
  height: 48,
  width: 48,
  fontSize: 24,
},
recommendedProduct: {
  backgroundColor: theme.palette.primary.main,
  color: theme.palette.common.white,
},
chooseButton: {
  backgroundColor: theme.palette.common.white,
},
}));

export default PricingPage;
```

We will not add any functionality here; it is just for aesthetics for our current app. But you can play around with it and change it according to your preference.

Updating the Routes

Okay, now it's time to update the routes to add the PricingPage and the AccountView. Add them below the login Route path and the calendar Route path, respectively, as shown in Listing 13-33.

Listing 13-33. Updating the routes.tsx

```
<Route
        exact
        path={'/pricing'}
        component={lazy(() => import('./views/pages/pricing/
        PricingPage'))}
      />

...

<Route
            exact
            path={path + '/account'}
            component={lazy(
              () => import('./views/dashboard/account/AccountView'),
            )}
          />
```

Summary

In this chapter, we have learned how to create our Profile Form and shown how easily we can sync it to another component in our application with the help of Redux. We also used a popular JavaScript library called jwt-decode that can be used to decode JWT tokens. We also created Login and Register Forms using Formik and JWT for authentication.

In the second part of this chapter, we will continue with updating the sidebar navigation.

CHAPTER 14

Updating the Dashboard Sidebar Navigation

We just finished building our Profile, Login, and Register Forms and ended the first part by updating the routes. We now move on to the second part of this three-part chapter series to update the dashboard sidebar navigation.

Now that we have updated the routes, we will now move on to the dashboard-sidebar-navigation.

Let's start with adding useDispatch and the useSelector from React-Redux and reducers, respectively. See Listing 14-1.

Listing 14-1. Updating the Named Components in the dashboard-sidebar-navigation

```
import { useSelector, useDispatch } from 'react-redux';
import {RootState} from 'store/reducers';
```

Let's use the useDispatch and the useSelector in the DashboardSidebarNavigation component, as shown in Listing 14-2.

Listing 14-2. Updating the DashboardSidebarNavigation

```
const DashboardSidebarNavigation = () => {
  const classes = useStyles();
  const dispatch = useDispatch();
  const {profile} = useSelector((state: RootState) => state.profile);
  const {claims} = useSelector((state: RootState) => state.auth);
  const { url } = useRouteMatch();
  const [open, setOpen] = useState(false);
```

© Devlin Basilan Duldulao, Ruby Jane Leyva Cabagnot 2021
D. B. Duldulao and R. J. L. Cabagnot, *Practical Enterprise React*, https://doi.org/10.1007/978-1-4842-6975-6_14

In Listing 14-2, we are getting the `profile` reducer profile and the `claims` from the `auth reducer`.

Next, import the named module getProfileAction from the profileAsyncActions. In the `useEffect`, we call the `dispatch` to send the `getProfileAction` with `claims.sub` to the reducer. This means we need to import the `getProfileAction`, as shown in Listing 14-3.

Listing 14-3. Dispatching the getProfileAction in the DashboardSidebarNavigation

```
...
import { getProfileAction } from 'features/profile/profileAsyncActions';
...

useEffect(() => {
    dispatch(getProfileAction(claims.sub));

  }, []);
```

getProfileAction: A function that we call to pass the `claims.sub` and get the user's id.

Let's add styling for the avatar and the additional components – Avatar, Box, and Typography – from Material-UI Core, as shown in Listing 14-4.

Listing 14-4. Adding the Avatar Style in the DashboardSidebarNavigation

```
import { Collapse, Divider, ListSubheader, Avatar, Box, Typography} from
'@material-ui/core';
...
const useStyles = makeStyles(theme =>
  createStyles({
    avatar: {
      cursor: 'pointer',
      width: 64,
      height: 64,
    },
...
```

Now, we are ready to update to the new UI. Replace the Toolbar containing the logo with the one in the following, as shown in Listing 14-5.

Listing 14-5. Updating the DashboardSidebarNavigation

```
{/* check first if profile.name is true before rendering what's inside the
Box, including the avatar */}
{profile.name && (
          <Box p={2}>
            <Box display="flex" justifyContent="center">
              <Avatar
                alt="User"
                className={classes.avatar}
                src={profile.avatar}
              />
            </Box>
            <Box mt={2} textAlign="center">
              <Typography>{profile.name}</Typography>
              <Typography variant="body2" color="textSecondary">
                Your tier: {profile.tier}
              </Typography>
            </Box>
          </Box>
        )}
```

Updating the db.json

Okay, before we refresh the browser, we need to update the db.json first and add the users-db.

Currently, we only have the users for authentication. Let's add that now. See Listing 14-6.

Listing 14-6. Adding the users-db in the db.json

```
"users-db": [
    {
      "id": "7fguyfte5",
      "email": "demo@acme.io",
      "name": "Mok Kuh",
```

```
    "password": "$2a$10$.vEI32nHFyG15ZACR7q/J.DNT/7iFC1Gfi2fFPMsGO9
    LCPtwkOq/.",
    "avatar": "/images/avatar_6.png",
    "canHire": true,
    "country": "United States",
    "city": "NY",
    "isPublic": true,
    "phone": "+40 777666555",
    "role": "admin",
    "state": "New York",
    "tier": "Premium",
    "subscription": {
      "name": "Premium",
      "price": 29,
      "currency": "$",
      "proposalsLeft": 12,
      "templatesLeft": 5,
      "invitesLeft": 24,
      "adsLeft": 10,
      "hasAnalytics": true,
      "hasEmailAlerts": true
    }
  }
]
```

Refresh the browser, and you should see the one shown in Figure 14-1.

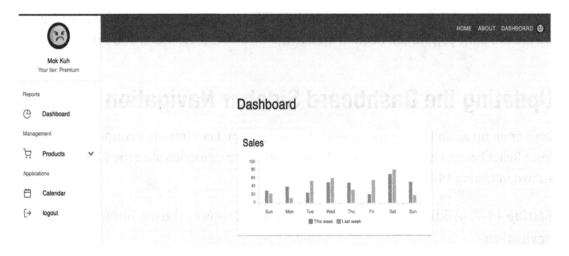

Figure 14-1. *Updating the UI*

You'll notice the sidebar navigation and the navigation bar are syncing; they are rendering the same image. They are getting the same state from the Redux Store.

Check the Redux DevTools and click the State, and you'll see the profile, which is now available in any part of the application, as shown in Figure 14-2.

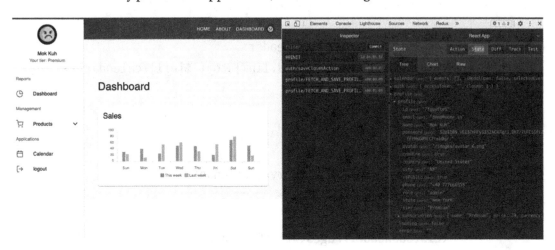

Figure 14-2. *Checking the Redux DevTools*

⚠ In real world application, we don't send back the password.
You would use a DTO in your web application or backend to restrict sensitive or limit unnecessary data over the network.

Okay, now we know that we can sync the profile of the user in any component. But we are not done yet; we still need to update the Dashboard, Account, and Pricing menus.

Updating the Dashboard Sidebar Navigation

Let's open up again the dashboard-sidebar-navigation. Let's import a couple of icons from React Feather and also add the Account and Pricing menus after the Calendar, as shown in Listing 14-7.

Listing 14-7. Adding the Account and Pricing Menus in the dashboard-sidebar-navigation

```
...
  User as UserIcon,
  DollarSign as DollarSignIcon,
  LogOut as LogOutIcon,
} from 'react-feather';

...

<ListSubheader>Applications</ListSubheader>
            <Link className={classes.link} to={`${url}/calendar`}>
              <ListItem button>
                <ListItemIcon>
                  <CalendarIcon />
                </ListItemIcon>
                <ListItemText primary={'Calendar'} />
              </ListItem>
            </Link>
            <ListSubheader>Pages</ListSubheader>
            <Link className={classes.link} to={`${url}/account`}>
              <ListItem button>
                <ListItemIcon>
                  <UserIcon />
```

```
      </ListItemIcon>
      <ListItemText primary={'Account'} />
    </ListItem>
  </Link>
  <Link className={classes.link} to={`/pricing`}>
    <ListItem button>
      <ListItemIcon>
        <DollarSignIcon />
      </ListItemIcon>
      <ListItemText primary={'Pricing'} />
    </ListItem>
  </Link>
  <a className={classes.link} href={'/'}>
    <ListItem button onClick={handleLogout}>
      <ListItemIcon>
        <LogOutIcon />
      </ListItemIcon>
      <ListItemText primary={'logout'} />
    </ListItem>
  </a>
</List>
```

Refresh the browser, and you'll see the two new additional menus in the sidebar. The Account is empty for now, but the Pricing has some styling on it, courtesy of the Material-UI components. See Figure 14-3.

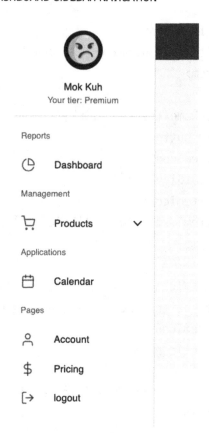

Figure 14-3. *Updated sidebar menus*

Click Pricing to see the same UI as shown in Figure 14-4.

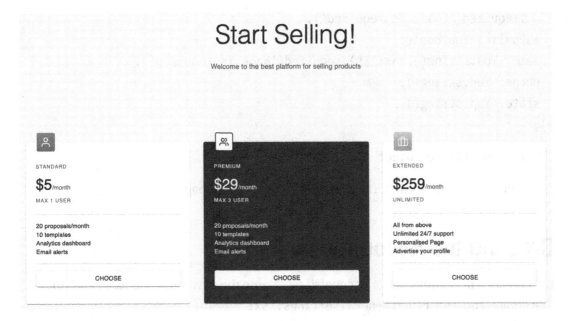

Figure 14-4. *Screenshot of the Pricing page*

If you had clicked Account, you'd see that it was just the bare minimum. So let's do something here. But before we do that, we need to create a Yup validation. It is an extensive profile validation, so it's better to write it in a separate file.

Creating the Yup Profile Validation

Create a new file: **features ➤ profile ➤ yup ➤ profile.validation.ts**.

Let's add the Yup profile validation, as shown in Listing 14-8.

Listing 14-8. Adding the Yup Profile Validation

```
import * as Yup from 'yup';

const profileYupObject = Yup.object().shape({
  canHire: Yup.bool(),
  city: Yup.string().max(255),
  country: Yup.string().max(255),
  email: Yup.string()
    .email('Must be a valid email')
    .max(255)
```

```
    .required('Email is required'),
  isPublic: Yup.bool(),
  name: Yup.string().max(255).required('Name is required'),
  phone: Yup.string(),
  state: Yup.string(),
});

export { profileYupObject };
```

After that, we can now start building the AccountView page.

Creating the AccountView Page

Let's create a new folder under AccountView. Name the new folder General, and under that create a new file called GeneralSettings.tsx:

account ➤ AccountView ➤ General ➤ GeneralSettings.tsx

Let's import the named components we need, as shown in Listing 14-9.

Listing 14-9. Importing the Named Components of the GeneralSettings

```
import React, { useState } from 'react';
import { useDispatch } from 'react-redux';
import clsx from 'clsx';
import { Formik } from 'formik';
import { useSnackbar } from 'notistack';
import Autocomplete from '@material-ui/lab/Autocomplete';
import {
  Box,
  Button,
  Card,
  CardContent,
  CardHeader,
  Divider,
  FormHelperText,
  Grid,
  Switch,
```

```
  TextField,
  Typography,
  makeStyles,
} from '@material-ui/core';

import { UserType } from 'models/user-type';
import { putProfileAction } from 'features/profile/profileAsyncActions';
import { profileYupObject } from 'features/profile/yup/profile.validation';
```

What's new here? We got the Autocomplete from Material-UI Lab. For our Autocomplete, we will be using the Country select component.

Aside from the other usual Material-UI components, we also imported the UserType, putProfileAction, and profileYupObject.

Next, we will create the shape of the GeneralSettings and the local states we will be returning, as shown in Listing 14-10.

Listing 14-10. Creating the Shape and Local States of the GeneralSettings

```
type Props = {
  className?: string;
  user: UserType;
};

const GeneralSettings = ({ className, user, ...rest }: Props) => {
  const dispatch = useDispatch();
  const classes = useStyles();
  const [error, setError] = useState('');
  const { enqueueSnackbar } = useSnackbar();
```

And then, let's use Formik in the return statement, as shown in Listing 14-11.

Listing 14-11. Creating the Formik Props

```
return (
    <Formik
      enableReinitialize
      initialValues={user}
      validationSchema={profileYupObject}
      onSubmit={async (values, formikHelpers) => {
```

```
      try {
        dispatch(putProfileAction(values));
        formikHelpers.setStatus({ success: true });
        formikHelpers.setSubmitting(false);
        enqueueSnackbar('Profile updated', {
          variant: 'success',
        });
      } catch (err) {
        setError(err);

        formikHelpers.setStatus({ success: false });
        formikHelpers.setSubmitting(false);
      }
    }}
  >
    {({
      errors,
      handleBlur,
      handleChange,
      handleSubmit,
      isSubmitting,
      touched,
      values,
      setFieldValue,
    }) => (
```

Inside Formik, we use the **enableReinitialize**, which allows us to update or edit the form. This is the Formik prop we need to use when we have an existing object or data and we want to edit it using Formik. We have this two-way data binding.

initialValues: We are passing the user, which is coming from the parent component of the GeneralSettings.

validationSchema: We are passing the profileYupObject.

onSubmit: We are dispatching the putProfileAction and passing the values of the user's inputs.

Now let's use the Formik props and build the different TextFields we need.

We shall create a TextField for Country, where we will integrate the Autocomplete. See Listing 14-12.

Listing 14-12. Using the Formik Props in the GeneralSettings

```
<form onSubmit={handleSubmit}>
        <Card className={clsx(classes.root, className)} {...rest}>
          <CardHeader title="Profile" />
          <Divider />
          <CardContent>
            <Grid container spacing={4}>
              <Grid item md={6} xs={12}>
                <TextField
        error={Boolean(touched.name && errors.name)}
                fullWidth
        helperText={touched.name && errors.name}
                label="Name"
                name="name"
                onBlur={handleBlur}
                onChange={handleChange}
                value={values?.name}
                variant="outlined"
              />
            </Grid>
            <Grid item md={6} xs={12}>
              <TextField
        error={Boolean(touched.email && errors.email)}
                fullWidth
                helperText={
                  touched.email && errors.email
                    ? errors.email
        : 'We will use this email to contact you'
                }
                label="Email Address"
                name="email"
                onBlur={handleBlur}
```

```
                        onChange={handleChange}
                        required
                        type="email"
                        value={values?.email}
                        variant="outlined"
                      />
                    </Grid>

                    <Grid item md={6} xs={12}>
                      <TextField
                  error={Boolean(touched.phone && errors.phone)}
                        fullWidth
                  helperText={touched.phone && errors.phone}
                        label="Phone Number"
                        name="phone"
                        onBlur={handleBlur}
                        onChange={handleChange}
                        value={values?.phone}
                        variant="outlined"
                      />
                    </Grid>
                    <Grid item md={6} xs={12}>
                      <Autocomplete
                        id="country"
                        options={countries}
                        value={values?.country}
                  getOptionLabel={option => option.toString()}
                    renderOption={option => <>{option.text}</>}
                        onChange={(e: any) => {
                  setFieldValue('country', e.target.innerText);
                        }}
                        renderInput={params => (
                          <TextField
                            {...params}
                            value={values?.country}
                            fullWidth
```

```
                label="Country"
                name="country"
                onChange={handleChange}
                variant="outlined"
                inputProps={{
                  ...params.inputProps,
                  autoComplete: 'country',
                }}
              />
            )}
          />
        </Grid>                          .

        <Grid item md={6} xs={12}>
          <TextField
  error={Boolean(touched.state && errors.state)}
            fullWidth
      helperText={touched.state && errors.state}
            label="State/Region"
            name="state"
            onBlur={handleBlur}
            onChange={handleChange}
            value={values?.state}
            variant="outlined"
          />
        </Grid>
        <Grid item md={6} xs={12}>
          <TextField
    error={Boolean(touched.city && errors.city)}
            fullWidth
     helperText={touched.city && errors.city}
            label="City"
            name="city"
            onBlur={handleBlur}
            onChange={handleChange}
```

```
                    value={values?.city}
                    variant="outlined"
                  />
                </Grid>

                <Grid item md={6} xs={12}>
            <Typography variant="h6" color="textPrimary">
                    Make Contact Info Public
                </Typography>
        <Typography variant="body2" color="textSecondary">Means that anyone
    viewing your profile will be able to see your contacts details
                </Typography>
                <Switch
                  checked={values?.isPublic}
                  edge="start"
                  name="isPublic"
                  onChange={handleChange}
                />
                </Grid>
                <Grid item md={6} xs={12}>
            <Typography variant="h6" color="textPrimary">
                    Available to hire
                </Typography>
        <Typography variant="body2" color="textSecondary">
Toggling this will let your teammates know that you are
            available for acquiring new projects
                </Typography>
                <Switch
                  checked={values?.canHire}
                  edge="start"
                  name="canHire"
                  onChange={handleChange}
                />
                </Grid>
              </Grid>
```

```
            {error && (
                <Box mt={3}>
        <FormHelperText error>{error}</FormHelperText>
                </Box>
              )}
            </CardContent>
            <Divider />
    <Box p={2} display="flex" justifyContent="flex-end">
              <Button
                color="secondary"
                disabled={isSubmitting}
                type="submit"
                variant="contained"
              >
                Save Changes
              </Button>
            </Box>
          </Card>
        </form>
      )}
    </Formik>
  );
};

const useStyles = makeStyles(() => ({
  root: {},
}));

export default GeneralSettings;
```

The TextField is bound to the property name, for example, name, email, phone, country, state region, city, etc.

The Autocomplete is bound to the country. We wrap the country in Autocomplete, and we got this API from Autocomplete of Material-UI, including the list of countries in Figure 14-5.

And after that, we will just hard-code down below the list of all the countries. The following is only a screenshot of it. You can copy-paste the complete list from this link:

https://github.com/webmasterdevlin/practical-enterprise-react/blob/ master/chapter-12/src/app/views/dashboard/account/AccountView/General/ GeneralSettings.tsx

```
const countries = [
  { text: 'Afghanistan', value: 'AF' },
  { text: 'Åland Islands', value: 'AX' },
  { text: 'Albania', value: 'AL' },
  { text: 'Algeria', value: 'DZ' },
  { text: 'American Samoa', value: 'AS' },
  { text: 'Andorra', value: 'AD' },
  { text: 'Angola', value: 'AO' },
  { text: 'Anguilla', value: 'AI' },
  { text: 'Antarctica', value: 'AQ' },
  { text: 'Antigua and Barbuda', value: 'AG' },
  { text: 'Argentina', value: 'AR' },
  { text: 'Armenia', value: 'AM' },
  { text: 'Aruba', value: 'AW' },
  { text: 'Australia', value: 'AU' },
  { text: 'Austria', value: 'AT' },
  { text: 'Azerbaijan', value: 'AZ' },
  { text: 'Bahamas', value: 'BS' },
  { text: 'Bahrain', value: 'BH' },
  { text: 'Bangladesh', value: 'BD' },
  { text: 'Barbados', value: 'BB' },
  { text: 'Belarus', value: 'BY' },
  { text: 'Belgium', value: 'BE' },
  { text: 'Belize', value: 'BZ' },
  { text: 'Benin', value: 'BJ' },
  { text: 'Bermuda', value: 'BM' },
  { text: 'Bhutan', value: 'BT' },
  { text: 'Bolivia', value: 'BO' },
  { text: 'Bosnia and Herzegovina', value: 'BA' },
  { text: 'Botswana', value: 'BW' },
  { text: 'Bouvet Island', value: 'BV' },
  { text: 'Brazil', value: 'BR' },
  { text: 'British Indian Ocean Territory', value: 'IO' },
  { text: 'Brunei Darussalam', value: 'BN' },
  { text: 'Bulgaria', value: 'BG' },
  { text: 'Burkina Faso', value: 'BF' },
```

Figure 14-5. *Adding the Autocomplete Country select in the GeneralSettings*

Creating the Profile Details

Still, under the General folder, we will create a new file called ProfileDetails.tsx. This new component is just a user avatar.

The named components we need to import are shown in Listing 14-13.

Listing 14-13. Adding the Named Components in the ProfileDetails

```
import React from 'react';
import { Link as RouterLink } from 'react-router-dom';
import clsx from 'clsx';
import {
  Avatar,
  Box,
  Button,
  Card,
  CardActions,
  CardContent,
  Link,
  Typography,
  makeStyles,
} from '@material-ui/core';

import { UserType } from 'models/user-type';
```

And then add the ProfileDetails React function component, as shown in Listing 14-14.

Listing 14-14. Adding the ProfileDetails Function Component

```
type Props = {
  className?: string;
  user: UserType;
};

const ProfileDetails = ({ className, user, ...rest }: Props) => {
  const classes = useStyles();

  return (
```

```jsx
    <Card className={clsx(classes.root, className)} {...rest}>
      <CardContent>
        <Box
          display="flex"
          alignItems="center"
          flexDirection="column"
          textAlign="center"
        >
          <Avatar className={classes.avatar} src={user?.avatar} />
          <Typography
            className={classes?.name}
            color="textPrimary"
            gutterBottom
            variant="h4"
          >
            {user?.name}
          </Typography>

          <Typography color="textPrimary" variant="body1">
            Your tier:{' '}
            <Link component={RouterLink} to="/pricing">
              {user?.tier}
            </Link>
          </Typography>
        </Box>
      </CardContent>
      <CardActions>
        <Button fullWidth variant="text">
          Remove picture
        </Button>
      </CardActions>
    </Card>
  );
};

const useStyles = makeStyles(theme => ({
```

```
  root: {},
  name: {
    marginTop: theme.spacing(1),
  },
  avatar: {
    height: 100,
    width: 100,
  },
}));
```

```
export default ProfileDetails;
```

The user object is coming from the parent component of the Profile Details. The user is called to render the avatar, the name, and the tier. We also have the ***Remove picture,*** but we're not going to put any functionality here. It is just for aesthetics.

Creating General Settings

Now we move on to create an index.tsx under the General folder:

account ➤ AccountView ➤ General ➤ index.tsx

Let's add first the named components, as shown in Listing 14-15.

Listing 14-15. Adding the Named Components in the index.tsx of the General Settings

```
import React from 'react';
import clsx from 'clsx';
import { useSelector } from 'react-redux';
import { Grid, makeStyles } from '@material-ui/core';

import ProfileDetails from './ProfileDetails';
import GeneralSettings from './GeneralSettings';
import { RootState } from 'store/reducers';
```

And then, let's create the shape of the component and the useSelector to access a piece of the Store state, as shown in Listing 14-16.

Listing 14-16. Creating the Shape and useSelector in the index.tsx of the General Settings

```
type Props = {
  className?: string;
};

const General = ({ className, ...rest }: Props) => {
  const classes = useStyles();
  const { profile } = useSelector((state: RootState) => state.profile);
```

In the return statement, we pass the profile state in `ProfileDetails` and General Settings' `user props`, as shown in Listing 14-17.

Listing 14-17. Using the Profile to Pass to ProfileDetails and General Settings

```
return (
    <Grid
      className={clsx(classes.root, className)}
      container
      spacing={3}
      {...rest}
    >
      <Grid item lg={4} md={6} xl={3} xs={12}>
        <ProfileDetails user={profile} />
      </Grid>
      <Grid item lg={8} md={6} xl={9} xs={12}>
        <GeneralSettings user={profile} />
      </Grid>
    </Grid>
  );
};

const useStyles = makeStyles(() => ({
  root: {},
}));

export default General;
```

Creating the Header

After that, we need to go back to `AccountView` to add some more components:

account ➤ AccountView ➤ Header.tsx

Let's add the named components, as shown in Listing 14-18.

Listing 14-18. Adding the Named Components of Header.tsx in AccountView

```
import React from 'react';
import { Link as RouterLink } from 'react-router-dom';
import clsx from 'clsx';
import {
  Typography,
  Breadcrumbs,
  Link,
  makeStyles,
  Box,
} from '@material-ui/core';
import NavigateNextIcon from '@material-ui/icons/NavigateNext';
```

So what's new here? We have the Breadcrumbs from Material-UI Core and the NavigateNextIcon from Material-UI Icons.

Breadcrumbs: Gives users the ability to select from a range of values.

And then, let's add the return statement for the Header component, as shown in Listing 14-19.

Listing 14-19. Creating the Header Component

```
type Props = {
  className?: string;
};

const Header = ({ className, ...rest }: Props) => {
  const classes = useStyles();

  return (
    <div className={clsx(classes.root, className)} {...rest}>
```

```
    <Breadcrumbs
      separator={<NavigateNextIcon fontSize="small" />}
      aria-label="breadcrumb"
    >
      <Link color="inherit" to="/app" component={RouterLink}>
        Dashboard
      </Link>
      <Box>
        <Typography variant="body1" color="inherit">
          Account
        </Typography>
      </Box>
    </Breadcrumbs>
    <Typography variant="h4" color="textPrimary">
      Settings
    </Typography>
  </div>
  );
};

const useStyles = makeStyles(() => ({
  root: {},
}));

export default Header;
```

Summary

In this chapter, we successfully sync data between the sidebar navigation and the navigation bar because the data is coming from the global store or the Redux store.

We also updated the Dashboard, Account, and Pricing menus and used Formik and the Yup validation schema to build them.

Next, we will continue to build on this three-part chapter series and add three more components, the Notification, Security, and Subscription pages, to complete the UI of our application.

CHAPTER 15

Creating the Notifications, Security, and Subscription Pages

This last part of the series will make the Notifications, Security, and Subscription pages using Redux, Formik, and the Yup validation schema.

Overall, the aim here is to complete the UI of our React application with basic real-world functionalities and consolidate our learnings of how Redux works and how to use Formik and the Yup validation schema in our application.

Creating the Notifications Page

We will first do the Notifications page. This page is just for the design or overall UI look of the application.

Under the AccountView, we will need to create a file called Notifications.tsx:

account ➤ AccountView ➤ Notifications.tsx

Here are the named import components, as shown in Listing 15-1.

Listing 15-1. Adding the Named Components of the Notifications.tsx

```
import React from 'react';
import clsx from 'clsx';
import {
  Box,
  Button,
  Card,
```

© Devlin Basilan Duldulao, Ruby Jane Leyva Cabagnot 2021
D. B. Duldulao and R. J. L. Cabagnot, *Practical Enterprise React*, https://doi.org/10.1007/978-1-4842-6975-6_15

```
  CardContent,
  CardHeader,
  Checkbox,
  Divider,
  FormControlLabel,
  Grid,
  Typography,
  makeStyles,
} from '@material-ui/core';
```

And the shape of the Notifications component, as shown in Listing 15-2.

Listing 15-2. Adding the Notifications Function Component

```
type Props = {
  className?: string;
};

const Notifications = ({ className, ...rest }: Props) => {
  const classes = useStyles();
```

And the return statement that returns elements, as shown in Listing 15-3.

Listing 15-3. Creating the Return Elements of the Notifications

```
return (
    <form>
      <Card className={clsx(classes.root, className)} {...rest}>
        <CardHeader title="Notifications" />
        <Divider />
        <CardContent>
          <Grid container spacing={6} wrap="wrap">
            <Grid item md={4} sm={6} xs={12}>
<Typography gutterBottom variant="h6" color="textPrimary">
                System
              </Typography>
              <Typography gutterBottom variant="body2"
                color="textSecondary">
                You will receive emails in your business email address
```

```
      </Typography>
      <div>
        <FormControlLabel
          control={<Checkbox defaultChecked />}
          label="Email alerts"
        />
      </div>
      <div>
        <FormControlLabel
          control={<Checkbox />}
          label="Push Notifications"
        />
      </div>

      <div>
        <FormControlLabel
          control={<Checkbox defaultChecked />}
          label="Text message"
        />
      </div>
      <div>
        <FormControlLabel
          control={<Checkbox defaultChecked />}
          label={
            <>
              <Typography variant="body1" color="textPrimary">
                Phone calls
              </Typography>
              <Typography variant="caption">
                Short voice phone updating you
              </Typography>
            </>
          }
        />
      </div>
    </Grid>
```

```
            <Grid item md={4} sm={6} xs={12}>
              <Typography gutterBottom variant="h6" color="textPrimary">
                Chat App
              </Typography>
              <Typography gutterBottom variant="body2"
              color="textSecondary">
  You will receive emails in your business email address
              </Typography>

              <div>
                <FormControlLabel
                  control={<Checkbox defaultChecked />}
                  label="Email"
                />
              </div>
              <div>
                <FormControlLabel
                  control={<Checkbox defaultChecked />}
                  label="Push notifications"
                />
              </div>
            </Grid>
          </Grid>
        </CardContent>
        <Divider />
        <Box p={2} display="flex" justifyContent="flex-end">
  <Button color="secondary" type="submit" variant="contained">
            Save Settings
          </Button>
        </Box>
      </Card>
    </form>
  );
};

const useStyles = makeStyles(() => ({
```

```
  root: {},
}));
```

```
export default Notifications;
```

Our Notifications component here is just for aesthetics. At this point, we are not going to use any additional functionality here. The General Settings should do for our purpose of understanding the implementation flow of Redux.

However, you can update it on your own just to practice and solidify your learnings.

Creating the Security Page

Another React component we need to add is Security. Also, under `AccountView,` create a new file and name it `Security.tsx.`

We will be using here simple HTTP requests without Redux Toolkit. We are creating this to remind you that we DON'T need to use Redux in every HTTP request, similar to what we did in Chapter 6.

 We only use Redux if it's necessary like if we need to use a state in different components, but if you only need to send a request to a json server or a web service.

Okay, now let's add the named components for the Security, as shown in Listing 15-4.

Listing 15-4. Importing the Named Components in Security

```
import React, { useState } from 'react';
import clsx from 'clsx';
import * as Yup from 'yup';
import { Formik } from 'formik';
import { useSnackbar } from 'notistack';
import { useSelector } from 'react-redux';
import {
  Box,
  Button,
  Card,
  CardContent,
  CardHeader,
```

```
  Divider,
  FormHelperText,
  Grid,
  TextField,
  makeStyles,
} from '@material-ui/core';

import { changePasswordAxios, ChangePasswordModel } from 'services/
authService';
import { RootState } from 'store/reducers';
```

We are using Yup and Formik and the usual bunch of other components we need. We also imported the changePasswordAxios and ChangePasswordModel from authService and the RootState from reducers. As you can see, no action will send a request or update anything to the Store.

Next, we add the type of the object and use some React Hooks, as shown in Listing 15-5.

Listing 15-5. Creating the Security Function Component

```
type Props = {
  className?: string;
};

type PasswordType = {
  password: string;
  passwordConfirm: string;
};

const Security = ({ className, ...rest }: Props) => {
  const { claims } = useSelector((state: RootState) => state.auth);
  const classes = useStyles();
  const [error, setError] = useState('');
  const { enqueueSnackbar } = useSnackbar();
```

claims: We are getting the claims from the auth reducer through the useSelector. And the return elements for the Security component, as shown in Listing 15-6.

Listing 15-6. Returning the Elements for the Security React Component

```
return (
    <Formik
      initialValues={
        {
          password: '',
          passwordConfirm: '',
        } as PasswordType
      }

      {/*validation schema for the password */}

      validationSchema={Yup.object().shape({
        password: Yup.string()
          .min(7, 'Must be at least 7 characters')
          .max(255)
          .required('Required'),
        passwordConfirm: Yup.string()
          .oneOf([Yup.ref('password'), null], 'Passwords must match')
          .required('Required'),
      })}
      onSubmit={async (values, formikHelpers) => {
        try {

          {/*Checking if the password matches or not */}

          if (values.password !== values.passwordConfirm) {
            alert('Must match');
            return;
          }

          {/* If it matches, return this object with the
            following args to change password */}
          const args: ChangePasswordModel = {
            id: claims.sub,
            email: claims.email,
            password: values.password,
          };
```

```
        await changePasswordAxios(args);

        formikHelpers.resetForm();
        formikHelpers.setStatus({ success: true });
        formikHelpers.setSubmitting(false);
        enqueueSnackbar('Password updated', {
          variant: 'success',
        });
      } catch (err) {
        console.error(err);
        formikHelpers.setStatus({ success: false });
        formikHelpers.setSubmitting(false);
      }
    }}
  >
    {formikProps => (
      <form onSubmit={formikProps.handleSubmit}>
        <Card className={clsx(classes.root, className)} {...rest}>
          <CardHeader title="Change Password" />
          <Divider />
          <CardContent>
            <Grid container spacing={3}>
              <Grid item md={4} sm={6} xs={12}>
                <TextField
                  error={Boolean(
                    formikProps.touched.password &&
                      formikProps.errors.password,
                  )}
                  fullWidth
                  helperText={
                    formikProps.touched.password &&
                    formikProps.errors.password
                  }
                  label="Password"
                  name="password"
                  onBlur={formikProps.handleBlur}
```

```
        onChange={formikProps.handleChange}
        type="password"
        value={formikProps.values.password}
        variant="outlined"
      />
    </Grid>

    <Grid item md={4} sm={6} xs={12}>
      <TextField
        error={Boolean(
          formikProps.touched.passwordConfirm &&
            formikProps.errors.passwordConfirm,
        )}
        fullWidth
        helperText={
          formikProps.touched.passwordConfirm &&
          formikProps.errors.passwordConfirm
        }
        label="Password Confirmation"
        name="passwordConfirm"
        onBlur={formikProps.handleBlur}
        onChange={formikProps.handleChange}
        type="password"
        value={formikProps.values.passwordConfirm}
        variant="outlined"
      />
    </Grid>
  </Grid>
  {error && (
    <Box mt={3}>
      <FormHelperText error>{error}</FormHelperText>
    </Box>
  )}
</CardContent>
<Divider />
```

```
            <Box p={2} display="flex" justifyContent="flex-end">
              <Button
                color="secondary"
                disabled={formikProps.isSubmitting}
                type="submit"
                variant="contained"
              >
                Change Password
              </Button>
            </Box>
          </Card>
        </form>
      )}
    </Formik>
  );
};

const useStyles = makeStyles(() => ({
  root: {},
}));

export default Security;
```

Creating the Subscription Page

The last component we will build in this chapter is the Subscription.tsx, which is still under the AccountView folder.

Let's add first the named components, as shown in Listing 15-7.

Listing 15-7. Adding the Named Components in the Subscription

```
import { Link as RouterLink } from 'react-router-dom';
import clsx from 'clsx';
import { useSelector } from 'react-redux';
import {
  Box,
  Button,
```

```
  Card,
  CardContent,
  CardHeader,
  Divider,
  Link,
  Paper,
  Typography,
  makeStyles,
} from '@material-ui/core';

import { RootState } from 'store/reducers';
```

Next, let's do the type or shape of the object, as shown in Listing 15-8.

Listing 15-8. Adding the Props and Using Hooks for Subscription.tsx

```
type Props = {
  className?: string;
};

const Subscription = ({ className, ...rest }: Props) => {
  const classes = useStyles();
  const {
    profile: { subscription },
  } = useSelector((state: RootState) => state.profile);
```

In Listing 15-8, we access the profile and then render the Manage your subscription in the UI in Listing 15-9.

For example, we can access the subscription.currency, subscription.price, and subscription.name – because the subscription is a deconstructed object of the profile. The nested destructuring is a valid syntax here.

Listing 15-9 is the return statement of the Subscription component.

Listing 15-9. Adding the Return Statement of the Subscription Component

```
return (
    <Card className={clsx(classes.root, className)} {...rest}>
      <CardHeader title="Manage your subscription" />
      <Divider />
```

```
<CardContent>
  <Paper variant="outlined">
    <Box className={classes.overview}>
      <div>
        <Typography display="inline" variant="h4"
         color="textPrimary">
          {subscription.currency}
          {subscription.price}
        </Typography>
        <Typography display="inline" variant="subtitle1">
          /mo
        </Typography>
      </div>
      <Box display="flex" alignItems="center">
        <img
          alt="Product"
          className={classes.productImage}
          src="/images/products/product_premium.svg"
        />
        <Typography variant="overline" color="textSecondary">
          {subscription.name}
        </Typography>
      </Box>
    </Box>
    <Divider />

    <Box className={classes.details}>
      <div>
        <Typography variant="body2" color="textPrimary">
          {`${subscription.proposalsLeft} proposals left`}
        </Typography>
        <Typography variant="body2" color="textPrimary">
          {`${subscription.templatesLeft} templates`}
        </Typography>
      </div>
      <div>
```

```jsx
      <Typography variant="body2" color="textPrimary">
        {`${subscription.invitesLeft} invites left`}
      </Typography>
      <Typography variant="body2" color="textPrimary">
        {`${subscription.adsLeft} ads left`}
      </Typography>
    </div>
    <div>
      {subscription.hasAnalytics && (
        <Typography variant="body2" color="textPrimary">
          Analytics dashboard
        </Typography>
      )}
      {subscription.hasEmailAlerts && (
        <Typography variant="body2" color="textPrimary">
          Email alerts
        </Typography>
      )}
    </div>
  </Box>
</Paper>

<Box mt={2} display="flex" justifyContent="flex-end">
  <Button size="small" color="secondary" variant="contained">
    Upgrade plan
  </Button>
</Box>
<Box mt={2}>
  <Typography variant="body2" color="textSecondary">
    The refunds don&apos;t work once you have the subscription,
    but you
    can always{' '}
    <Link color="secondary" component={RouterLink} to="#">
      Cancel your subscription
    </Link>
```

·

```
        </Typography>
      </Box>
    </CardContent>
  </Card>
  );
};
```

And lastly, the styling for this component, as shown in Listing 15-10.

Listing 15-10. Styling Components for the Subscription.tsx

```
const useStyles = makeStyles(theme => ({
  root: {},
  overview: {
    padding: theme.spacing(3),
    display: 'flex',
    alignItems: 'center',
    flexWrap: 'wrap',
    justifyContent: 'space-between',
    [theme.breakpoints.down('md')]: {
      flexDirection: 'column-reverse',
      alignItems: 'flex-start',
    },
  },
  productImage: {
    marginRight: theme.spacing(1),
    height: 48,
    width: 48,
  },
  details: {
    padding: theme.spacing(3),
    display: 'flex',
    alignItems: 'center',
    flexWrap: 'wrap',
    justifyContent: 'space-between',
    [theme.breakpoints.down('md')]: {
      flexDirection: 'column',
```

```
      alignItems: 'flex-start',
    },
  },
}));
```

```
export default Subscription;
```

Updating the AccountView

Before we wrap up this chapter, we need to update the AccountView one more time.

First, let's update the import named components, as shown in Listing 15-11.

Listing 15-11. Import Named Components of AccountView

```
import React, { useState, ChangeEvent } from 'react';
import {
  Box,
  Container,
  Divider,
  Tab,
  Tabs,
  makeStyles,
} from '@material-ui/core';

import Header from './Header';
import General from './General';
import Subscription from './Subscription';
import Notifications from './Notifications';
import Security from './Security';
import Page from 'app/components/page';
```

What's new here? **Tabs** is from Material-UI; specifically, we will be using Simple Tabs.

Tabs: Allows us to organize and navigate between groups of related content at the same hierarchy level.

Next, let's build the AccountView React function component, as shown in Listing 15-12.

Listing 15-12. Updating the index.tsx of the AccountView

```tsx
const AccountView = () => {
  const classes = useStyles();

  /*initialize the useState to 'general' - we will use that */

  const [currentTab, setCurrentTab] = useState('general');

  /*handleTabsChange -for setting or updating the value of the current tab */

  const handleTabsChange = (event: ChangeEvent<{}>, value: string): void => {
    setCurrentTab(value);
  };

  return (
    <Page className={classes.root} title="Settings">
      <Container maxWidth="lg">
        <Header />
        <Box mt={3}>
          <Tabs

            {/*handleTabsChange - for the clicking and selection of tabs */}

            onChange={handleTabsChange}
            scrollButtons="auto"
            value={currentTab}
            variant="scrollable"
            textColor="secondary"
          >

            {/*we're going to iterate or loop on the tabs here */}

            {tabs.map(tab => (
              <Tab key={tab.value} label={tab.label} value={tab.value} />
            ))}
          </Tabs>
        </Box>
        <Divider />
        <Box mt={3}>
```

```
      {/*current tab by default is the General component.
       The rest is not displayed until clicked or selected */}
      {currentTab === 'general' && <General />}
      {currentTab === 'subscription' && <Subscription />}
      {currentTab === 'notifications' && <Notifications />}
      {currentTab === 'security' && <Security />}
    </Box>
   </Container>
  </Page>
 );
};

const useStyles = makeStyles(theme => ({
  root: {
    minHeight: '100%',
    paddingTop: theme.spacing(3),
    paddingBottom: theme.spacing(3),
  },
}));

/* an array of objects with value. to be used in the
tabs for navigating between components*/
const tabs = [
  { value: 'general', label: 'General' },
  { value: 'subscription', label: 'Subscription' },
  { value: 'notifications', label: 'Notifications' },
  { value: 'security', label: 'Security' },
];

export default AccountView;
```

Refresh

Now time to refresh the browser.

In the sidebar navigation, click Account, and you'll see the default Settings page is the General page.

Click the other tabs such as the Subscription, Notifications, and Security.

To appreciate the power of using Redux in our app and how easily we can access or share a state of one component to another component, try to edit something in Settings ➤ General.

For example, edit the name and change it to Mok Kuh JR and save it. Once it's saved, you'll see the immediate update in the sidebar navigation also.

Figure 15-1. *Screenshot of the updated Settings*

So that's the power of Redux – making the whole application reactive to any changes.

Summary

That's it for this three-part series. In this last chapter, we finished the UI of our application, and hopefully we get into a complete understanding of how Redux works and how to use it in our applications whenever necessary. Hopefully, you have also deepened your knowledge and understanding of Formik and the Yup validation schema to build forms in applications.

Also, just keep in mind that Redux is good, but you DON'T need to use it everywhere in your application because it still adds complexity. For simple CRUD apps or if you don't need to reuse the state in other components, you don't need to use Redux.

But if you anticipate building an extensive application or an enterprise-level app, I would suggest setting up Redux in your application right from the get-go.

The setup would probably just take you an hour or two, and what's good about this is that it is just there waiting to be used whenever you need it. You can then access the state in the reducer from any component.

In the next chapter, we will see how to make our React app mobile-friendly.

CHAPTER 16

Making the App Mobile-Friendly

This chapter will update our React application to the latest current version (as of this writing) in the first quarter of 2021 and then make our application mobile-friendly. It will ensure that our application can also perform well on a small screen such as that of a mobile device or a tablet.

Mobile-friendly apps is another term for responsive design or adaptive design apps. In short, the display page is automatically adjusted based on the size of the device screen.

Getting Started

Let's go to the package.json, and to use the latest version available for each library we are using, we need to use a VS Code extension called Version Lens. We installed this in a previous chapter, but feel free to install it now if you have not done so.

© Devlin Basilan Duldulao, Ruby Jane Leyva Cabagnot 2021
D. B. Duldulao and R. J. L. Cabagnot, *Practical Enterprise React*, https://doi.org/10.1007/978-1-4842-6975-6_16

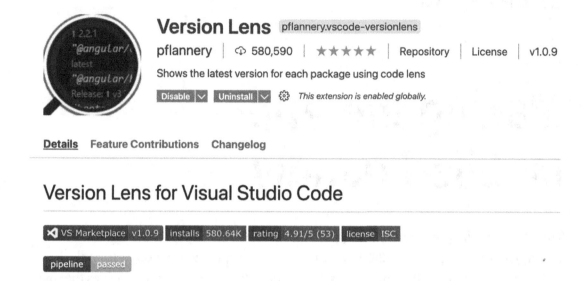

Figure 16-1. *Using Version Lens*

So how to check the latest version of each library we are using? Open the package.
json and click the V icon that you see in the upper-right corner, as shown in Figure 16-2.

```
ig.json        dashboard-default-content.tsx        index.tsx src        package.json ×   V

package.json > { } jest > [ ] collectCoverageFrom
  1  {
  2      "name": "react-enterprise-app",
  3      "version": "0.1.0",
  4      "private": true,
  5      "dependencies": {

  6        "@date-io/moment": "1.3.13",
```

Figure 16-2. *Version Lens library*

Updating a Package Library Safely

We are going to do a safe upgrade of React and of the libraries we are using. To upgrade,
just click the up arrow sign, as shown in Figure 16-3.

```
{
    "name": "react-enterprise-app",
    "version": "0.1.0",
    "private": true,
    "dependencies": {
        fixed 1.3.13 | latest: ↑ 2.10.8
        "@date-io/moment": "1.3.13",
        latest
        "@fullcalendar/core": "5.5.1",
        latest
        "@fullcalendar/daygrid": "5.5.0",
        latest
        "@fullcalendar/interaction": "5.5.0",
        latest
```

Figure 16-3. *Safe update of libraries*

The latest version of **date-io/moment** is 2.10.8, a major version update from the 1.3.13 version we are using. We are NOT going to update this because the major version means there are potentially breaking changes. The **1.3.13** is the version that is compatible with the Calendar component that we are using here.

- Be careful of breaking changes when upgrading to a major version. Minor version and patch upgrades are usually okay.

Upgrade all the minor versions and patches in your app using Version Lens, or if you want to be sure, compare your versions first with the ones we have at the time of this writing. You can check out the package.json in my GitHub:

```
https://github.com/webmasterdevlin/practical-enterprise-react/blob/
master/chapter-13/package.json
```

We updated the minor versions and patches in this app, including the following major versions, as shown in Listing 16-1.

Listing 16-1. Updated Major Versions

```
//major versions that were updated

@types/react
@types/react-dom
concurrently
```

```
prettier
react
react-dom
react-test-renderer
sanitize.css
ts-node
typescript
```

Okay, after doing that, we need to delete the **package-lock.json** and the **Node modules**. And then do

```
npm install
npm start:fullstack
```

If you encounter a problem or an error after running the npm start:fullstack, check your version of NPM. At this time of writing, we are using NPM version 6 because there's a compatibility problem with version 7.

Speaking of versions, one of the more noticeable changes in React 17 is that you don't need to explicitly type **import React from 'react'** when creating a component. Try to delete one of the components and see if it's still working. At the moment, though, I would not recommend deleting it yet because some React developers might not be familiar with this change. I'm just mentioning it so you won't get confused if you see components with the explicitly written import React statement.

Besides, the snippets we used in VS Code or WebStorm still automatically include the import React statement. Nevertheless, we need to upgrade to React 17 in preparation for the upcoming features in React.

Once you have checked that your app is still working, we can now start to make our app mobile-friendly.

Updating the HomePage

Let's start with the Home Page component and make it responsive. We will need style components from Material-UI Core and also the Page template we created, as shown in Listing 16-2.

Listing 16-2. Making the Home Page Mobile-Friendly

```
import React from 'react';
import { Box, Container, Typography, useMediaQuery } from '@material-ui/core';
import Page from 'app/components/page';

const Home = () => {
  const mobileDevice = useMediaQuery('(max-width:650px)');

  return (
    <Page title="Home">
      <Container>
        <Box
          height={mobileDevice ? '50vh' : '100vh'}
          display={'flex'}
          flexDirection={'column'}
          justifyContent={'center'}
          alignItems={'center'}
        >
          <Typography variant={mobileDevice ? 'h4' : 'h1'}>
            Welcome to Online Shop ☙
          </Typography>
        </Box>
      </Container>
    </Page>
  );
};

export default Home;
```

What's new here?

useMediaQuery: A CSS media query Hook for React. It will detect if the browser is small, like a mobile app or a tablet browser. We are setting the max-width to 650 pixels, and if it is below that, we are setting it to mobileDevice.

We have the Page template and the Container and Box from Material-UI in the return elements.

height: We are setting the height to the following: if it's a mobile device, then set the height to 50 vh (view height) or 50 percent of the browser's size; otherwise, the height is 100 vh.

typography: If a mobile device is detected, the size is h4; otherwise, set it to h1.

We are also using a shopping bag emoji here. And to get that kind of emojis and just straight away copy-paste it to your code, go to this website emojipedia.org. Search for "shopping bag" and copy and paste this emoji to your code.

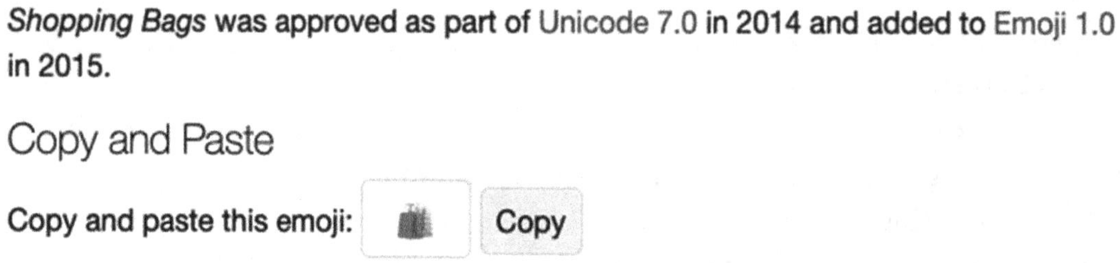

Shopping Bags was approved as part of Unicode 7.0 in 2014 and added to Emoji 1.0 in 2015.

Copy and Paste

Copy and paste this emoji: 🛍   Copy

Figure 16-4. Emojis from emojipedia.org

Refresh your browser and drag the window to make it smaller. You can also check it from a Simulator if you're using Mac or Android Studio on Windows.

Figure 16-5. *Mobile screenshot of the Home Page using MediaQuery*

Updating the About Page

Next, let's update the About Page component. We would be doing pretty much the same thing here, as shown in Listing 16-3.

Listing 16-3. Making the About Page Mobile-Friendly

```
import React from 'react';
import { Box, Container, Typography, useMediaQuery } from '@material-ui/
core';

import Page from 'app/components/page';

const AboutPage = () => {
  const mobileDevice = useMediaQuery('(max-width:650px)');
```

```
  return (
    <Page title="About">
      <Container>
        <Box
          height={mobileDevice ? '50vh' : '100vh'}
          display={'flex'}
          flexDirection={'column'}
          justifyContent={'center'}
          alignItems={'center'}
        >
          <Typography variant={mobileDevice ? 'h4' : 'h1'}>
            About us 👨👨👨
          </Typography>
        </Box>
      </Container>
    </Page>
  );
};

export default AboutPage;
```

It is just practically the same as the Home Page, except for the emojis, as shown in Figure 16-6.

Figure 16-6. *Mobile screenshot of the About Page using MediaQuery*

Updating the Not Found Page

The next one we will update is the Not Found Page. Again, we are doing the same except for the emoji used, as shown in Listing 16-4.

Listing 16-4. Updating the NotFoundPage Using Media Query

```
import React from 'react';
import { Box, Container, Typography, useMediaQuery } from '@material-ui/core';
import Page from 'app/components/page';

const NotFoundPage = () => {
  const mobileDevice = useMediaQuery('(max-width:650px)');
```

```
  return (
    <Page title="Not Found Page">
      <Container>
        <Box
          height={mobileDevice ? '50vh' : '100vh'}
          display={'flex'}
          flexDirection={'column'}
          justifyContent={'center'}
          alignItems={'center'}
        >
          <Typography variant={mobileDevice ? 'h4' : 'h1'}>
            404 Page Not Found ☹
          </Typography>
        </Box>
      </Container>
    </Page>
  );
};

export default NotFoundPage;
```

To test it, just go to a `localhost` page that does not exist, for example, "localhost:3000/not-found," as shown in Figure 16-7.

Figure 16-7. Making the Not Found Page mobile-friendly

Making the Navbar Mobile-Friendly

We will need to make the dashboard sidebar navigation mobile-friendly. In Figure 16-8, you'll note that the sidebar navigation is taking up more than 50 percent of the screen size.

Figure 16-8. *Mobile screenshot of the UI before using media query*

Let's go to the navigation-bar.tsx, and we will incorporate the useMediaQuery, as shown in Listing 16-5.

Listing 16-5. Importing useMediaQuery in dashboard-sidebar-navigation

```
//add the useMediaQuery
import { AppBar, Toolbar, Button, useMediaQuery, colors, } from '@material-
ui/core';

...
//add the Media Query hooks
const mobileDevice = useMediaQuery('(max-width:650px)')

//return elements. we will hide the logo if its not a mobile device
return (
```

```
<div className={classes.root}>
  <AppBar position="static">
    <Toolbar>
      <Link className={`${classes.link} ${classes.title}`} to={'/'}>
        {!mobileDevice && 'LOGO'}
      </Link
```

But we are not done yet. If you look at the app in your Simulator or a mobile device, there's only a slight change. The dashboard navigation is still not responsive, as shown in Figure 16-9, which shows the current state of the sidebar in a mobile device.

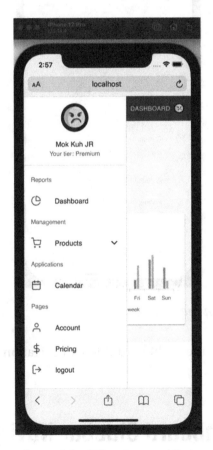

Figure 16-9. *Mobile screenshot of the UI using media query*

There are several ways we could do to make the navigation bar responsive. First, remove the entire sidebar navigation on a mobile device and create a drop-down menu list or a burger menu in the upper-right corner, as shown in Figure 16-10.

Figure 16-10. *Drop-down menu list*

Another way is to shrink the dashboard sidebar navigation. We will do the second option.

Making the Dashboard Sidebar Navigation Mobile-Friendly

Go to dashboard-sidebar-navigation.tsx and add useMediaQuery from Material-UI Core, as shown in Listing 16-6.

Listing 16-6. Adding the Media Query Hooks and Style Components in Dashboard Sidebar Navigation

```
import {
  Collapse,
  Divider,
  Drawer,
  List,
  ListItem,
  ListItemIcon,
  ListItemText,
  ListSubheader,
  Avatar,
  Box,
  Typography,
  useMediaQuery,
} from '@material-ui/core';

...
//add the Media Query hooks

const mobileDevice = useMediaQuery('(max-width:650px)');

//add the styling components in the useStyles component
// mobile style
    drawerClose: {
      transition: theme.transitions.create('width', {
        easing: theme.transitions.easing.sharp,
        duration: theme.transitions.duration.leavingScreen,
      }),
      overflowX: 'hidden',
      width: theme.spacing(7) + 1,
      [theme.breakpoints.up('sm')]: {
        width: theme.spacing(9) + 1,
      },
    },
```

Next, we will update the className drawer and classes paper. And also, import the named component clsx, as shown in Listing 16-7.

Listing 16-7. Updating the Drawer Elements

```
...
import clsx from 'clsx';
...
<Drawer
         className={clsx(classes.drawer, mobileDevice && classes.
         drawerClose)}
         variant="permanent"
         classes={{
           paper: clsx(
             classes.drawerPaper,
             mobileDevice && classes.drawerClose,
           ),
         }}
         anchor="left"
```

Then we will change the profile.name. We will not display the avatar if it's on a mobile screen. We created another drawer container for the mobile or smaller screen, as shown in Listing 16-8.

Listing 16-8. Updating the Avatar Elements

```
{profile.name && !mobileDevice && (
           <Box p={2}>...

         )}
         <Divider />

         {/*drawer container for the mobile screen */}

         {mobileDevice ? (
          <div className={classes.drawerContainer}>
             <List>
             <Link className={classes.link} to={`${url}`}>
```

```
    <ListItem button>
      <ListItemIcon>
        <PieChartIcon />
      </ListItemIcon>
    </ListItem>
  </Link>
  <Divider />
  <ListItem button onClick={handleClick}>
    <ListItemIcon>
      <ShoppingCartIcon />
    </ListItemIcon>
    {open ? <ChevronUpIcon /> : <ChevronDownIcon />}
  </ListItem>
  <Divider />
  <Collapse in={open} timeout="auto" unmountOnExit>
    <List component="div" disablePadding>
      <Link className={classes.link} to={`${url}/list-
      products`}>
        <ListItem button className={classes.nested}>
          <ListItemIcon>
            <ListIcon />
          </ListItemIcon>
        </ListItem>
      </Link>

      <Link className={classes.link} to={`${url}/create-
      product`}>
        <ListItem button className={classes.nested}>
          <ListItemIcon>
            <FilePlusIcon />
          </ListItemIcon>
        </ListItem>
      </Link>
    </List>
  </Collapse>
  <Divider />
```

```jsx
        <Link className={classes.link} to={`${url}/calendar`}>
          <ListItem button>
            <ListItemIcon>
              <CalendarIcon />
            </ListItemIcon>
          </ListItem>
        </Link>
        <Divider />
        <Link className={classes.link} to={`${url}/account`}>
          <ListItem button>
            <ListItemIcon>
              <UserIcon />
            </ListItemIcon>
          </ListItem>
        </Link>
        <Divider />
        <Link className={classes.link} to={`/pricing`}>
          <ListItem button>
            <ListItemIcon>
              <DollarSignIcon />
            </ListItemIcon>
          </ListItem>
        </Link>
        <Divider />

        <a className={classes.link} href={'/'}>
          <ListItem button onClick={handleLogout}>
            <ListItemIcon>
              <LogOutIcon />
            </ListItemIcon>
          </ListItem>
        </a>
      </List>
      <Divider />
    ) : (
```

```
    {/*drawer container for the web browser */}

    <div className={classes.drawerContainer}>
          <List>
             ...
          </List>
        </div>
      )}
    </Drawer>
  </div>
</>
);
};
```

Now we have two drawer containers, one for a mobile screen and another for a web browser.

We wrap the return elements in an if-else statement. If it's not a mobileDevice, show the avatar. Otherwise, don't show it.

Making the Dashboard Layout Mobile-Friendly

After doing that, we also need to use the media query Hooks in the index.tsx of the dashboard layout. We also need to import clsx.

And lastly, add another styling property in the useStyles, as shown in Listing 16-9.

Listing 16-9. Making the Dashboard Layout Mobile-Friendly

```
//import the useMediaQuery

import { Grid, useMediaQuery} from '@material-ui/core';
import clsx from 'clsx';
...

//add the Media Query hooks

const mobileDevice = useMediaQuery('(max-width:650px)')

//update the className
<DashboardSidebarNavigation />{' '}
```

```
    <div className={classes.wrapper}>
      <div className={classes.contentContainer}>
        <div
          className={clsx(classes.content, mobileDevice && classes.
          leftSpace)}
        >
          {children}
        </div>
      </div>
    </div>

//add a new style element

leftSpace: {
   paddingLeft: '3rem',
 },
```

Now recheck your mobile screen. It should be mobile-friendly now, as shown in Figure 16-11.

Figure 16-11. *Mobile friendly dashboard*

FOR YOUR ACTIVITY

The mobile screen is now mobile-friendly. However, there's still room for improvement. For
your activity

1. With useMediaQuery Hooks, adjust the ample space between the navigation bar
   and the dashboard pages' content when viewing them on a mobile device.

2. Figure 16-12 is a screenshot of the Dashboard (L) and the Dashboard
   Calendar (R).

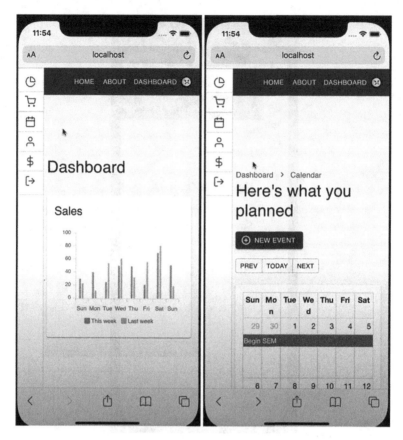

Figure 16-12. *Screenshot of the Dashboard (L) and the Dashboard Calendar (R)*

Summary

To summarize, we updated our React application to the latest current version (as of this writing) in the first quarter of 2021. We then made our application mobile-friendly with the help of media query Hooks.

In the next chapter, we will tackle the various popular styling methods for React components.

CHAPTER 17

Styling Methods for React Components

In the previous chapter, we made our app mobile-friendly with the help of media query Hooks. Now our app is almost ready to be deployed. However, before we proceed to do that, I think we should briefly pay attention to other styling methods for React components.

Throughout the application, we used the Material-UI library as our styling preference. But there are several other popular methods out there. We will not be diving deeply into each styling method but rather inform you of your other options.

There are various ways we can style React components. For many of us, choosing one over the other depends on different factors such as the architectural or design goals of our current project, a particular use case, and, of course, personal preferences.

For example, in some cases, when you just need to add a few style properties in a particular file, then maybe inline styling is the best option. And in the case of when you find yourself reusing some style properties in the same file, then styled-components are perfect. For other complex applications, you could look into CSS Modules or even the regular CSS.

Inline Styling

Developers typically use inline styling to prototype a component or test the component's CSS styling. This styling is also a way to brute-force an element to see the outcome of any CSS inline style we write and remove. Inline styling is perhaps the most straightforward styling method we can use, albeit not recommended for large-scale applications.

One thing to remember is that in React, inline styling is specified as an object, not as a string. The key value is the CSS property name and should be written in camelCase, and the style's value is usually a string.

417

© Devlin Basilan Duldulao, Ruby Jane Leyva Cabagnot 2021
D. B. Duldulao and R. J. L. Cabagnot, *Practical Enterprise React*, https://doi.org/10.1007/978-1-4842-6975-6_17

So let's try that.

In the components folder, let's create a new file and name it InlineStyle.tsx.

Listing 17-1. InlineStyle.tsx

```
import React from "react";

const heading = {
  color: "orange",
  fontSize: "50px",
};

function InlineStyle() {
  return (
    <div>
      {/* style attribute to equal to the object it is calling */}
      <h1 style={heading}> Inline Style</h1>
    </div>
  );
}

export default InlineStyle;
```

Plain CSS

This is just your standard plain CSS. Easy and straightforward to use. No dependencies and has native browser support. However, this is not typically used in React projects, especially large-scale ones.

Let's do a button example using this styling method. We are creating a button class with the following properties. We're also adding a background color for the hover class.

Create a file and name it Plain.css, as shown in Listing 17-2.

Listing 17-2. Plain CSS Styling

```
.button {
    align-items: center;
    display: inline-flex;
    justify-content: center;
```

```
    padding: 6px 16px;
    border-radius: 3px;
    font-weight: 50;
    background: rgb(43, 128, 77);
    color: rgb(241, 240, 240);
    border: 1px solid rgb(249, 200, 200);
    box-shadow: rgba(0, 0, 0, 0.1) 0px 1px 2px;
    width: auto;
    margin-top: 500px;
    margin-bottom: 1px;
    cursor: pointer;;
}
.button:hover {
    background-color: #d4bd54;
}
```

I added a few styling properties for aesthetic purposes, but the main focus is creating the CSS file. We have the named elements that are using classes. This allows us to reuse the elements in our components.

And then let's use this button styling. We just imported the CSS file and then used the button class. And since this is React, we need to use className because the word *class* is a reserved keyword in JavaScript.

Listing 17-3. Plain CSS Styling in your React component

```
import React from "react";
import "./Plain.css";

const Button = () => {
  return (
    <>
      <Container>
        <button className="button"> Log in </button>
      </Container>
    </>
  );
};
```

Global CSS

Essentially, they are written the same as plain CSS. The main difference is that global CSS is ideal for using shared layout components such as Header components, navigation bar, dashboard, and other shared sites.

We can also create global CSS in our root index directory, as in the following case. We made an index.css and imported it into our root index file.

Listing 17-4. Global CSS in index.css

```
body {
  margin: 0;
  font-family: -apple-system, BlinkMacSystemFont, 'Segoe UI', 'Roboto',
  'Oxygen', 'Ubuntu', 'Cantarell', 'Fira Sans', 'Droid Sans',
  'Helvetica Neue', sans-serif;
  -webkit-font-smoothing: antialiased;
  -moz-osx-font-smoothing: grayscale;
}

code {
  font-family: source-code-pro, Menlo, Monaco, Consolas, 'Courier New',
    monospace;
}
```

And then import it in the index.tsx to be used globally.

Listing 17-5. Global CSS in index.tsx

```
.GlobalButton-root {
    background-color: #792b78;
    box-shadow: 0 4px 6px rgba(50, 50, 93, 0.11), 0 1px 3px
    rgba(0, 0, 0, 0.08);
    padding: 7px 14px;
}
.GlobalButton-root:hover {
    background-color: #d49254;
}
```

```
.GlobalButton-label {
    color: #fff;
}
```

In this case, we are applying the styling of index.css on all our app components.

CSS Modules

All the class names by default are locally scoped or apply only to a particular component. This means that each React component has its own CSS file, which is scoped locally to that file and component, thus preventing name collisions or specificity issues.

For dependencies, css-loader is used. Create-react-app supports CSS Modules out of the box.

Listing 17-6. Button.module.css

```
.button {
  background-color: #406040;
  box-shadow: 0 4px 6px rgba(50, 50, 93, 0.11), 0 1px 3px rgba(0, 0, 0,
  0.08);
  padding: 7px 14px;
}
.button:hover {
  background-color: #a08884b;
}
```

Let's create another stylesheet using button and name it another-stylesheet.css, as shown in Listing 17-7.

Listing 17-7. another-stylesheet.css

```
.button {
    color: #f4f466;
}
```

We can use the same CSS class name in different files in our app without worrying about name clashes. Let's see how it works as shown in Listing 17-8 in ButtonModule.tsx.

Listing 17-8. ButtonModule.tsx

```
import React from 'react';

// import css modules stylesheets as styles

import styles from './Button.module.css';
import "./another-stylesheet.css";

export default function ButtonModule() {
  return (
    <div>

      <button className={`${styles.button} button`}> Button Module</button>
    </div>
  );
}
```

We used template literal or the backtick plus dollar sign to put the style object from the modules.css. The plain or regular CSS is used as a string.

See Figure 17-1.

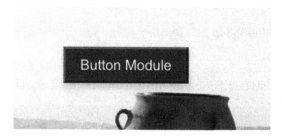

Figure 17-1. *Screenshot of the Button Module UI*

CSS-in-JS

Styled-components allow us to style React components and restyle existing components. We use props if we want to make changes in object styling.

Emotion in React, on the other hand, supports both string and object styles. The syntax is also more like CSS.

Styled-Components Library

Styled-components allow us to write regular CSS and pass functions and props in our application. We can use styled-components to any component as long as it accepts a className prop.

Styled-components use tagged template literals – the CSS code is written between two backticks – to style the components.

Listing 17-9. ButtonStyled Style Class

```
import styled from "styled-components";

//you can rename your classes however you want.

export const ButtonStyled = styled("button")`
  align-items: center;
  display: inline-flex;
  justify-content: center;
  padding: 6px 16px;
  border-radius: 3px;
  font-weight: 50;
  background: rgb(49, 85, 77);
  color: rgb(241, 240, 240);
  border: 1px solid rgb(249, 200, 200);
  box-shadow: rgba(0, 0, 0, 0.1) 0px 1px 2px;
  width: auto;
  margin-top: 500px;
  margin-bottom: 1px;
  cursor: pointer;

  &:hover {
    background-color: #95503a;
  }
`;
```

```
export const Container = styled.div`
  display: flex;
  justify-content: center;
  align-items: center;
  height: 1px;
  color: #5a3667;
`;
```

Next, use the Button style class. The mapping between components and styles is removed; this means you just create a standard React component and attach your styles to it – you only directly used <ButtonStyled> instead of using a <div> with a className.

We can also use props to style our styled-components, like how props are passed to regular React components.

Listing 17-10. Button.tsx Using ButtonStyled Styling Class

```
import React from "react";
import { ButtonStyled, Container } from "./styles";

const Button = () => {
  return (
    <>
      <Container>
        <ButtonStyled>Log in</ButtonStyled>
      </Container>
    </>
  );
};

export default Button;
```

Emotion in React

I have to emphasize "Emotion in React" here because there are two methods of using Emotion – one is framework agnostic and the other is with React.

This means the installation is also different. For more info on this, you can check out the official documentation here:

https://emotion.sh/docs/introduction

We will, of course, focus on the React method.

But within the React method, there are also two main approaches of styling elements – with CSS prop or using styled-components. We will just cite an example of the latter.

Using styled-components in Emotion, the package is @emotion/styled.

For the CSS prop, read more on the documentation here: https://emotion.sh/docs/css-prop.

Listing 17-11. Emotion Styling Component

```
import styled from "@emotion/styled";

export const ButtonEmotion = styled("button")`
  align-items: center;
  display: inline-flex;
  justify-content: center;
  padding: 6px 16px;
  border-radius: 3px;
  font-weight: 50;
  background: rgb(85, 49, 74);
  color: rgb(241, 240, 240);
  border: 1px solid rgb(249, 200, 200);
  box-shadow: rgba(0, 0, 0, 0.1) 0px 1px 2px;
  width: auto;
  margin-top: 500px;
  margin-bottom: 1px;
  cursor: pointer;

  &:hover {
    background-color: #134f0e;
  }
`;
```

```
export const Container = styled.div`
  display: flex;
  justify-content: center;
  align-items: center;
  height: 1px;
  color: #5a3667;
`;
```

The styled-component uses the `styled.div` style API for creating components.

Summary

As we have stated at the beginning of this chapter, there are different ways or methods to style React components. There are a lot of factors for choosing one over the other. We have outlined just a few of them here, from the most basic such as inline styling to CSS Modules and popular styling libraries including styled-components and Emotion.

The next chapter is essentially the culmination of our project app as we deploy it using two different ways: Netlify and Docker.

CHAPTER 18

Deploying React in Netlify and in Docker

After making our application mobile-friendly in a previous chapter with the media query hooks' help, we are now ready to deploy our front-end application.

We are going to deploy our app in two different ways.

First, we will use Netlify to build, deploy, and host our static site or app. Developers love Netlify because of its drag-and-drop interface that allows for continuous integration and delivery from GitHub or Bitbucket. In this instance, we will be deploying to Netlify using GitHub.

Our next deployment strategy is with the use of a popular container technology called Docker. One of the most significant advantages of using Docker is to package our applications in "containers." Hence, our application becomes "portable" for any systems running the Windows OS or the Linux OS.

Keep in mind that we are just using a fake local server (using an external CLI tool that runs in a terminal to create a fake server), so we don't really have a back-end code to compile for the back-end service. It means that the local server or localhost that we have been using will not work with Netlify or Docker.

However, we will still be able to see the application live. Our goal here is to learn how to deploy our front-end application, not the back end, specifically using Netlify and Docker.

Now, let's go to the package.json because we will need to update our build script. Edit the build script as shown in Listing 18-1.

© Devlin Basilan Duldulao, Ruby Jane Leyva Cabagnot 2021
D. B. Duldulao and R. J. L. Cabagnot, *Practical Enterprise React*, https://doi.org/10.1007/978-1-4842-6975-6_18

Listing 18-1. Updating the Build Script in package.json

```
"scripts": {
    "start": "react-scripts start",
    "build": "CI= react-scripts build NODE_ENV=production",
    "test": "react-scripts test",
    "eject": "react-scripts eject",
    "test:generators": "ts-node --project=./internals/ts-node.tsconfig.json
    ./internals/testing/test-generators.ts",
    "cypress:open": "cypress open",
    "start:prod": "npm run build && serve -s build",
    "checkTs": "tsc --noEmit",
    "eslint": "eslint --ext js,ts,tsx",
```

Now, let's start setting up the tools we need before we can start deploying our app. The first one up is GitHub.

GitHub

Before we begin, let's talk about GitHub and what it is used for.

To understand what GitHub is all about, you should know Git, which is an open source version control system. The versioning system allows us to store files efficiently, collaborate more effectively with other developers, make changes, and upload the newest revision.

So what is GitHub? Git is a command-line tool, but the "Hub" in GitHub is where all things come together for everyone as far as Git is concerned and where developers store their projects and other files. To deploy to Netlify, there are some requirements we need to do. We can do several ways, but we would go with the most straightforward path through our GitHub.

Go to this website www.github.com and create your account if you don't have one yet.

Figure 18-1. *GitHub website*

You can save all your sample codes or sample projects in your GitHub account; no need to keep them locally in your machine.

Go to your project app and save it in your GitHub account.

To do this, you need to click Initialize Repository.

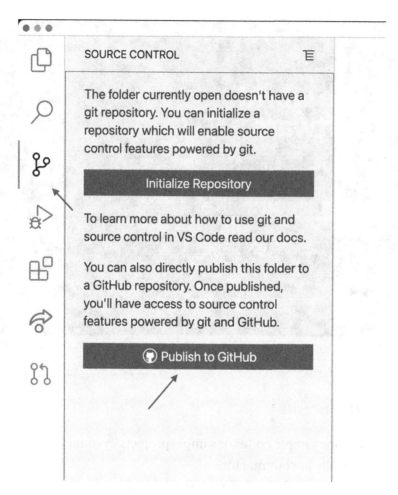

Figure 18-2. *Initialize Repository or Publish to GitHub*

Commit any changes; if there are any, Save, and then Publish to GitHub. Choose the option private repository.

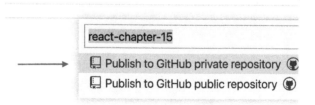

Figure 18-3. *Commit the GitHub private repository*

Next, go to your GitHub account to check if your project has been saved in your private repository. After confirming it, head off to www.netlify.com and create an account if you don't have one yet.

Netlify

Netlify is a web development hosting platform that allows developers to build, test, and deploy websites. Main features include hosting, serverless functions, forms, split testing, continuous deployment, and other add-ons.

Figure 18-4. *Netlify website*

You can also log in using your GitHub account.

Figure 18-5. *Login options for Netlify*

After creating an account, we are going to create a new site from Git.

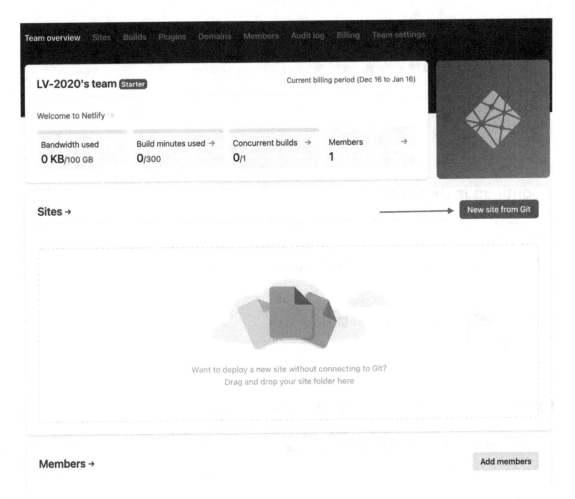

Figure 18-6. *Adding new site*

After clicking the New site from Git button, here's what you'll see. Choose GitHub for our continuous deployment.

Create a new site

From zero to hero, three easy steps to get your site on Netlify.

1. Connect to Git provider   2. Pick a repository   3. Build options, and deploy!

Continuous Deployment

Choose the Git provider where your site's source code is hosted. When you push to Git, we run your build tool of choice on our servers and deploy the result.

You can unlock options for self-hosted GitHub/GitLab by upgrading to the Business plan.

Figure 18-7. *Choose GitHub for continuous deployment*

Then, you'll see the Create a new site page.

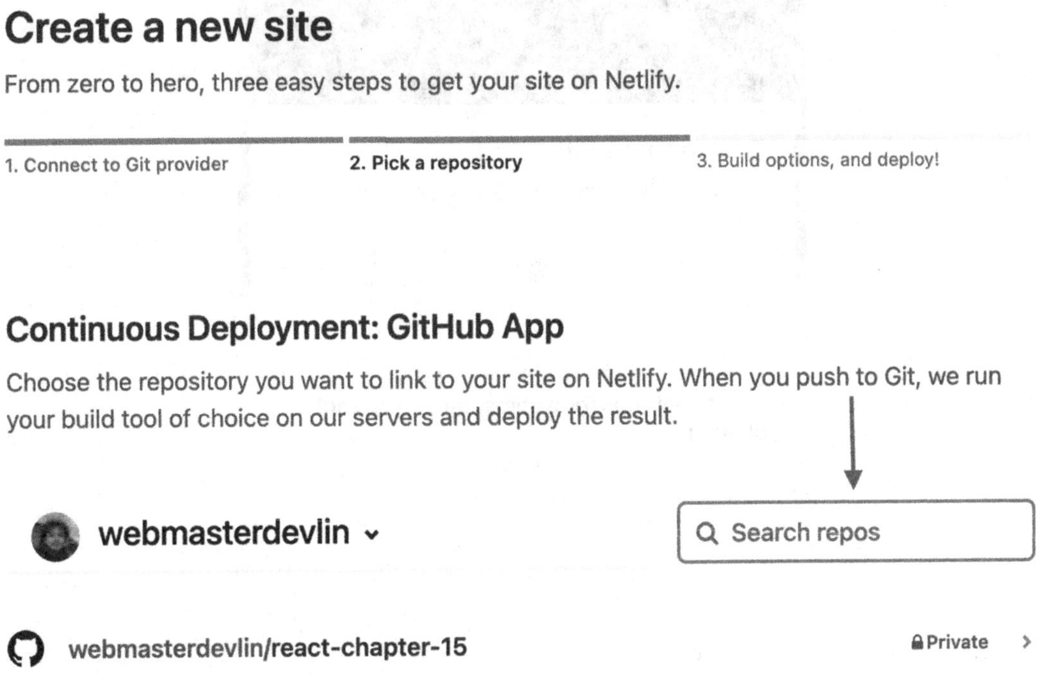

Create a new site

From zero to hero, three easy steps to get your site on Netlify.

1. Connect to Git provider   **2. Pick a repository**   3. Build options, and deploy!

Continuous Deployment: GitHub App

Choose the repository you want to link to your site on Netlify. When you push to Git, we run
your build tool of choice on our servers and deploy the result.

webmasterdevlin ⌄   Q Search repos

 webmasterdevlin/react-chapter-15   🔒 Private   >

Figure 18-8. *Search for your repo*

Search for the name of your repository.

Once you find it, just click it, and you'll be directed to the following. Check if you
have the same settings, and click the button Deploy site.

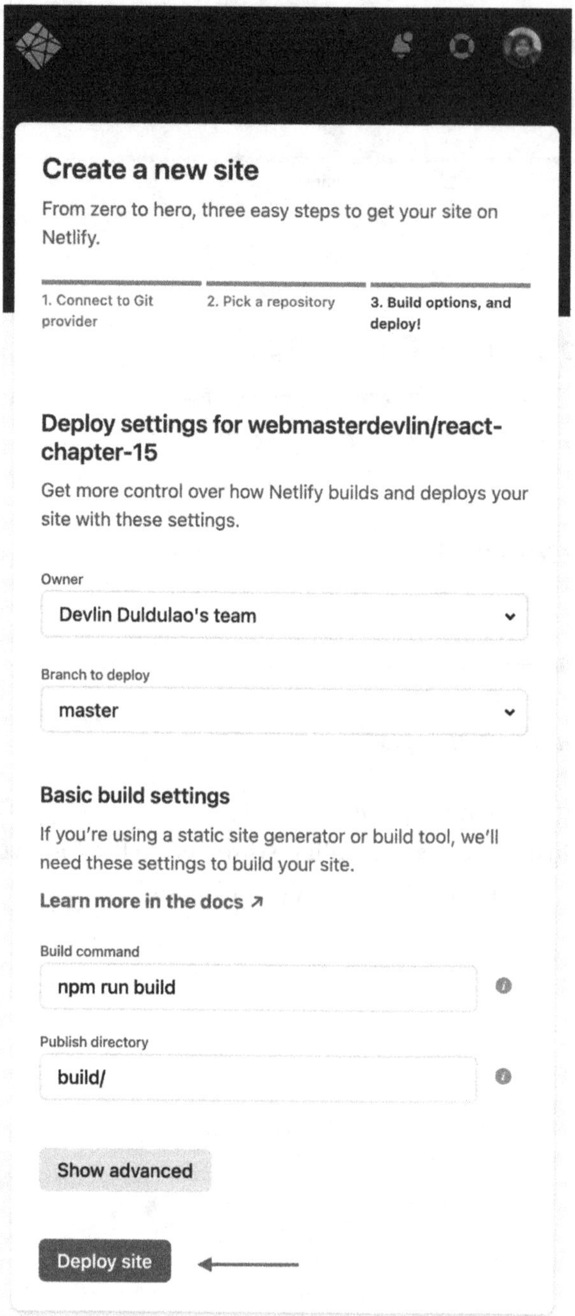

Figure 18-9. *Deploy site page*

After clicking the button, the process takes a few minutes, so just sit back and relax for a moment. You'll see the message "Deploying your site," which is the first step.

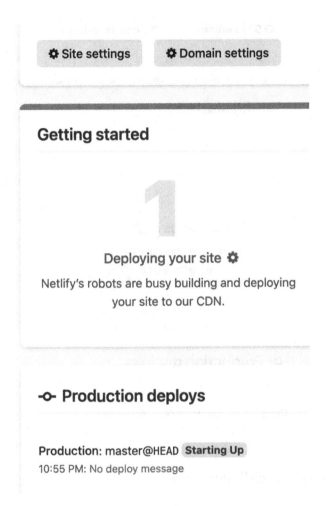

Figure 18-10. *First step: Deploying the site*

If the deployment is successful, you should see the message "Your site is deployed."

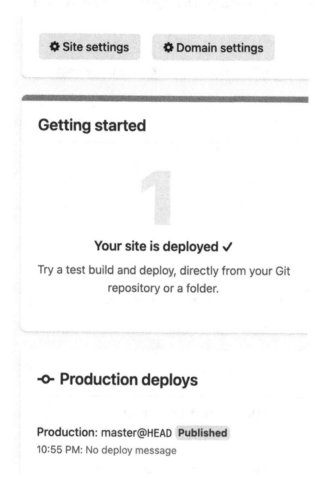

Figure 18-11. *Site successfully deployed*

Once you have successfully deployed, you should see the following.

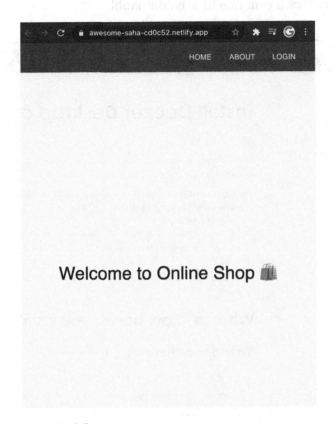

Figure 18-12. *App on Netlify*

Now that the app has been deployed, click the free domain name that Netlify has given you. Yes, it's free, but you cannot customize or change it, although there are paid options wherein you can customize your URL.

Docker

First, let's discuss what Docker is. Simply, it is a tool to enable developers to create, deploy, and run apps through containers. In containers, we can package up our application with all its parts – from libraries to dependencies – and then deploy it in one package.

Next, let's try Docker.

We will start first with Docker Desktop on Windows. You'll see here also the system requirements, and check if your machine is compatible.

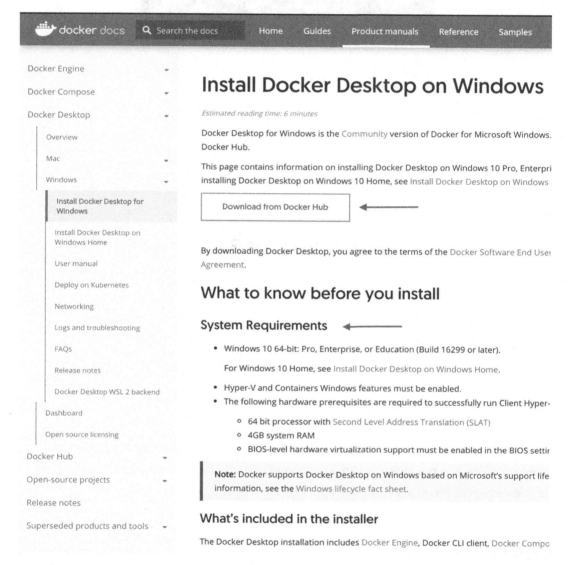

Figure 18-13. *Installing Docker Desktop on Windows. Source:* `https://docs.docker.com/docker-for-windows/install/`

After clicking the button Download from Docker Hub, you'll be redirected to the following page. Click the Get Docker button to start the installation process.

Docker Desktop
for Windows

By Docker

The fastest and easiest way to get
started with Docker on Windows

Edition   Windows   x86-64

**Get Docker Desktop
for Windows**

Docker Desktop for
Windows is available for
free.

Requires Microsoft
Windows 10 Professional
or Enterprise 64-bit, or
Windows 10 Home 64-bit
with WSL 2.

By downloading this, you
agree to the terms of
the Docker Software End
User License Agreement
and the Docker Data
Processing Agreement
(DPA).

Figure 18-14. *Get Docker button. Source:* `https://hub.docker.com/editions/`
`community/docker-ce-desktop-windows`

For Mac, the installation process is pretty much the same.

Install Docker Desktop on Mac

Figure 18-15. *Installing Docker Desktop on Mac. Source:* $https://docs.docker.$
$com/docker-for-mac/install/$

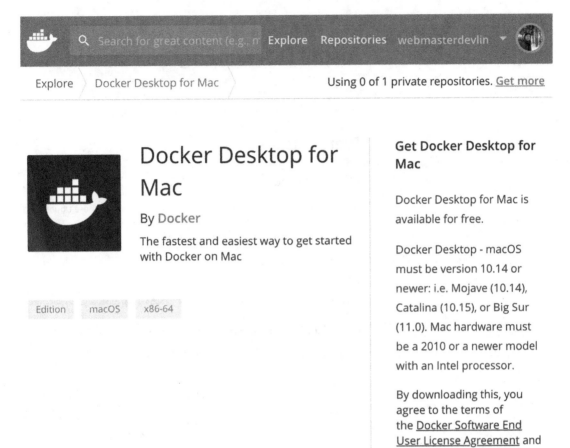

Figure 18-16. *Get Docker Desktop on Mac*

And here's how to download the Docker Engine on Ubuntu.

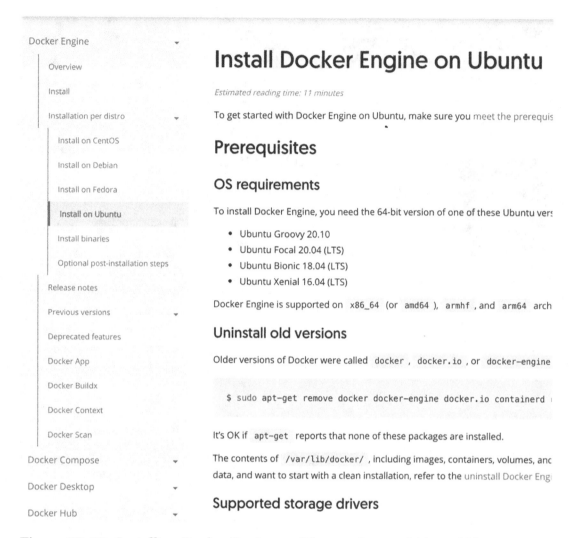

Figure 18-17. *Installing Docker Engine on Ubuntu. Source:* $https://docs.$
$docker.com/engine/install/ubuntu/$

The only difference between Ubuntu and the other two, Mac and Windows, is that Ubuntu does not have a Docker client. A Docker client is the GUI or UI for Docker for managing your containers.

After installing Docker, Figure 18-18 shows the Docker client's dashboard appearance for Windows or Mac if you have containers running. Otherwise, you'll see a dashboard message: No containers running.

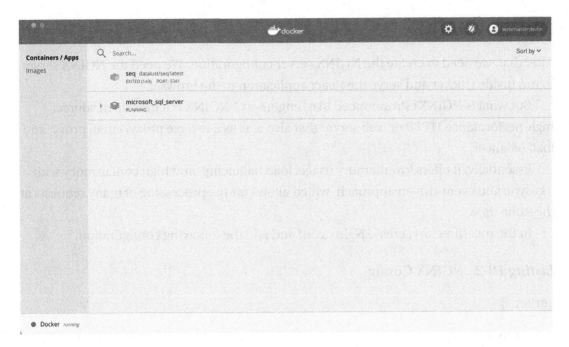

Figure 18-18. *Docker client dashboard*

Docker Ignore

Next, let's go to our source code because we need to add the Docker ignore file. In the root directory, create .dockerignore.

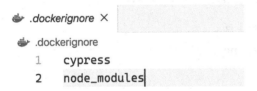

Figure 18-19. *Docker ignore file*

We are ignoring or not committing the cypress for the tests and the Node modules.

NGINX Config

After that, we need to create the NGINX server configuration. We need the NGINX server to run inside Docker and serve the React application to the browser.

But what is NGINX? Pronounced like "engine-ex," NGINX is a free, open source, high-performance HTTP or web server that also acts as a reverse proxy, email proxy, and load balancer.

Essentially, it offers low memory usage, load balancing, and high concurrency with its async and event-driven approach, which allows for the processing of many requests at the same time.

In the root directory, create Nginx.conf and add the following configuration.

Listing 18-2. NGINX Config

```
server {

  listen 80;

  location / {
    root    /usr/share/nginx/html;
    index   index.html index.htm;
    try_files $uri $uri/ /index.html;
  }

  error_page    500 502 503 504   /50x.html;

  location = /50x.html {
    root    /usr/share/nginx/html;
  }

}
```

Dockerfile

Next, let's add the Dockerfile.

Listing 18-3. Dockerfile

```
# Stage 1
FROM node:15-alpine as build
WORKDIR /app
ENV PATH /app/node_modules/.bin:$PATH
COPY package.json ./
COPY package-lock.json ./
RUN npm install
COPY . ./
RUN npm run build

# Stage 2
FROM nginx:stable-alpine
COPY --from=build /app/build /usr/share/nginx/html
COPY nginx.conf /etc/nginx/conf.d/default.conf
EXPOSE 80
CMD ["nginx", "-g", "daemon off;"]
```

In Listing 18-3, we are using the Alpine version 15 to build Docker images and other small, container-like uses. The **WORKDIR** (working directory) is like "cdying" or going to the cd directory inside the Docker container.

We are also specifying the **ENV PATH.** We are copying the package.json and the package-lock.son and dump them in Docker. This is being done in the **COPY**.

The left side (package.json) is part of your repository, while the right side is part of Docker. We are merely copying the package.json and package-lock.json and dumping them to the root file ./ of Docker.

RUN npm install

This is not being run inside your directory but in the Docker container's app directory. The app directory is the same root directory where we dumped a copy of the package. json and package-lock.json files.

Copy . ./

Note the space also between the dot and the dot slash. The first dot pertains to your application's whole repository being copied and then pasted to the ./ or the app directory.

If you're going to ask me why we're copying the whole application, why do we need to copy the package.json and package-lock.json early on?

It's because we need to npm run it first, and another reason has something to do with the optimization of the application.

Docker creates layers for each command such as COPY, ADD, RUN, etc. As per the current configuration, Docker does not need to npm install or rebuild all layers, including the package.json. Doing so will take a lot of time and resources whenever there are changes in our source code, which could happen frequently.

npm install will only be executed if there are changes in the package.json, such as removing or adding something.

Meanwhile, in Stage 2, note the three parameters in the COPY, the first two parameters being copied or dumped into the third or last parameter.

Docker Hub

Now, let's try our Docker deployment. But before that, log in to your Docker Hub account so you can upload or push your Docker images and publish them to your Docker Hub.

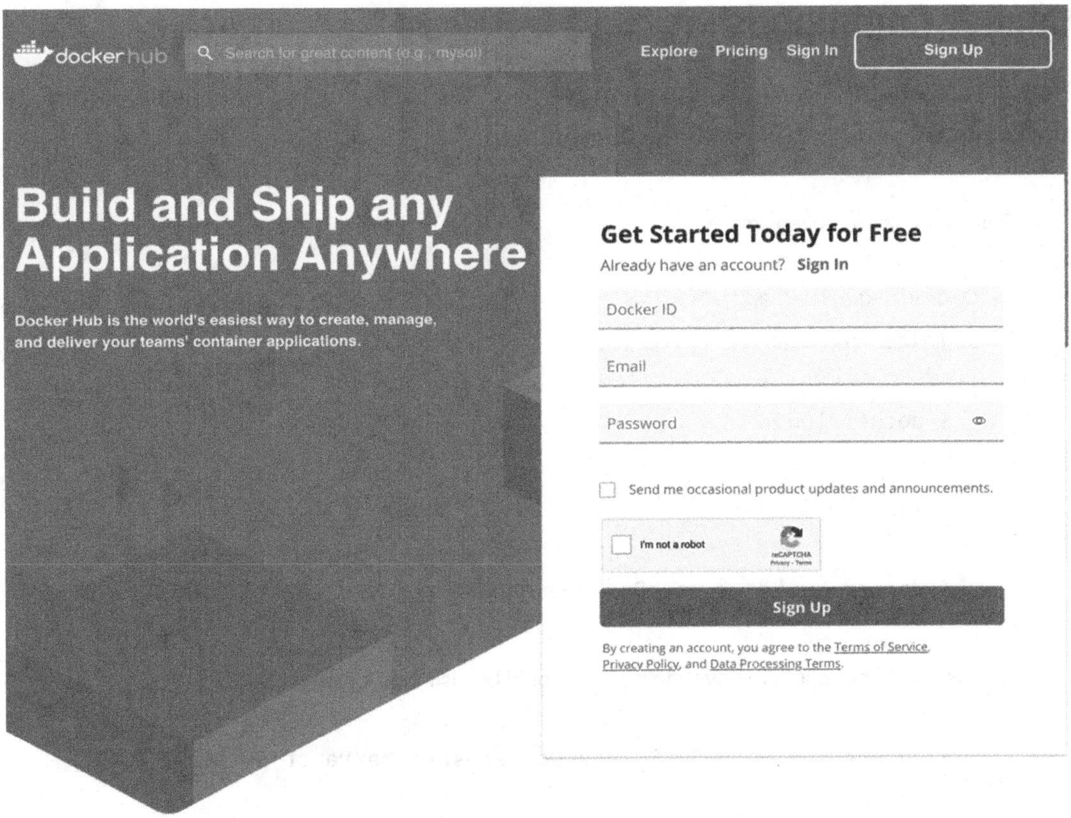

Figure 18-20. *Docker Hub Sign Up/Login page. Source:* `https://hub.docker.com/`

Docker Commands

Now, let's begin the Docker deployment process. The following is a screenshot of the Docker commands starting with the docker login.

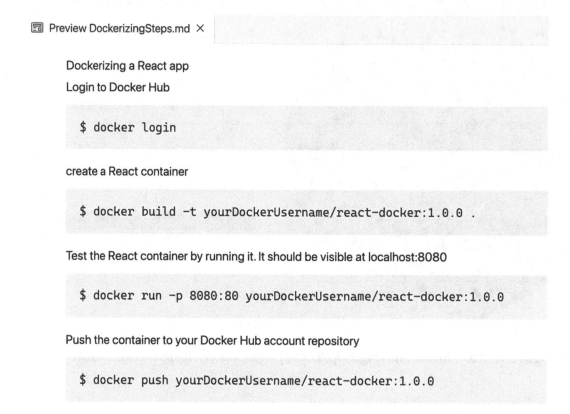

Figure 18-21. *Docker commands*

Make sure that your Docker is running, and then write the Docker build. The following is a screenshot of a successful Docker build (FINISHED). Depending on your computer, this could take a few minutes to finish.

```
[1] % docker build -t webmasterdevlin/react-docker:1.0.0 .
[+] Building 117.9s (16/16) FINISHED
 => [internal] load build definition from Dockerfile
 => => transferring dockerfile: 37B
 => [internal] load .dockerignore
 => => transferring context: 61B
 => [internal] load metadata for docker.io/library/nginx:stable-alpine
 => [internal] load metadata for docker.io/library/node:15-alpine
 => [build 1/7] FROM docker.io/library/node:15-alpine@sha256:deac0ca3214e4fd
 => [internal] load build context
 => => transferring context: 2.52MB
 => [stage-1 1/3] FROM docker.io/library/nginx:stable-alpine@sha256:7ae8e5c3
 => CACHED [build 2/7] WORKDIR /app
 => CACHED [build 3/7] COPY package.json ./
 => CACHED [build 4/7] COPY package-lock.json ./
 => CACHED [build 5/7] RUN npm install
 => [build 6/7] COPY . ./
 => [build 7/7] RUN npm run build
 => CACHED [stage-1 2/3] COPY --from=build /app/build /usr/share/nginx/html
 => CACHED [stage-1 3/3] COPY nginx.conf /etc/nginx/conf.d/default.conf
 => exporting to image
 => => exporting layers
 => => writing image sha256:fbdc72c27eb8e77ed9719a1f1edd952fdb9e546348a88675
 => => naming to docker.io/webmasterdevlin/react-docker:1.0.0
```

Figure 18-22. *Docker build*

Once you have successfully built it and pushed it to Docker Hub's repository, I think it's better to run it first in our local machine. Run a Docker command:

```
$ docker run -p 8080:80 yourDockerUserName/react-docker:1.0.0
```

The following is a screenshot of the Docker run on my machine. Your username would be different.

```
[0] % docker run -p 8080:80 webmasterdevlin/react-docker:1.0.0
/docker-entrypoint.sh: /docker-entrypoint.d/ is not empty, will attempt
/docker-entrypoint.sh: Looking for shell scripts in /docker-entrypoint.(
/docker-entrypoint.sh: Launching /docker-entrypoint.d/10-listen-on-ipv6-
10-listen-on-ipv6-by-default.sh: Getting the checksum of /etc/nginx/con+
10-listen-on-ipv6-by-default.sh: info: /etc/nginx/conf.d/default.conf d:
/docker-entrypoint.sh: Launching /docker-entrypoint.d/20-envsubst-on-ter
/docker-entrypoint.sh: Configuration complete; ready for start up
```

Figure 18-23. *Docker run*

Check the Docker client to see if it's running on your specified port 8080. The name hungry_raman is randomly generated two words, joined by an underscore. In short, it is sort of the UUID or universally unique identifier of your container.

Figure 18-24. *Containers in Docker client dashboard*

Go to the localhost:8080 to check your application.

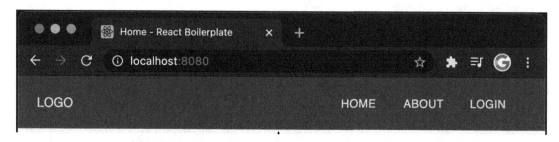

Figure 18-25. *Running on port 8080*

Ok, now that we've seen that everything is working, we can push it to our Docker Hub:

```
-$ docker push yourDockerUsername/react-docker:1.0.0
```

```
[0] % docker push webmasterdevlin/react-docker:1.0.0
The push refers to repository [docker.io/webmasterdevlin/react-docker]
1510f2cf390e: Pushed
f10693328243: Pushed
aa9a1fbe2932: Mounted from library/nginx
f07d8248da8b: Mounted from library/nginx
c4e38c3b23b3: Mounted from library/nginx
816ad72dad7c: Mounted from library/nginx
0fcbbeeeb0d7: Mounted from library/node
1.0.0: digest: sha256:554b658d0a2f936f6dfb0f5042ffd3da8b4403b2287ab827d
```

Figure 18-26. *Docker push*

After this, open your own Docker Hub, so you should be able to see your app.

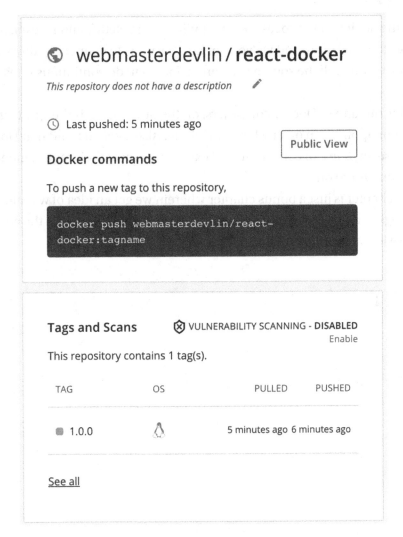

Figure 18-27. *Docker Hub after a successful deployment*

You can download or deploy it anywhere you want, for example, in Kubernetes, Azure, or AWS using their services or instances for containers.

If you want to know more about Kubernetes, you can go to their website: `https://kubernetes.io/`.

If you want to know more about Azure, you can go to their website: `https://azure.microsoft.com/`.

If you want to know more about AWS, you can go to their website: `https://aws.amazon.com/`.

Summary

That's it for the deployment process of our application in Netlify and Docker. Netlify is perfect for static websites, and we've seen how easy it is to connect Netlify with our GitHub repository to pull the source code and allow us to do continuous integration and deployment.

Deploying our app to Docker containers, on the other hand, is the way to go if we need to run our application on any Linux machine. Also, keep in mind that Docker is open source, so anyone can contribute and extend it to meet their requirements, such as adding features and so on.

The next chapter is just a bonus chapter wherein we get an idea of ways to reuse our React learnings and expand to other related platforms and frameworks the concepts and skills we have learned while building our project application.

Index

A

AccountView components, 389
    images, 340
    index.tsx, 390–392
    named component, 389
    PricingPage creation, 340, 342–346
    standard page, 339
    styling components, 347, 348

ApexCharts
    dashboard, 111
    dashboard-layout, 116, 117
    dashboard-sidebar-navigation, 118, 119
    definition, 110
    feather icons, 117
    index.tsx, 113, 114
    layout component, 112
    main-layout directory, 113, 115
    Material-UI core library, 110
    navigation-bar.tsx, 114
    page component, 110, 111
    useStyles component, 117

Axios instance
    api endpoints, 99
    approaches, 100
    components folder, 105
    configuration, 98
    endpoints, 225–227
    fetchSales Function, 103
    forwarding refs, 105
    getSalesAxios() method, 102

    implementation, 98
    local state creation, 104
    option configurations, 99
    page component, 106
    setSales method, 104
    styling component, 106, 107, 109
    type array, 100
    TypeScript configuration, 100
    useEffect() method, 103
    useStyles/useTheme styles, 109

B

Boilerplate, 39
    cloning process, 42, 43
    competent/efficient developer, 41
    cons, 41
    CRA template, 43
    create-react-app (CRA), 44–51
    disadvantages, 42
    GitHub project, 42
    package/dependency, 40
    package.json, 39
    pros, 40, 41
    VS code extension, 52

C

Cascading Style Sheets (CSS) file
    ButtonModule.tsx, 422
    Button Module UI, 422

455

N, O

Printed in the United States
by Baker & Taylor Publisher Services